ST ANTONY'S/MACMILLAN SERIES

General editors: Archie Brown (1978–85) and Rosemary Thorp (1985–), both Fellows of St Antony's College, Oxford

Roger Owen (*editor*) STUDIES IN THE ECONOMIC AND SOCIAL HISTORY OF PALESTINE IN THE NINETEENTH AND TWENTIETH CENTURIES

Ilan Pappé BRITAIN AND THE ARAB–ISRAELI CONFLICT, 1948–51

D. C. M. Platt and Guido di Tella (*editors*) ARGENTINA, AUSTRALIA AND CANADA: STUDIES IN COMPARATIVE DEVELOPMENT, 1870–1965

Irena Powell WRITERS AND SOCIETY IN MODERN JAPAN

Alex Pravda (*editor*) HOW RULING COMMUNIST PARTIES ARE GOVERNED

T. H. Rigby and Ferenc Fehér (*editors*) POLITICAL LEGITIMATION IN COMMUNIST STATES

Hans Rogger JEWISH POLICIES AND RIGHT-WING POLITICS IN IMPERIAL RUSSIA

Marilyn Rueschemeyer PROFESSIONAL WORK AND MARRIAGE

A. J. R. Russell-Wood THE BLACK MAN IN SLAVERY AND FREEDOM IN COLONIAL BRAZIL

Nurit Schleifman UNDERCOVER AGENTS IN THE RUSSIAN REVOLUTIONARY MOVEMENT

Amnon Sella and Yael Yishai ISRAEL THE PEACEFUL BELLIGERENT, 1967–79

Aron Shai BRITAIN AND CHINA, 1941–47

Lewis H. Siegelbaum THE POLITICS OF INDUSTRIAL MOBILIZATION IN RUSSIA, 1914–17

David Stafford BRITAIN AND EUROPEAN RESISTANCE, 1940–45

Nancy Stepan THE IDEA OF RACE IN SCIENCE

Jane E. Stromseth THE ORIGINS OF FLEXIBLE RESPONSE

Marvin Swartz THE POLITICS OF BRITISH FOREIGN POLICY IN THE ERA OF DISRAELI AND GLADSTONE

Rosemary Thorp (*editor*) LATIN AMERICA IN THE 1930s

Rosemary Thorp and Laurence Whitehead (*editors*) INFLATION AND STABILISATION IN LATIN AMERICA

Rosemary Thorp and Laurence Whitehead (*editors*) LATIN AMERICAN DEBT AND THE ADJUSTMENT CRISIS

Rudolf L. Tökés (*editor*) OPPOSITION IN EASTERN EUROPE

Toshio Yokoyama JAPAN IN THE VICTORIAN MIND

Series Standing Order

If you would like to receive future titles in this series as they are published, you can make use of our standing order facility. To place a standing order please contact your bookseller or, in case of difficulty, write to us at the address below with your name and address and the name of the series. Please state with which title you wish to begin your standing order. (If you live outside the UK we may not have the rights for your area, in which case we will forward your order to the publisher concerned.)

Standing Order Service, Macmillan Distribution Ltd, Houndmills, Basingstoke, Hampshire, RG21 2XS, England.

Legal Opposition Politics under Authoritarian Rule in Brazil

The Case of the MDB, 1966-79

Maria D'Alva G. Kinzo
Assistant Professor of Political Science
University of Campinas, Brazil

M
MACMILLAN
PRESS

in association with
ST ANTONY'S COLLEGE
OXFORD

First published 1988

Published by
THE MACMILLAN PRESS LTD
Houndmills, Basingstoke, Hampshire RG21 2XS
and London
Companies and representatives
throughout the world

Phototypeset by STYLESET LIMITED · Warminster, Wiltshire

Printed in Hong Kong

British Library Cataloguing in Publication Data
Kinzo, Maria D'Alva G.
Legal opposition politics under authorit-
arian rule in Brazil: the case of the MDB,
1966–79.—(St Antony's/Macmillan series).
1. Movimento Democrático Brasileiro—
History
I. Title   II. St Antony's College
III. Series 324.281'072   JL2498.M6
ISBN 0-333-41852-2

Contents

v

List of Tables and Figures

Tables

vii

Figure

Preface

This book deals with the problems of opposition in authoritarian regimes. It attempts to examine in detail a specific case of opposition to military-authoritarian rule: the legal opposition embodied in the Brazilian Democratic Movement – MDB. This party was created in 1966 after the Brazilian military government had dissolved the political parties of the 1945–64 democratic period and had imposed new regulations for the creation of a two-party system. This artificially created party system – a government party and an opposition party – developed in a way that eventually posed problems for the institutionalization of the regime, leading to the dissolution of the two-party system in 1979 when, once again, a party reform was promoted by the military. Although the experience of military rule lasted from 1964 to 1985, this study deals basically with the 1966–79 period, during which the two-party system operated and the MDB was a single opposition party. As such, this work does not examine in detail opposition party politics either during the first two years of military rule or after the party reform of 1979 when the MDB was reorganized under the new name of PMDB, and other opposition parties were created. Nor does this study deal with the other kinds of opposition to the regime undertaken by outlawed left-wing parties and guerrilla organizations, and by institutions, organizations and associations in civil society. Their participation in the period was certainly important in influencing the political process in one way or another. However, the evaluation of their role would require research of a different kind; in particular it would have to look outside the institutional framework created by the government. The limitation of this study to the period mentioned and to the MDB is due to its specific aim of evaluating the role of a legal opposition party operating under the constraints of a military–authoritarian regime which allowed the functioning of only two political parties.

Another point to note in clarification of the scope of this work is that its main focus is on the MDB, treated as a political organization (despite its ambiguous nature) and on the relationship between the MDB and the regime in so far as the latter affected and was affected by the opposition party. In this analysis, then, the class nature of the post-1964 state will not be discussed. Nor will the MDB be examined in terms of its class origin. Several works dealing with the class nature of the state on which the military regime was based have been produced, and bibliographic reference is provided where appropriate. It would be inappropriate to study the MDB in terms of the class interests that it expressed or represented, as it was primarily a movement in opposition to the regime and, as such, included politicians of diverse ideological positions. Moreover, by having operated under a closed political system which barred the opposition from power, the MDB's performance was mainly oriented towards questioning the very existence of the military regime, rather than towards representation of class interest. The MDB's action was against the regime as such, and to some extent, against the socio-economic problems caused by the policies adopted by the military governments. But the primary aim that the party fought for, was the re-establishment of democracy. This is the basic feature of this party-movement, and the one which made possible the unification of diverse groups into this single channel for opposition. There has been much theoretical speculation about the nature of authoritarianism but relatively few studies of the organization of opposition within such regimes. The emphasis of this work is therefore to verify or disprove current arguments on the nature of Brazilian authoritarianism by detailed empirical research. In this way I hope to contribute to the understanding of the nature and dynamics of the political process under authoritarian rule.

This book is composed of two parts. Part I deals with the creation, organization and electoral performance of the MDB. In Chapter 1 the creation of the MDB is examined through an analysis of the political background that influenced the establishment of the party. Thus, the major features of the post-1964 regime as well as the events that led to the government's 1965 decision to dissolve the existing multiparty system and replace it by a two-party arrangement are discussed. In Chapter 2 an analysis of the organizational aspect is developed by focusing on the MDB's initial weakness as an organization and its evolution over its thirteen years of existence. A description of the party structure, its functioning and its programme, as well as an examination of the groups within the party are provided. Chapter 3 deals with the voting trends over the period through an analysis of electoral data and surveys of electoral behaviour. This chapter emphasizes the growth of the MDB's electoral support since 1974, its remarkable electoral strength in the urban areas of the country and among the electorate of low socio-economic status, and the emergence of a partisan identification with the MDB. This work focuses mainly on the MDB at the national level, since it was at the national level that the party had some impact on the political system, but it also provides some information on the MDB's experience at the state level by looking at the creation, organization and electoral performance of the MDB in São Paulo State.

With the aim of evaluating the role played by the opposition party in the political process over the period, Part II examines the MDB's performance in Congress and in electoral campaigns. This section is composed of five chapters which cover the development of phases of repression and liberalization that the military–authoritarian regime went through. Chapter 4 examines the period between 1966 and 1968, which starts at the initiation of the MDB's parliamentary activities and ends when the Institutional Act Number 5 (AI–5) was decreed and Congress was forcibly adjourned. Chapter 5 deals with the 1969–74 period which includes the events following the AI–5, the period of General Medici's government up to the 'election' of General Geisel in January 1974. Chapter 6 examines the period initiated by Geisel's policy of 'gradual and secure' political relaxation and ended by the break in this process of political decompression in 1977 when Geisel put Congress into forced recess and decreed a series of restrictive political measures. Chapter 7 deals with the last period of the MDB's experience as a single opposition party: the period following the so-called 1977 April Package and the liberalization measures implemented during Geisel's last year in power. As a conclusion to the historical reconstruction of the MDB's experience, Chapter 8 examines the political party reform of 1979 and the subsequent dissolution of the two-party system and creation of new political parties; it also offers some information for the 1980–5 period so as to show the reorganization of the renamed PMDB (Party of the Brazilian Democratic Movement) and the role that it played in the presidential succession which finally marked the re-establishment in 1985 of civilian rule in Brazil. Finally, Chapter 9 considers some aspects of the experience of military-authoritarian rule in Brazil, and of the legal opposition politics within it.

This study is the result of empirical research based not only on secondary sources but primarily on the compilation of electoral data, newspaper articles, memoirs, and extensive interviews with politicians and party militants. The quotations appearing in the text of this work were translated into English by this author, who has tried to remain as faithful as possible to the original Portuguese. While the reader may find the use of quotations from interviews and other sources rather extensive, this does not merely indicate that I was affected by the vivacity of political discourse. Rather it should reflect my intention to share with the actors and participants this attempt to record the history of the Brazilian Democratic Movement (MDB). This does not imply however that the interpretations offered in this book are not the exclusive responsibility of the author.

This book is a revised version of my D.Phil. thesis which was presented at the University of Oxford in May 1985. I am indebted to many helpers during the long period that I spent researching and, writing the thesis. My gratitude goes to many people in Brazil, too numerous to mention here, who were of great assistance in the logistics of my research. I am particularly grateful to those politicians and party militants who gave so much of their time to answer my interminable questions. I also wish to acknowledge here the great debt I owe to Bolivar Lamounier who introduced me to the intricacies of political research and has since stimulated and supported my efforts to understand politics.

In Oxford, my thanks go first of all to my supervisor, Alan Angell, without whose unfailing inspiration and support in my moments of despair I would never have finished my thesis. I am grateful to him also for having recommended the thesis for publication thus providing me with the opportunity to have a book published in England. I also owe a great deal to Laurence Whitehead and Leslie Bethell (my thesis examiners) who encouraged me to publish this work and whose critical suggestions helped me in revising the thesis for publication. My gratitude extends to my friends in Oxford for their invaluable support. I would like to thank in particular Mark Dodsworth, Saul Dubow, Rui Feijó, Nancy Gillespie, Anita Isaacs, Antonieta Leopoldi, Betty Lin and David Robinson. An especial gratitude goes to Mourad Wahba who not only read every page of this work making valuable comments, but also gave me that much needed support during the painful phase of completing my thesis.

Finally, I am glad to acknowledge the *Coordenadoria de Aperfeiçoamento de Pessoal do Ensino Superior* (CAPES), whose financial support made it possible for me to spend four years studying in Oxford.

São Paulo, Brazil   MARIA D'ALVA G. KINZO

To Antonia Gil Kinzo,
a remarkable woman
and my mother

Part I
The Creation, Organization and Electoral Performance of the MDB

1 The Birth of the Legal Opposition in 1966: The Movimento Democrático Brasileiro (MDB)

In October 1965 the military government dissolved the multi-party system which consisted of the thirteen political parties in existence since democratization in 1945. Rules for the creation of new political groupings were then laid down in the Complementary Act Number 4 (AC–4) issued by President Castelo Branco on 20 November 1965. The AC–4 established that the creation of new political organizations, a task to be carried out by the members of the Congress within forty-five days, would require the support of one-third of the Federal Deputies and one-third of the Senators. This requirement, however, did not imply that the desired outcome was to be a three-party system. Rather, it implied the possibility of creating a majority of two-thirds for the government, the remaining third being left for a symbolic opposition. These regulations in fact reflected the regime's intention to create a political arrangement in which there would be a sizeable and cohesive party extending legal support to the government and a small formal opposition party merely guaranteeing a democratic facade. Yet this was the final outcome of a political crisis the roots of which lay in the peculiar way in which the Brazilian military–authoritarian regime was constructed. In order to understand the creation of the two-party system it is important, therefore, to examine the major features of the Brazilian military–authoritarian regime and the process that led to the dissolution of the previous multi-party system.

THE PARTICULARITIES OF THE BRAZILIAN MILITARY-AUTHORITARIAN REGIME

Peculiarly, the military – authoritarian regime established after the 1964 coup which overthrew João Goulart and severed almost twenty years of attempted representative democracy in Brazil, sought to maintain some formal mechanisms of democracy. The 'Revolution' did not abolish the legislature and the judiciary, although their power was to be restricted later on. It did not dispense with periodic elections, although these would become controlled. It did not, initially, dissolve the existing political parties, although their 'anti-revolutionary' elements were purged. Nor did it, at first, abrogate the 1946 constitution; it remained in effect until 1967, although it was modified as a result of the Institutional Acts of the 'Revolution'. We could also say that the first impression for almost everyone, was that it was just another military intervention to add to the already long list in Brazilian political history. The fact that following Goulart's overthrow the Revolutionary Supreme Command called upon the president of the Chamber of Deputies, Deputy Ranieri Mazzili, to assume the Presidency of the Republic,[1] thus respecting the constitution's procedure, seemed to indicate that things would happen as before. This impression, however, rapidly vanished. The 'revolutionaries' hastened to choose a new President to complete Goulart's term clearly showing their preference for a general.[2] Nonetheless, an electoral process was not dispensed with, so as to 'legitimize' the 'revolutionary' government: Congress was summoned to elect the new President, General Humberto de Castelo Branco[3] who, on this occasion greeted the Congress by promising the reinvigoration of democracy:

> by accomplishing entirely the higher aims of the victorious April Movement in which all the people and the Armed Forces joined together around the same aspiration of restoring legality, [I hope] to reinvigorate democracy, to re-establish peace and to promote progress and social justice. I also hope that, when the year of 1966 starts, I can pass to my successor, legitimately elected by the people through free elections, a cohesive nation still more confident in its future, no longer assaulted by the fears and anxieties of the present time.[4]

An evaluation of the degree of authoritarianism of the political order established after 1964 is not, however, the aim of this work.[5] Despite the authoritarian character of the regime, the mechanisms of a democratic system were maintained. Our intention is to explain why these were not suppressed and the consequences of this contradictory arrangement for the party political process. In other words, we will try to show that the abolition of the multi-party system, its replacement by two parties and their eventual dissolution in 1979 all resulted from unsuccessful attempts on the part of the Brazilian military–authoritarian regime to institutionalize itself as a hybrid regime. One can ask why the 1964 'revolutionaries' built such a hybrid regime; that is, why did they keep open some channels of political participation, although peripherally, while at the same time constructing an extremely closed political system?

One explanation may lie in the need to preserve Brazil's international image: belonging to the liberal capitalist world's periphery, the establishment of an overt dictatorship following the overthrow of a constitutional government is not easily palatable to international opinion, particularly when the major slogan of the 1964 Movement was the defence of democracy. As President Castelo Branco argued in a letter addressed to the armed forces command, warning about the danger of a military dictatorship, the country could not be exposed to a regime which would be condemned by world democratic opinion and could imply the loss of external credit and suspension of loans essential for national development.[6] Furthermore, Brazil's strong ties with the United States and the latter's indirect participation in the 1964 coup[7] strengthened the view that the Brazilian case was not one to be confused with the many other Latin American military dictatorships.[8]

Perhaps a more important explanation lies in the nature of the coup. Other than the desire to end a political situation which was seen as threatened by 'communism and corruption', there were no clear ideological or political objectives which were shared by the diverse victorious forces.[9] The ease and rapidity with which the movement to overthrow Goulart was successful brought into the open a plurality of leaders and factions with different aspirations and even contradictory views of the new order. In this respect, two problems must have certainly influenced the building of the new regime. The first problem has to do with the role of civilian politicians. We must remember that the 1964 coup was in fact both a military and civilian movement. Among the civilians who backed the coup there was almost total consensus that it should only seek to remove Goulart and cleanse the system of 'subversive' and 'corrupt' elements. To some extent, the need for a short term of military rule was also accepted, as the task of 'cleansing democracy' might involve a heavy cost to politicians, if they attempted to do this on their own.[10] Moreover, among civilian participants of the 'Revolution', the UDN

(National Democratic Union's Party) had a crucial role not only in creating support for the movement in Congress, but also in participating actively in plotting the coup, particularly through its influential governors of the states of Guanabara and Minas Gerais, Carlos Lacerda and Magalhães Pinto. But the UDN was a party which was born in opposition to the Vargas dictatorship, and defended liberal democratic ideology (although in a very elitist version). Moreover, a political party whose history was marked by unsuccessful attempts to reach power through the electoral process and for whom military intervention had become the only way of defeating the strong PSD–PTB electoral alliance (which represented the Vargas heritage), had seen in the 1964 'Revolution' its final victory. The 'revolutionary' movement was thus supposed to make it possible for the party eventually to form the government, after being in the opposition for most of the period since the 1945 democratization.[11] Although military leadership of the first 'revolutionary government' was seen as a necessary and convenient step to restore 'democracy', it was expected that direct presidential elections in 1965 would take place as scheduled, and Carlos Lacerda had already made public his intention to be UDN's candidate for the Presidency. If among the civilian supporters of the 1964 movement there was obviously no desire to leave control of government to the military alone, it would not be easy for the military either, to opt for the complete marginalization of those civilians who had so actively participated in the coup; particularly those – such as the UDN politicians – who had developed close links with sectors of the military and were thought capable of undermining the unity of military institutions.[12] These factors thus created additional problems for an option which would have closed all representative channels.

The second problem was related to the role of the military as an institution which was now assuming the reins of government, in contrast to its traditional role of moderator. The armed forces did not participate in the coup as a cohesive force based on an ideology and with a clear and precise policy. On the contrary, beyond feeling that the military organization had been threatened as an institution in the final months of the Goulart government, there existed only a low level of agreement based on the rejection of communism, corruption, political mobilization and a desire for economic growth. Although this agreement was able to unify the military to overthrow Goulart, it was insufficient to maintain institutional unity for policy implementation. Two groups, which were to have an active role during the entire period of military rule, very soon emerged from the armed forces. On the one hand there were the moderates with several factions. Among them, the most prominent group – characterized by Alfred Stepan as the 'liberal internationalist' – was the one which ruled during the first 'revolutionary' government led by General Castelo Branco and representing the *Escola Superior de Guerra* (ESG) (War School).[13] Created by those sectors of the Army which had participated, together with American forces, in the Second World War through the Brazilian Expeditionary Force, this school had built a project for Brazil based on the motto *segurança e desenvolvimento* (security and development) and had formulated a pro-American position and a commitment, albeit peculiar, to democracy.[14] On the issue of democracy, and based on interviews with several representatives of the group, Stepan observes that 'they felt that in a democracy there should be a high degree of consensus, little political conflict, and an informed citizenry which would be immune to demagogic appeals of politicians.'[15]

On the other hand, there was the 'hard-line' group within the armed forces, which had functioned as a strong pressure group during military governments and was a key force in initiating crises including that which led to the abolition of the multi-party system. Some confusion remains regarding the character of this group which, as Stepan comments, 'was not an entirely fixed one, but one whose composition and passions changed according to the political pressures of the day'.[16] In any case, it did not share the ideas and policies defended by the ESG intellectuals. It was composed of authoritarian nationalists who were opposed to the government's economic-financial policy which they saw as aggravating the country's foreign dependence, and the hard-liner officers proper who, in charge of the Police–Military Investigations (IPMs) created for the 'revolutionary purges', opposed what they considered a soft and legalist line followed by Castelo Branco's government.[17]

As there were divergent groups within the armed forces, and the military was convinced that they must take power into their own hands – at least until the new order was consolidated – the dilemma for the armed forces as an institution became one of avoiding the erosion of military cohesion – the basic spring that sustains the institution's unity – that would emerge with the task of governing. In other words, the problem was to render the selection of the Head of State acceptable to the entire institution, thus favouring the direct participation of one military faction and their associated social interest groups and policies, without causing the disintegration of the institution which might result from intramilitary conflict. Because of the need to preserve the unity of the military institution some political – ideological mechanisms of liberal democracy were therefore stressed; such as that of the impersonality of the Army and the state, and that government was run not by a *caudilho* general but by the institution whose representative was an officer chosen by some universal and legal mechanism. This mechanism, this universal imperative, would be elections albeit unrepresentative ones. The preservation of some form of party organization, Congress and elections, aside from maintaining favourable international opinion and the support of civilian politicians would also serve to legitimate one faction, and one soldier, as head of state, to the detriment of others within the institution.[18] This would become quite evident during the crisis of 1968–9 when Congress which had been under imposed recess for ten months was summoned to ratify the appointment of General Médici as President to replace the temporary government of the military junta which took power after President Costa e Silva's illness.[19]

Because of all these complex problems, the military never considered closing Congress, even though it was 'purified' by the *cassações* (cancellation of mandates and suspension of political rights) and functioned solely to sanction laws formulated within the restricted circles of the executive. Also, the parties of the old regime were supposed to continue operating as before. In fact, the ratification by Congress in early 1965 of a Bill proposed by the executive, introducing a new code of political parties to regulate party organization, confirmed this intention.[20] A regime of a hybrid nature, in which old constitutional procedures were mixed with arbitrary executive powers, thus emerged. Successive political crises resulted from the creation of such a contradictory regime. Although the opposition took advantage of the small operating space left by the government – i.e. Congress and the press – to denounce the arbitrariness of the regime, the hard-liners applied strong and powerful pressures demanding increased 'revolutionary' action by the government. This situation created crises which led, up to the end of the Médici government, to an increasingly repressive and arbitrary regime. The first of these crises resulted in the decreeing of the Institutional Act Number 2 (AI–2) which among other things, dissolved the political parties of the former regime. The next section will deal, therefore, with the crisis which led to the AI–2.

THE 1965 POLITICAL – MILITARY CRISIS AND THE SUPPRESSION OF THE MULTIPARTY SYSTEM

A Brief Note on the Previous Multi-party System

Before discussing the crisis of 1965 a brief consideration of the nature of political competition during the multi-party system which existed in the period prior to 1964 is necessary to understand the subsequent development of the new political order.

Before 1964 the party system comprised thirteen parties of which three were dominant. The PSD (Social Democratic Party) was established by the group in power during the *Estado Novo*,[21] that is, by those who controlled the government machines in the federal states during Getulio Vargas' dictatorship. The UDN (National Democratic Union) was formed by oligarchical factions and other groups, in opposition to Getulio Vargas; while the PTB (Brazilian Labour Party) was created by the trade union and welfare system controlled by the Ministry of Labour in an effort to co-opt the emerging urban masses. Thus the three major parties competing for political power were created either by government initiative or in opposition to the faction which was in power during the *Estado Novo*.[22]

One feature that characterized inter-party competition at the national and state level was the dispute over bureaucratic power distribution. In the very centralized government structure which had existed in Brazil, control over bureaucratic machinery not only conferred some measure of influence on decision making, but also, and perhaps even more importantly, enabled traditional political factions to maintain their electoral support through patronage. In other words, a patron-client relationship, rather than a political system based upon interest-group representation was reinforced.

Although this pattern remained at the core of the political system, another cleavage – this one ideological – began to divide the parties even within themselves, towards the end of the period. In the early 1960s, more controversial issues were added to the political agenda, forcing the parties to assume more rigorously defined ideological positions. At the time, the electoral trend was towards the decline of the conservative parties, namely the PSD and UDN, and the rise of the *trabalhista* and reformist parties. This trend was due largely to the incorporation of wage-earning urban masses (whose number grew along with urbanization and industrialization), into the electoral process. In addition, the increasingly reformist posture assumed by the central Executive from Janio Quadro's government onwards, and the heightened political mobilization of Brazilian society, contributed to this cleavage and gave rise to an ideological polarization in party competition.[23]

Thus, there were two cleavages dividing the parties and their factions in the early 1960s: one was ideological, the other a product of the struggle between oligarchical factions over control of the government machine. As will be discussed later, these two cleavages would have an impact on the political system which emerged after 1964 and on the party realignment which occurred after 1966.

The 1965 Political-Military Crisis: Consequences for the Party System

The political – military crisis of October 1965 became manifest following Castelo Branco's decision to respect the electoral schedule and hold gubernatorial elections in eleven Brazilian states. The President's determination to allow the scheduled elections was resisted by hard-line officers who saw these as unwise and an unnecessary risk for a revolution which had not as yet been consolidated. In this respect, Governors Carlos Lacerda and Magalhães Pinto – the two obstinate aspirants for presidential office – played an important role inciting the hard-liners to pressure the President not to go forward with the elections. In a letter to Castelo Branco, Governor Magalhães Pinto showed his entire agreement with the hard-liners when he asked for 'revision of the revolutionary process' and criticized Castelo Branco's government for its legalist and soft posture which was not allowing it to accomplish the 'task of purging all of those who had threatened internal security, the political institutions and, above all, the military institution.[24] He then suggested the prorogation of the gubernatorial term, pointing out the inconvenience of an electoral test before the process of establishing the revolution had been concluded. He argued:

> The elections are bound to be, as is always the case with electoral contests following revolutionary events, a judgement of the Revolution. . . . Moreover, the elections will interfere with the execution of the difficult programme of the government, particularly with respect to the country's economic and financial recovery. . . . And we will take the risk of, if misinterpreted by the people, witnessing the return to power of many of those who

contributed to the creation of that situation which caused the revolutionary movement.[25]

The possibility of losing the important position of governor to the opposition was the major concern of Magalhães Pinto and Carlos Lacerda. If this should happen it would mean their loss of control over the states' government machines which were crucial for assuring the UDN's victory in the presidential elections that were to take place in 1966. Carlos Lacerda who had already been nominated by the UDN's Convention as the party's candidate for the Presidency[26] defended the postponement of the gubernatorial elections more vehemently. His obstinate presidential ambitions had made him gradually move away from Castelo Branco, and close ranks with the hard-liners. Disagreements between the self-proclaimed civilian leader of the Revolution, Carlos Lacerda, and President Castelo Branco had started since the latter had his presidential term extended for nearly fourteen months, through a constitutional amendment passed by Congress in July 1964. Lacerda was vehemently against the prorogation of Castelo Branco's term and tried hard to persuade his party's colleagues of what he considered a threat to the realization of his long awaited aspirations to presidential office.[27] As Lacerda was not successful in blocking the amendment extending Castelo Branco's term in office, he wanted to avoid the risk of losing his electoral resources which he hoped to use in his rise to power. In a letter to Castelo Branco in February 1965, Lacerda showed clearly his intention to ensure for himself the control of his state's government machine by arguing against the coming gubernatorial elections while defending the presidential elections planned for 1966. Manifesting his opposition even to the proposed option of having the governors elected by the State Assemblies, he wrote to the President:

I consider the 1964 [presidential] elections indispensable. Regarding the gubernatorial elections, it seems risky to replace these elections by subterfuges. I am sure that your Exellency will present to the Nation reasons capable of convincing it that the elections are inconvenient while preventing the people from thinking that the Revolution was made to abolish the people's right to choose their government.... In 1966 I will make democracy unite with the Revolution, promoting through the people's electoral support the transformation of the country.[28]

In another letter addressed to Castelo Branco in April 1965 he tried again to persuade the President to postpone the elections and to opt instead for the prorogation of the gubernatorial mandates – that is his own mandate – by defiantly alluding to the procedure used in the President's own case: 'the solution is the pure and simple adoption of the formula which Congress adopted regarding the presidential mandate: prorogation'.[29]

Despite the pressures of the two governors and their new allies in the army, Castelo Branco was determined to carry out the planned elections in the eleven states. In order to appease his opponents, the President sent Congress a bill which further defined and amplified ineligibilities for the elections, and thus prevented all disaffected politicians ('corrupts and subversives') from entering the gubernatorial contest. In the words of an opposition deputy, the bill of ineligibilities was: 'rather than a Bill, it is a family album ... where in each article, in each paragraph, in each line, it is not difficult to discover a clear, perfect, photograph in close-up of those who will be proscribed from Brazilian political life'.[30] Despite the opposition's inflamed speeches denouncing the government's manoeuvres to prohibit the candidacy of those it considered 'non-revolutionaries', the government did not face great difficulty in securing congressional support. Congress, pleased with the President's determination to guarantee that the elections would be carried out, overwhelmingly passed the bill of ineligibilities.

Given the government's manoeuvres to ensure that 'corrupt and subversive' elements were not returned to power, the elections on 3 October 1965 were carried out in perfect calm ... until the votes were counted. The victory of the opposition alliance (PSD–PTB) was verified in two important states: Guanabara and Minas Gerais. These states were precisely those where Carlos Lacerda and Magalhães Pinto had been the heads of the government.[31] This fact was enough to provoke the most serious military and political crisis since the coup. Although both of the victorious PSD–PTB candidates were not at all 'dangerous' opposition elements – on the contrary, they would easily adapt and collaborate later on with Castelo Branco's government – they were seen by the hard-liners as Juscelino Kubitchek's men. Ex-President Kubitchek, much disliked by the radical sectors, had returned to the country after sixteen months of exile in Paris, on the very morning of polling-day.

On the night of 5 October, at the Rio de Janeiro military head-quarters, a movement to remove Castelo Branco from office began to be mounted by the commander of the First Army, General Albuquerque Lima, together with hard-line colonels. Only the inter-vention of General Costa e Silva, Minister of War, who went to talk to the rebels and managed to establish a compromise guaranteeing the 'reinvigoration of the Revolution' prevented the success of the army revolt.[32] On 9 October, Carlos Lacerda resigned his candidacy for the Presidency, making his final break with Castelo Branco.

The request for legal support from Congress for a set of very restrictive measures was sought by Castelo Branco in an attempt to quiet the animus of nonconformist sectors of the armed forces. The broadening of executive powers over the legislature, increased central control over state governments, severe restrictions on freedom of expression and action for those who had had their political rights suspended (the *cassados*), the amplification of military juris-diction over subversion and national security matters, and the guaranteeing of the government's control over the Supreme Court by increasing the number of judges, were the main measures embodied in the Constitutional Amendment Bill and the statute of the *cassados*. Thus, by reiterating that the results of the elections would be respected and, guaranteeing that the new governors' inauguration would take place, Castelo Branco sought to secure from Congress the legaliza-tion of a move towards the closing of the regime.

The measures solicited by the government, however, went beyond what a submissive Congress would passively accept. Until then, the government had not lost any battle in Congress, given its parliamen-tary support built under the leadership of the UDN. In fact, since the beginning of 1965, a 'revolutionary – parliamentary' bloc had been functioning in Congress to gather support for the government. This bloc – the *Bloco Parlamentar Renovador* – was originally engineered by the government in order to ensure the victory of the UDN's can-didate (Bilac Pinto) for the presidency of the Chamber of Deputies against the PSD Deputy Ranieri Mazzili who stood for re-election. It was also designed to guarantee a solid parliamentary basis of support in Congress to endorse the government's actions. Formed by the UDN, the *Bloco Parlamentar Renovador* also counted on the support of 48 deputies from the PSD and 23 from the PTB, mostly in exchange for public sinecures. The government had earlier on secured approval of several controversial measures which were passed thanks not only to the support of the *Bloco Parlamentar Renovador* but also to representatives from the opposition who were intimidated by the possibility of a reaction by the 'radical – revolutionary' sectors should the government's requests be denied.

Castelo Branco's new demands, nonetheless, encountered strong resistance among members of Congress. The unsuccessful results of the Justice Minister's attempt to negotiate with the PSD leadership (the major party), the inflamed debates in the Federal Chamber's sessions,[33] and the premature death of the promising *Bloco Parlamentar Renovador*, were evidence of the difficulties faced in passing the executive's measures. Aside from stressing the fact that Congress had already conceded too much to the government, the criticisms presented during the parliamentary debates pointed out the consequences which the approval of such bills would entail: 'the break up or annihilation of the Brazilian Federation', 'the castration of the Supreme Court', 'the transformation of Brazil into barracks by extending military jurisdiction to every crime', 'the creation of local exile by determining restricted domicile for the *cassados*'.[34] Congressmen denounced the political crisis as a reflection of internal divisions within the Armed Forces, arguing that the measures put to Congress for approval represented hard-line demands. It is worth reproducing here some parts of the speech of Deputy Andrade Lima Filho, a combative PTB representative, criticizing the government's Bills, the 'Revolution' and the subservient position that Congress had assumed since 1964:

> I start this speech ... asking myself with perplexity and astonishment: is this country governed by the Constitution, or is it governed by the Ku-Klux-Klan? Because ... since the presidential Bills on the so-called 'laws of compression' arrived in this Congress, or more precisely, since the votes ... were counted, the days we have lived in this House, under veiled or open threats of radical nonconformism, carry, undoubtedly, those names by which the members of that American terrorist organization are known.... How sad and hopeless this world is, which the Revolution wants to impose on us! ... What is intended by these measures? To practically suppress the autonomy of the states by means of preventive intervention in order to subjugate them better to Central power? It is the end of the Federation. To incorporate into the Constitution the arbitrariness of the

Institutional Act . . . ? It is the end of the juridical order. To revive the fascism buried in the Piazza Loreto, through the re-creation among us, of 'confined domicile', to confine citizens as in the Duce's Italy or in the Führer's Germany? It is the end of democracy . . . [We, parliamentarians] are no longer politicians: we are firemen. We do not legislate: we extinguish fires. But after the crisis, which is a single one, institutional, deep, endemic, it comes out again, graver than before . . . Under the same pressures of circumstances, we legitimized here the Institutional Act, with all its disfiguration of our juridical order, as we accepted, without a murmur, the *cassação* of mandates, or approved more recently, the monstrous law of ineligibilities. . . . Thanks to this obstinate suicidal vocation, Congress has become, through the continuing ratification of discretionary powers, a vast room of wasted efforts, in which the people no longer see themselves represented. . . . Because here . . . nothing is created and nothing is lost, but transformed . . . through a system of accommodation or artificial adaptation to the conjuncture, so as to allow the continuation of the many who . . . are satisfied to remain here, even as pensioners of the Exchequer. Like liquids, we take the shape of the vases which we occupy . . . Because, in fact, we have been the Emergency Hospital of the Revolution – of a Revolution which has lost itself in the streams of violence to which it has subjugated the citizenry, or in the maelstrom of hunger, to which it has subjected the people.[35]

The measures requested by Castelo Branco, however, were not submitted to a vote in Congress. In light of the pessimistic forecasts about a congressional vote, Castelo Branco decreed the Institutional Act Number 2 on the morning of 27 October 1965. This new Institutional Act, aside from implementing measures which would probably have been rejected by Congress, granted the President the power to suspend Congress, to govern by decree, to decree a state of siege, to dismiss government employees, to cancel mandates and suspend political rights and greatly increased the executive's control over government expenditure. The new Act also eased the constitution's amendments, provided for the indirect election of the President of the Republic by Congress and finally, dissolved the existing political parties. The regime's attempt to work with the political parties of the former regime had failed to secure a solid and stable basis in Congress for the government, since the main political force supporting the 'revolution' – the UDN – was not numerous enough to provide that indispensable basis alone. Moreover, the problems which had emerged with the presidential candidacy of Carlos Lacerda who had openly opposed Castelo Branco, made it indispensable to dissolve even the political party – the UDN – which had provided the major civilian support for the 1964 movement.

ENGINEERING A NEW PARTY SYSTEM: THE CREATION OF THE ARENA AND THE MDB

While the promulgation of the Institutional Act Number 2 (AI–2) did not close down Congress, silence reigned within its walls for several days. Except for the occasional speeches either condemning or defending the new Institutional Act, the fear of having their mandates cancelled encouraged most opposition members to opt for silent protest. The next task confronting the deputies involved the organization of a new party life, as stated in the AI–2. The government, however, did not heed appeals from members of Congress and even from government parliamentary leaders that Congress be entrusted with establishing the rules for a new party system. A new decree was issued – the Complementary Act Number 4 (AC–4) – which established a compulsory two-party system. This party system, advocated primarily by the Minister of Justice, Juracy Magalhães (who insisted on the promulgation of the AC—4), seemed to be the ideal formula for achieving a solid and stable parliamentary majority. The journalist Carlos Castello Branco reported on 25 November 1965 the President's intentions regarding the party reorganization:

> The government is not interested in the creation of two parties to support the Presidency. A united, cohesive, and as large as possible a parliamentary basis, which gives the government security in legislative and political procedures of interest to it, is the Executive's concern. The President does not intend to continue to be at the mercy of eventual majorities which are formed for every particular proposed measure, with the erosion of the president's political and administrative authority.[36]

Furthermore, a two-party system (given the rejection of a one-party model for its negative connotations), was the only way to avoid the resurrection of the former parties under different labels, particularly the dominant and electorally strong PSD and PTB which the UDN politicians wanted to see definitively buried. This preoccupation was evident in this account of the ex-Minister and ex-UDN politician, Juracy Magalhães regarding the engineering of the new party arrangement:

> There was actually an intention of forcing the creation of a bi-partisan system: a valid, democratic system which flourishes in Anglo-Saxon democracies such as England and the United States.... I influenced this decision ... It was politically convenient. If the PSD and the PTB had continued, there would have been a conservative party along with a progressive or properly socialist party. These two parties together would always win the elections. Political leaders were consulted, I listened to my colleagues of the UDN. I saw the UDN's death with sorrow, because this party had been a great part of my life.... But as the pragmatic politician which I have always been, I reached the conclusion that, for the Revolution to have the possibility of electoral victory, it needed to start from an entirely new basis. If the old parties were left alive with their links, the PSD–PTB 'entente' would continue, and the UDN would always lose'.[37]

The intention was thus to create a party framework organized in terms of support – or lack thereof – for the government: to group in a single party all members of Congress endorsing political tendencies which supported the regime; those remaining political forces were to set up a weak opposition party. Alluding to the negotiations involved in setting up the new organizations, Luis Viana Filho reports that after the promulgation of the AC-4:

> the President started to work for the creation of the ARENA – the label adopted for *Aliança Renovadora Nacional*. Adauto Lucio Cardoso had insisted that the President take command of the negotiations which would not be easy given the deep divergences, mistrust and grievances which separated the elements of the several former organizations, particularly the PSD and the UDN. In some states the old enmity seemed to be irreconcilable. But, before such discord was overcome, the impossibility faced by the opposition for several days ... of gathering together 20 senators ... was the gravest problem.[38]

There were real difficulties which hampered the formation of the *Movimento Democratico Brasileiro* (MDB)[39] for an opposition party in an authoritarian regime would not be very attractive to those who wanted either to have at least some proximity to power, or not to risk having their mandates cancelled for a somewhat imprudent speech. It is known that President Castelo Branco persuaded a member of the Senate to join the opposition party so as to make the creation of a second political organization possible.[40] Furthermore, many of the politicians who had opposed the 1964 Coup were already excluded from politics. The first Institutional Act decreed by the Revolutionary Supreme Command had cancelled the mandates and suspended the political rights of fifty Federal Deputies and nine alternates: among them 25 were from the PTB and 12 from the small *trabalhista* and reformist parties.[41] This left Congress with few members actually on the opposition side. The MDB, however, overtook ARENA, and by mid-December 1965 it had already accomplished the requirements for its creation. This came about once the ex-PTB Senator Aarão Steinbruck agreed to be the 20th member of the Senate to sign the founding document of the party.

In fact, it was ARENA which faced the more serious problems, although these were the opposite of the opposition's: the difficulty here was to assemble the diverse tendencies formed on a local and regional basis which had chosen to enter the government party. The deadline which had been set had to be extended for two months, in order to find a way of reconciling divergent forces. This was possible only by resorting to a mechanism whereby permission was granted to create opposing groups within the party – the *sublegenda* – to run in local elections. As the ex-UDN and ex-Minister Mem de Sá narrated:

> The reconciliation of electoral and partisan interests of the remnants of previously adversary organizations . . . was the most difficult problem faced by the government. How to put them together in the same boat, and particularly, how to choose among them the candidates for the next legislative elections in 1966? . . . I defended them as the solution – and I think the only possible one – the establishment of the system of *sublegendas* following the example of Uruaguay where for a century this practice has produced so many positive results.[42]

On 10 February 1966 Deputy Vieira de Mello, the MDB's first leader in the Chamber of Deputies, read the opposition's manifesto approved in the first plenary meeting of the MDB national directorate and executive commitee. This manifesto, addressed to the

Brazilian people, stated the party's aim to fight for the reestablishment of the representative democratic system with direct elections at all levels and legislative and judicial autonomy, as well as criticizing the government's anti-democratic practices and its economic and financial policy, and finally, called upon all sectors of the Brazilian society 'to proclaim their disagreement with violence, arbitrariness and subversion of the democratic order. We are all certain that without a democratic order we will never have peace, development and progress'.[43]

On 24 March 1966, ARENA and the MDB were granted legal status by decision of the Electoral Tribunal. Their names did not contain the word *party* probably owing to the terms of the AC–4 which alluded to the creation of 'provisional organizations' to contest the 1966 legislative elections. This arrangement enabled the government to test the viability of the new framework and, above all, the ARENA's ability to provide the electoral and parliamentary support it desired. If the outcome of the 1966 elections favoured the government – as in fact happened – the two-party system would be given its full credentials for as long as the regime found it convenient.[44]

The main characteristic of both of the then recently created parties was the confluence of the most varied tendencies which, in order to survive politically, were compelled to cohabit the same party. The way in which the dissolved thirteen political parties entered the new party framework is a good illustration of this. Table 1.1 shows how the federal deputies from the previous political parties were distributed between ARENA and the MDB soon after the setting up of the two-party system. In the table the party labels are classified according to a very loose ideological division between conservative and reformist lines. This is a very rough classification, since the political parties of the period 1945–64 were far from being clearly oriented ideologically, undermined as they were by clientelism, populism, and regional politics. The political parties were used to making electoral alliances at the regional and local level independently of the parties' national lines, thus resulting in the most diversified party alliances. Furthermore, the legislation allowed parliamentarians to change their party affiliation. Thus, in the inauguration of a new legislature, a deputy recently elected through party *A* for example could announce that he/she would be joining and following party *B*. We must also point out that the parties' representation in Congress at the time of the creation of the two-party system had been altered as a consequence of the political purges which followed the 1964 coup. Up to the promulgation of the AI-2, the deputies who had their mandates cancelled could be replaced by alternates. Given the extensive use of party alliances in the 1962 legislative elections, the alternates, who were next on the party list, were not necessarily from the same party to which the purged deputy belonged, but from any of the parties which formed the electoral alliance.

Table 1.1   Affiliation to ARENA and the MDB by the members of the former parties, in the Federal Chamber, 1966

| Former Parties | New Parties | | |
	ARENA	MDB	TOTAL
Conservative			
UDN (National Democratic Union)	86	9	95
PSD (Social Democratic Party)	78	43	121
PSP (Social Progressive Party)	18	2	20
PR (Republican Party)	4	–	–
PL (Liberator Party)	3	–	3
PRP (Popular Representation's Party)	5	–	5
'Trabalhista'/Reformist			
PTB (Brazilian Labour Party)	38	78	116
PDC (Christian Democratic Party)	13	6	19
PTN (National Labour Party)	8	4	12
PST (Social Labour Party)	2	–	2
PRT (Republican Labour Party)	2	2	4
MTR (Renovating Labour Movement)	–	3	3
PSB (Brazilian Socialist Party)	–	2	2
Non-affiliated	–	–	3
Total	257	149	409

Source: Anais da Camara dos Deputados, list of the members of the Federal Chamber, sessions of 2–10 February 1966 and of 13 December 1966 to 5 January 1967, 5th Legislature (1963–1967).

By looking at Table 1.1 we may notice that the affiliation to ARENA and to the MDB did not result from a clear-cut rift between, on the one hand, conservative parties, and on the other, *trabalhista* and reformist parties which roughly made up the former party system. It is true that the ARENA could count among its members almost the totality of ex-UDN deputies who had to coexist with a similar number of Congressmen of PSD origin – UDN's adversary in the past. But 40 per cent of the members of the so-called *trabalhista* and reformist parties also joined ARENA, accounting for 24 per cent of ARENA's representation in the Chamber of Deputies. On the MDB's side, although 64 per cent of its members in the Federal Chamber originated from *trabalhista* and reformist parties (lagerly from the PTB), 29 per cent of the MDB representation in that House was made up of ex-PSD members. Nor was there an absence of ex-UDN members in the opposition party.

The diversity of party origins which characterized both the ARENA and the MDB was not only the natural consequences of the artificial way in which the two-party system was established, but reflected the lack of clarity in the ideological and representative character of the former political parties. Moreover, it reflected the special way in which inter-party competition had taken place in the previous party system, as we have mentioned before. This factor would in turn, influence the creation of the new political parties, and particularly explain the initial weakness of the MDB. The potential core of the parliamentary opposition to the military was seriously weakened by the expulsion from politics of a large number of those who had opposed the 1964 coup. At the same time, the rival oligarchical factions in the federal states preferred to coexist 'peacefully' within the government party rather than join the MDB which was bound to be permanently excluded.

The realignment of political groups after the dissolution of the multi-party system meant that the MDB had difficulty building up its organization throughout the country. As the new organizations were created from above, that is, by the federal parliamentarians, only in those states where the MDB managed to gather significant numbers of politicians from the old dominant parties was it able to structure its organization. Table 1.2 shows affiliation to ARENA and the MDB by representatives from the ex-parties in each state of the Federation. As can be seen in the table, the MDB had a proportionately larger representation than ARENA in only the state rep-

Table 1.2   Affiliation to ARENA and the MDB by representatives from the ex-parties, by state, Federal Chamber, 1966

State		MDB	ARENA	State	
Acre	PTB	3	–	Alagoas	PTB
	PSD	–	4		PSD
					PSP
Amazonas	PTB	3	1		UDN
	PSD	–	2		PTN
	PDC	1	–		
				Sergipe	PTB
Para	PSD	2	2		PSD
	UDN	–	3		UDN
	PTB	–	2		
	PSP	–	1	Bahia	PTB
					PSD
Maranhão	PSD	4	2		UDN
	PTB	2	5		PSP
	PSP	–	3		PTN
					PL
Piaui	PTB	2	–		
	PSD	1	2	Espirito Santo	PTB
	UDN	–	3		PSD
					UDN
Ceará	PTB	2	4		PTN
	PSD	2	5		PRP
	UDN	–	6		
	PTN	–	2	Rio de Janeiro	PTB
					PSD
Rio Grande do	PTB	–	1		UDN
Norte	PDC	1	1		PSP
	PSD	–	2		PSB
	UDN	–	1		PDC
	PSP	–	1		
				Guanabara	PTB
Paraiba	PTB	1	1		PSD
	PSD	4	1		UDN
	UDN	–	6		PDC
Pernambuco	PTB	3	6	Minas Gerais*	PTB
	PSD	1	4		PSD
	UDN	–	8		UDN
	PDC	–	1		PR
	PST	–	1		PRP
					PSP

* Non-affiliated deputies: Minas Gerais 1(UDN), São Paulo 1 (PSP) and Rio Grande do Sul 1 (PL)

Source: Anais da Camara dos Deputados, 5th Legislature, 1966.

MDB	ARENA	State	MDB	ARENA
3	–	São Paulo* PTB	7	5
–	1	PSD	5	5
1	–	UDN	1	7
–	3	PTN	4	2
–	1	MTR	2	–
		PDC	2	4
1	–	PRT	2	2
2	1	PSP	–	8
–	3	PST	–	1
		PRP	–	1
3	7			
9	1	Goias PTB	1	1
–	8	PSD	4	3
–	1	UDN	–	3
–	1	PSP	–	1
–	1			
		Mato Grosso PTB	1	–
1	–	PSD	–	3
1	1	UDN	2	2
–	2			
–	2	Paraná PTB	7	2
–	1	PSD	–	6
		PDC	1	3
8	1	UDN	–	5
2	3	PRP	–	1
1	2			
1	–	Santa Catarina PTB	2	–
2	–	PSD	–	6
–	1	UDN	1	5
10	–	Rio Grande do PTB	14	–
2	1	Sul* PSD	–	7
2	4	UDN	–	1
1	1	MTR	1	–
		PDC	–	2
4	2	PL	–	2
4	16	PRP	–	1
2	13			
–	4	Territorio Amapa PSP	–	1
–	1			
–	1	T. Rondonia PSP	–	1
		T. Roraima UDN	–	1

resentations of Rio de Janeiro, Guanabara, Rio Grande do Sul and the small representation of Amazonas; owing largely to the almost massive adhesion of the ex-PTB deputies. This certainly helps to explain why in the states of Rio de Janeiro, Guanabara and Rio Grande do Sul the MDB managed to defeat ARENA in the first legislative elections of 1966, and, except for the 1970 elections, why its support increased significantly in all ensuing elections.[45] Moreover, the fact that in these states there were significant numbers of MDB members from the ex-PTB made it possible for the MDB to structure its organization on a more stable basis. In the case of São Paulo, where the dispersion of party representation during the pre-1964 period is remarkable (as we can see in Table 1.2., it is the only case in which ten parties shared the Federal Chamber's seats), no pattern in the affiliation to the new parties is verified. This made it very difficult for the MDB to establish its organization in this state, since the opposition could not count on organizational resources from the old dominant parties. The São Paulo case will nonetheless be discussed in Chapter 2.

Finally, we end this chapter by quoting the comments of a founding member of the MDB:

Even if we admit that the rules for the creation of new parties was a product of a dictatorship, those rules did not demand that a second party should be created. I think this is the injustice, at a historical level, that has been done against the MDB. It is obvious that the MDB was created in a very elitist way. It is obvious that it was created according to a rule established by a dictatorship. I have no doubt about that. But between two and zero, there is a third possibility: the creation of just one party; that is, not to create any opposition party. The second was born, I would say, by a synthesis of two factors. On the one hand, because of certain parliamentarians who had popular roots and had managed to survive the wave of purges of the Institutional Act Number 1. On the other hand, because of certain concessions and encouragement by the regime which was interested in the creation of the MDB. . . . In any case, the creation of the MDB was predominantly the fruit of a reaction which had existed since 1964. The MDB was not born by an act of the dictatorship. On the contrary, it was born because some people reacted against the dictatorship. The elitist character of the dictatorial rules for the creation of the parties was the dramatic problem of the MDB. Since the creation of the party was carried out by parliamentarians, the MDB acquired many of the vices of an exclusively parliamentarian existence. By being created by parliamentarians, it is obvious that its structure, its organization was made for the benefit of those who had created it. This is a natural consequence of a political process which is vicious in its origin.[46]

2 The MDB's Organization, Structure and Programme[1]

This chapter will discuss three main questions: first, the manner in which the MDB set up its national organization and the functioning of the party structure; second, the nature of the MDB as an opposition front, that is the nature of the groupings within the party; and third, what the MDB defended, that is the basic issues of the party programme.

THE MDB ORGANIZATION AND STRUCTURE

The Creation of the MDB Organization

Initially the MDB could hardly be considered as having a party structure such as the presence of different levels in a hierarchical organization. As the MDB was created by parliamentarians, its organization was obviously set up from above. A provisional directorate was then created, being composed of all parliamentarians who signed the manifesto of the party's foundation. These parliamentarians were also the ones who, with the help of state deputies who joined the MDB, would carry out the task of creating regional directorates in their respective states.

Out of the national directorate, a national executive committee composed of 11 members was also formed so as to carry out the major functions of organizing and deciding the party's activities. As the MDB was created by parliamentarians from the dissolved parties, particularly from the Brazilian Labour Party (PTB) and the Social Democratic Party (PSD), the composition of the MDB's first national executive committee largely reflected the relative weight of the two old parties. The MDB's first national president (the highest position in the party) was Oscar Passos who was a PTB Senator from the Northern state of Acre and, not by coincidence, was a general in

26

the army reserve.[2] The positions of first vice-presidency and treasurer were also held by ex-PTB parliamentarians, respectively Deputy Oswaldo Lima Filho and Senator José Ermirio de Moraes, both from the state of Pernambuco. On the other hand, parliamentarians from the ex-PSD were nominated for the position of general-secretary (Deputy José Martins Rodrigues from Ceará state), for the second vice-presidency (Deputy Ulysses Guimarães from São Paulo state) and for the position of leader in the Federal Chamber (Deputy Vieira de Mello from Bahia state). Apart from these two major ex-political parties, the ex-PDC (Christian Democratic Party) was granted the third . vice-presidency which was held by Franco Montoro (then deputy from São Paulo), and the ex-PSB (Brazilian Socialist Party) received the position of MDB leader in the Senate with the appointment of Senator Aurelio Vianna from Alagoas state. The four remaining places on the Executive (voting members) were shared between ex-PSD and ex-PTB representatives. Among the ex-PTB parliamentarians who were nominated for the positions in the executive committee, there was not a single parliamentarian from the states of Rio Grande do Sul, Rio de Janeiro and Guanabara, in spite of the fact that almost half the number of ex-PTB parliamentarians who joined the MDB was from these states. This was interpreted at the time as a deliberate move to dissociate the new opposition party from the PTB group of parliamentarians who were identified with the ousted President Goulart and with the ex-governor Leonel Brizola.[3]

The MDB national leadership would be modified several times in the course of the party's thirteen years of existence as a single opposition party. Rather than a sign of renovation, most of the changes in the party's national leadership were due to two events. The first was the political purges that followed the promulgation of the Institutional Act Number 5 (AI–5) in 1968, and the second was the electoral defeat suffered by the MDB in 1966 and 1970.

Owing to the wave of purges of 1968 and 1969, the MDB national executive committee lost six members who had their mandates cancelled and their political rights suspended by the AI–5. Among the important position in the party national leadership, the MDB lost its general-secretary Jośe Martins Rodrigues, the first vice-president Oswaldo Lima Filho and the party leader in the Federal Chamber, Deputy Mario Covas, and fourteen out of the twenty-one vice-leaders. On the other hand, several of the original party leaders resigned from their positions after having suffered electoral defeat.

In 1966, the leader of the Federal Chamber, Deputy Vieira de Mello, was defeated in his attempt to obtain a seat in the Senate. In 1970, the party national president, Senator Oscar Passos, and three other senators who also belonged to the executive committee were not re-elected in that year's legislative elections. As a consequence of these events, from 1971 onwards, only two members of the original executive committee remained holding positions: Deputy Ulysses Guimarães who became national president and Senator Franco Montoro who, since then, has occupied different positions on the executive committee. Another consequence of the political purges and of the electoral defeat of several prominent MDB politicians was that the party national leadership became predominantly composed of parliamentarians who originally belonged to the PSD. Ex-PSD politicians such as Ulysses Guimarães, Tancredo Neves, Amaral Peixoto, Thales Ramalho and Nelson Carneiro were major figures of the MDB's moderate group which held the party national leadership. From 1971 onwards, some changes in the composition of the executive committee occured given the pressures from new elements elected in 1970 and 1974 demanding change. But the most important positions in the party leadership were not changed frequently, as we can confirm by the fact that the MDB had only two national presidents, Senator Oscar Passos and Deputy Ulysses Guimarães, and only three general-secretaries (Deputy Martins Rodrigues, the ex-UDN Deputy Adolfo de Oliveira and the ex-PSD Deputy Thales Ramalho).

The setting up of the MDB organization all over the country was quite a difficult task given the unfavourable conditions faced by the opposition party. According to the Political Party Organization Law of 1965 (*Lei Orgânica dos Partidos Politicos*), in order to acquire permanent status, the political parties had to create regional directorates in half the country's states. A regional directorate could only be established if the party had created local organizations in at least a quarter of the state's number of municipalities. Moreover, for the creation of a municipal directorate the party needed to have affiliated members whose minimum number was fixed according to the size of the municipality's electorate. Finally, in order to have legal status, every municipal branch had to hold a local convention which had to be attended by at least 20 per cent of the local party's affiliated members, so as to elect the local directive board and delegates for the regional convention. Also, regional conventions and a national convention had to be held for the election of their respective regional and national directive boards.[4] All these requirements were supposed to be attained by the two political parties by 1968 when the conventions were to take place. Nonetheless, as a consequence of the 1968 political crisis and the political compression that followed, the structuring of the parties was postponed until 1969. In any case, it was in 1969, that is, when Congress and several State Assemblies were under imposed recess, that the ARENA and the MDB were supposed to organize their structure in accordance with those political party regulations mentioned above.

The MDB started to establish its organizational structure just at a time when several of its parliamentarians had been purged by the regime and several of its regional leaders who were setting up the party in their states had also suffered the same fate. Apart from this problem, there was little receptivity from local politicians, and among the population in general, to the idea that they should join in the MDB's effort to create its local organizations. Fear of joining an opposition party at a time of high political repression was not the only element acting against the MDB; two kinds of prejudice also harmed the party at least until 1974. Among the electorate of the interior where conservatism is much more rooted, the MDB was identified with subversion (communism), making it difficult for the party to recruit local politicians who could undertake the task of organizing the party at the local level. In the more urbanized and industrialized areas, particularly in the states' capital where the influence of the left tended to be stronger, the MDB was seen with discredit. Aside from the pro-Moscow Brazilian Communist Party (PCB) which supported the MDB since its creation, the other left-wing organizations had as little respect for the MDB as for ARENA, since both were seen as a product of the regime which wanted to save itself from being openly called a dictatorship.

Apart from all these problems, it should be also remarked that, traditionally, the political parties in Brazil had never built a solid nationwide organization.[5] The activity of organizing the party and promoting political participation through the party organization had always been neglected. The politicians' contact with the electorate had been, in general, restricted to periods of elections and even this kind of contact was not undertaken via the party organization, but predominantly as individuals competing for votes. It became common sense to refer to the political parties which existed before and after 1964 as seasonal organizations, since, aside from parliamentarian activity, they only came out to the population during electoral campaigns.

Therefore, with the lack of a rooted experience in party organization, and under an authoritarian system, the MDB organization in most of the states was restricted to the minimum conditions which allowed the party to accomplish the requirements determined by the law. Later, when the country's political situation became less constrained and after the MDB's electoral success in 1974, the MDB managed to extend its organizational network. Up to 1974 the MDB had local directorates created in 1100 municipalities: that is, its organization covered only 28 per cent of the total of the country's municipalities. One year later, by July 1975, as a consequence of the euphoria caused by the party's electoral success in 1974, and with the aim of preparing the grounds for the 1976 municipal elections, the MDB was in the process of covering almost 80 per cent of the country's municipalities.[6] By 1977, the opposition party had established its organization in 3208 municipalities, that is, in just three years, the MDB had almost tripled its number of local directorates.[7]

In order to have a better account of the organization of the MDB it is worthwhile to examine the process of creation of the MDB in São Paulo State. This state is quite an interesting case, since the MDB there was initially very weak, but afterwards became one of the strongest electoral bases for the party.

The Creation of the MDB Organization in São Paulo

One of the major problems faced by the MDB in establishing its organization in São Paulo state was the fact that the party could not count on the organizational resources of any of the old dominant political parties of the period prior to 1965. In contrast with the case of the states such as Rio Grande do Sul, Guanabara and Rio de Janeiro where a significant number of ex-PTB politicians joined the MDB, making it much easier to establish the opposition party in those states, in São Paulo, the realignment of the members of the old parties did not follow a clear pattern for the support of the MDB. This actually reflected the relative weakness of the nationally dominant parties in the state and, in turn, the very fragmented party system that characterized the São Paulo political picture prior to 1964.

The distinct pattern of party politics in São Paulo was certainly related to the great significance of its urban electorate which had to be taken into account in the parties' strategy.[8] Moreover, strictly political events which occurred on the São Paulo political scene during the 1945–64 period, significantly influenced the emergence of this distinct party politics that marked São Paulo's political life. The most important of these events was undoubtedly the emergence of Adhemar de Barros, a populist leader who built up a very structured party machine through his Social Progressive Party (PSP) in the state and contributed to obstructing the development of the national dominant parties in São Paulo.[9] Another factor was the weak role played by the PTB, whose development in São Paulo was obstructed by the PTB's national leadership, particularly by Getulio Vargas who feared to lose control over the PTB in a state with large electoral potential for the party. Adhemar's populist appeal and his alliance with the Brazilian Communist Party in 1947, facilitated his penetration into the PTB's potential base and, as a consequence, obstructed the development of the PTB in São Paulo. A third factor was the emergence of Janio Quadros, Adhemar's rival counter-part. Janio Quadros started his career strictly through municipal politics in São Paulo, and, adopting party labels to suit the opportunity, he became successively mayor, state governor and later President of the Republic. The populist Janio, with his charisma and more reformist appeal, was the only politician able to compete with Adhemar and his party. Nevertheless, Janio's lack of commitment to any political party left the *janismo* phenomenon without any channel in terms of party organization.

When the two-party system was established in 1966, *adhemaristas* and *janistas* would be on opposite sides of the new realignment. But neither group actually dominated the new party organizations in the state. Adhemar's followers joined ARENA, and remained there in spite of the fact that Adhemar de Barros was purged by the regime in 1966, losing his governor's mandate and having his political rights suspended.[10] But Adhemar's PSP lost its strength as a party machine after Adhemar's forced exit from the political scene. Moreover, the *adhemaristas* had to share the same party with the politicians from the ex-UDN which wanted to keep for themselves the control over ARENA in the state.

On the other hand, the *janistas* joined the MDB, but without Janio (who had also been purged by the regime), and moreover, without the support of any party organization, something that Janio, in contrast to Adhemar, had never been interested in creating. We must point out however that the influence of Janio Quadros' followers in the initial organization of the MDB was quite strong. The creation of the first Executive Committee in São Paulo involved a heated dispute between Janio's followers and politicians from the other parties, particularly from the PDC (Christian Democratic Party) and PSD (Social Democratic Party). Although the MDB's first constitution (1966) determined that in the composition of the regional executive committee, there should be at least one representative of every political group which contributed to the creation of the party in the state, the predominance in the executive committee of politicians linked to Janio Quadros was quite evident. This produced the protest of the other groups who succeeded in cancelling the elections which had nominated the executive committee. A second election was held. However, the list led by *janistas* managed to win again. Thus, although all the ex-parties were represented in the first executive committee, the positions of president, first and second vice-presidents were held by elements linked by Janio Quadros.

The presidency of the MDB in São Paulo was held by Senator Lino de Mattos who, although belonging to Janio's group (he had been elected Senator in 1962 through the PTN–MTR alliance, that is, the *janista* coalition), he was originally from the PSP (Adhemar's party).[11] For having contributed to the organization of the PSP, Lino de Mattos was possibly the only politician in the MDB who had had some experience in party organization. Senator Lino de Mattos actually contributed a great deal to the setting up of the MDB organization in the state. In any case, the MDB faced many difficulties in creating its organization in the state. Apart from the fact that most of the MDB politicians who joined the party lacked a solid party basis, the opposition party lost a significant number of politicians who either defected from the party to join ARENA or were purged by the regime in 1968-9.

With regard to the defections, an important event which aggravated the weak position ot the MDB occured after the 1966 elections. The mayor of São Paulo city, Faria Lima, who was close to Janio's group, and had not until then opted to join any of the two parties, ended up affiliating to ARENA in 1967. As a consequence, four federal parliamentarians and several state deputies and municipal councillors who were linked to Janio and Faria Lima, left the MDB to join ARENA. In this wave of defections the MDB lost even the party's first vice-president. Yet again, after the 1968 municipal elections when the MDB managed to have 63 mayors elected in the state's municipalities, most of them ended up joining the government party. In 1971, with the alterations in the Political Party Organization Law which established the prohibition of changing party affiliation for those holding a legislative mandate, the MDB suffered another wave of defections: MDB members, particularly municipal councillors, decided to join ARENA before the new regulation came into effect. After 1971, although the MDB would not suffer defections regarding its legislative representation given the prohibition established by the law, it would still have to face the problem of mayors who, after being elected under the MDB label, moved to ARENA as a consequence of the government's actions to attract them to ARENA by offering advantages or by exerting pressure and intimidation.

Regarding the purges suffered by the party in São Paulo in the wave of repression in 1968-9, 12 out of the 27 federal deputies from São Paulo elected in 1966 had their mandates cancelled and their political rights suspended. Several MDB deputies of the State Assembly were also purged. Because of its nature as a party which depended upon parliamentarians for the setting up of its organization, all these problems faced by the MDB resulted in the initial structure of the party in São Paulo being composed of the minimum number of local branches necessary for the legal functioning of the party. In 1969 the MDB had created local directorates in 204 out of the 506 municipalities in the state.[12] In 1973 the MDB still managed to cover only half the municipalities of the state.[13] It was only after 1973 that the MDB witnessed a considerable expansion of its organization. In 1974 the party increased the number of directorates to a total of about 371, and in 1975 the MDB had set up municipal branches in 468 municipalities out of the 572 in the interior of the state and had 37 district directorates in the state capital.[14]

A more accurate indication of the initial weakness of the MDB organization and its subsequent improvement can be obtained by examining the party's participation in local elections during the period. Tables 2.1 and 2.2 show the percentages of municipalities in which the MDB and ARENA ran candidates in the 1968, 1972 and 1976 elections for municipal mayors and for councillors, as well as the parties' electoral performance in the elections. We can see that while ARENA had participated since 1968 in local elections in the majority of the municipalities of the state, only in the 1976 elections did the MDB manage to put up candidates in more than two thirds of the municipalities. The low level of the MDB's participation in the 1968 and 1972 elections clearly demonstrates that the party organization at local level was so fragile that even in some places where the party had formally set up a local directorate it was not able to run candidates for lack of cadres.

It was only after 1973 that the MDB managed to expand its organization. This great expansion was largely due to the work developed by Orestes Quercia. By 1972, as mayor of the important city of Campinas (from 1969–73), Quercia started to create MDB directorates in the towns where the party had not yet been organized. Bidding for the nomination at the MDB regional convention as candidate for the Senate in 1974, he helped to establish almost two hundred municipal directorates. Most of these new branches were actually created on a very formal and provisional basis, and it is known that in most of the cases Quercia took advantage of local dissensions within the ARENA, thus managing to attract dissident elements from this party in order to create the MDB in the town. Thus, most of these local branches merely reflected local disputes and had little to do with opposition attitudes towards national politics. In any case, Quercia's enterprise in organising the MDB in the interior of the state helped him to win the nomination for the senatorial candidacy, since he had ensured the support at the convention of a large number of delegates, most of them, from the municipal directorates that his group had set up. Quercia's work also helped him in his overwhelming victory in the 1974 senatorial contest. Afterwards, his influence in the MDB in São Paulo allowed him to oppose the ruling group in the party's regional executive committee, which was still under the presidency of Lino de Mattos, and guarantee the nomination for the MDB presidency, at the regional convention of 1975, of an element from his group.[15] In terms of helping the consolidation of the MDB organization, the work developed by Quercia was quantitative rather than qualitative, and there is some doubt about the actual effectiveness of his work.

In any case, the strengthening of the MDB organization in São Paulo was a process which in fact began to develop only *after* 1974. One of the consequences of the MDB electoral victory in 1974 was that the opposition party finally gained credibility as a means of participation in politics. Thus after 1974 the MDB became an attractive instrument not only for those who were willing to increase their chance of being elected for a political mandate, but also for those from the left who saw the possibility of using the MDB's legal

Table 2.1 Percentage of municipalities in which the MDB and ARENA put up candidates and in which they won the elections for mayorship, 1968, 1972 and 1976, São Paulo State

	1968	1972	1976
% Municipalities in which the MDB put up candidates	37.6	31.2	71.3
% Municipalities in which ARENA put up candidates	99.6	99.8	100.0
% Municipalities the MDB won in the elections	12.9	10.5	18.3
% Municipalities the ARENA won in the elections	87.1	89.5	81.7
Total number of municipalities (=100)*	490	551	551

* The total of municipalities does not coincide with the total number of them in the state, since municipal elections for mayor were not allowed to be held in about 20 municipalities.
Source: My own calculations based on statistics provided by the Regional Electoral Tribunal (TRE) of São Paulo.

Table 2.2 Percentage of municipalities in which the MDB and ARENA put up candidates for municipal councillor elections and percentage of councillors elected by each party, 1968, 1972 and 1976, São Paulo state

	1968	1972	1976
% Municipalities in which the MDB put up candidates	52.2	41.2	82.1
% Municipalities in which ARENA put up candidates	99.6	99.8	100.0
Total number of municipalities	506	571	571
% of candidates elected from the MDB	18.4	14.1	28.3
% of candidates elected from ARENA	81.6	85.9	71.7
Total of candidates elected	5077	5735	5897

Source: My own calculations based on statistics from the Regional Electoral Tribunal (TRE–SP).

organization as means to mobilize popular participation (*trabalho de base*). Left-wing groups such as the remnants of the guerrilla organizations which had earlier refused to support the MDB, began to join the party and create local directorates, particularly in the districts of São Paulo city, as an attempt to develop political activity with the population as well as to create conditions for putting up candidates committed to their particular idealogical lines. The number involved were small, though of course exact figures are impossible to obtain.

By 1979 when the two-party system was dissolved, the MDB had already created conditions for the development of a much stronger party organization with some grass roots participation. This experience would be developed later with the reorganisation of the party which after 1979 was renamed PMDB.

The Structure and Functioning of the MDB

The party structure of the MDB can be described in formal terms as determined by the MDB constitution (party statute).[16] Its skeletal form is shown in the diagram. According to the MDB statute, the national convention is the highest organ of the party, playing the deliberative role at the party's national level. Also the regional and municipal conventions formally hold deliberative power at their respective levels. The national convention is composed of the members of the national directorate, party delegates from the states (and territories), and the party's representative members in the Congress. The main functions of the national convention are: to elect the members of the national directorate, to decide on alterations in the party constitution and on political and party matters, and to nominate the party's candidate for the Presidency of the Republic. At the state level, the regional convention has similar functions: it elects the members of the regional directorate and the state delegates for the national convention; it chooses the candidates to contest the elections for the state assembly, federal chamber, senate and state governorship; and it can decide on the platform of the party's. candidate for governor. The regional convention is composed of the members of the regional directorate, the federal parliamentarians who represent the state, the party's representatives in the state assembly, and the delegates from the municipal directorates. At the local level, the municipal convention is held to elect the municipal directorate's members and the delegates for the regional convention.

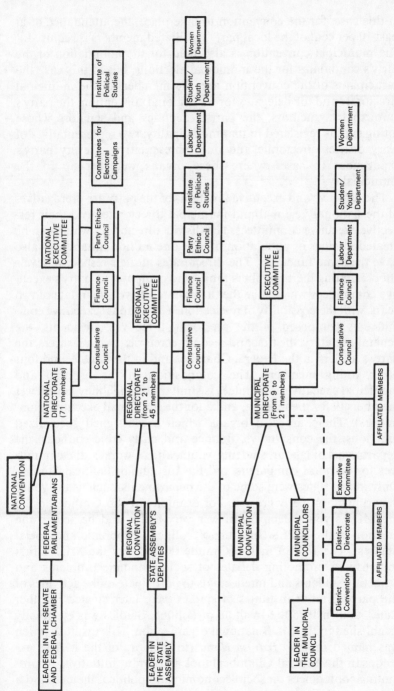

Figure 2.1 Diagram of the MDB's party structure

In this case, for the convention to take place, the attendance of at least 10 per cent of the local party's affiliated members is required.[17] The municipal convention is also held for the nomination of the party's candidates for the municipal elections, but in this case the participants of the convention are: the members of the municipal directorate and the delegates for the regional convention; the party's municipal councillors; the party's deputies and senators whose voting card is registered in that municipality; two representatives of every district directorate and one representative of every party's department in cases where these organs were set up in the municipality.[18]

The directive and executive functions of the party are prerogatives of the national, regional and municipal directorates and their respective executive committees. The district directorates which can be created in cities of population of over one million inhabitants also have the same functions. The directorates at their respective levels choose among their members those who compose the party's executive committees which, like the directorates, have a mandate of two years, with the possibility of re-election. The national executive committee is composed of the president, three vice-presidents, the general-secretary, the first and second secretaries, two treasurers, the party's leaders in the Federal Chamber and in the Senate, and four other voting members. The composition of the regional and municipal executive committees is similar although they have fewer members (9 for the regional and 5 for the municipal executive committees). There are also organs which are assigned specialized functions: the consultative, finance and party ethic councils, the departments of labour, students, youth, and of women, the committees for electoral campaigns and the Institute of Political Studies. Only in few states were some of the departments, such as the youth department, properly created. For example, in Rio Grande do Sul the MDB's youth department was very active and helped in the creation of the IEPES (Institute of Political, Economic and Social Studies). The IEPES in Rio Grande do Sul was the MDB's first initiative in promoting debates of socio-economic problems and attracting students and intellectuals to participate in the activities of the party. Similar institutes of studies were later created in other states, and in 1975 the Institute of Political Studies was eventually established in the MDB national organization. This institute which was named *Instituto Pedroso Horta* (in memory of the MDB's ex-leader in the Federal Chamber) took important initiatives in promoting conferences on socio-economic and political themes, and a series of publications on specific issues which the party had defended in Congress, on the symposia promoted by the party, and on the electoral platforms.

During the period in which the MDB was a very weak organisation, the actual functioning of its structure was quite precarious. The role of the conventions was merely a formality to accomplish the requirements of the Political Party Organization Law. This was particularly the case with respect to the organization at the local level, given the difficulties of recruiting elements to set up the party. In any case, in the elections for the national, regional and municipal directorates, the normal procedure was that a list of the members composing these organs as well as of those who would compose the executive committees was previously prepared so as to be put to the vote at their respective conventions. In most cases, at the convention, there were not opposing groups willing to contest the list prepared by the party leadership. When there were dissensions – actually these were more frequent at the national and regional levels with regard to the dispute for the major positions in the executive committee – the party leadership usually tried to negotiate by including in its list some of the elements from the dissenting groups, so as to ensure that only one list was presented to the convention. However, there were some cases when the negotiations failed, such as in the elections for the national directorate in 1972 when an opposing group went to the national convention to contest the official list proposed by the party leadership. After 1974, dissensions within the party regarding the elections for the national and regional directorates became quite frequent and sometimes very acute, although the party leadership – at least at the national level – was successful in keeping its control over the party organization. The emergence of dissensions actually reflected the increase of the MDB representation in parliamentarian terms, and consequently the emergence of new groupings demanding changes in the party leadership, programme and parliamentary action.

With regard to the conventions for the nomination of candidates for the legislative elections, the practice was very similar to that in the conventions for the election of the directorate's members. For the elections for the Federal Chamber, State Assemblies and Municipal Chambers (which are based on the PR system), the party executive committee (in each state or municipality) selected the candidates who were to be included on the party list and the convention's participants voted, in general, to ratify these lists. Up to 1974, the selection of candidates was quite a simple process, since there were not many aspirants willing to run for a political mandate with the MDB label. In several states the MDB did not manage to recruit enough candidates to compose the party list with as many names as there were seats in contest. After 1974, however, the MDB became an attractive party due to its electoral success in that year's elections. As a consequence, the process of selection of candidates became more problematic with the increase in the number of aspirants. Since the selection of candidates continued to be controlled by the party executive committee and, since there were no rules providing objective criteria for selection, the process of selection could be very arbitrary. Certainly the executive committee as a general rule tried to select candidates who represented or had strong possibilities of representing distinct areas of the state or specific sectors of civil society, so as to increase the party's chances in the elections. Thus, a postulant who, for example, had the support of a professional association, or had been working in trade union activities or was linked to some popular movement such as neighbourhood associations, had good chances of being included in the party list, since he/she could attract the vote of this sector. With respect to regions of the state, it was more complicated if there were several postulants who claimed to represent the same area. Moreover, those who had a political mandate were automatically included in the list if they wanted to try re-election; obviously the parliamentarians tried to ensure that nobody else would enter on their electoral base. This left less space for new postulants who had possibilities of harming the chances of established deputies, and was sometimes the cause for arbitrariness in the selection of candidates.

However, according to party legislation, opposing groups have the right to contest the nomination at the convention by proposing an alternative list. If it obtains at least 20 per cent of the vote in the convention, a proportional number of candidates from this alternative list is bound to be included in the party's official list. In practice it was rare that two lists were presented at the convention. Cases of dispute at the convention occured for the nomination of the candidate for the Senate. When this happened, usually there were previous negotiations between the executive committee and the aspirants for the senatorial candidacy regarding the composition of the party list for the Federal Chamber and State Assembly elections. This means that a single list would be submitted to the vote at the

Convention and the dispute remained only for the nomination of the senatorial candidacy. For example, in São Paulo, in 1974 the MDB convention was already quite competitive. Three candidates contested the nomination for the MDB's senatorial candidacy: the Deputy Freitas Nobre, who was supported by the party leadership, the municipal councillor João Cunha, and the ex-mayor Orestes Quercia. The latter, who was not supported by the leadership, won by obtaining 361 votes against 59 for Freitas Nobre and 14 for João Cunha. At that convention, an alternative list of candidates for the Federal Chamber and State Assembly was put up by a small number of party members who were dissatisfied with the official list. The second list obtained only one per cent of the votes.[19]

In 1978 in São Paulo, the convention was again quite competitive for the nomination of the senatorial candidate. In that year the *sublegenda* system for the senatorial elections was in force. This meant that each party could contest a senatorial seat by running three candidates. Thus if the aspirants for the nomination for the party's candidacies for the Senate obtained at least 20 per cent of the votes at the convention, they could get into the contest for the senatorial election in *sublegenda*, thereby competing also with other candidates from the same party. In 1978 there were initially four contenders for the nomination: Senator Franco Montoro who was the leading contestant, the sociologist Fernando Henrique Cardoso, the Deputy João Paulo Arruda and the councillor from São Paulo's municipal chamber, Samir Achoa. Senator Franco Montoro was the only one whose chances of winning were unquestionable. The possibility of the three others to obtain the necessary 20 per cent was quite uncertain, although Fernando Henrique Cardoso had the best chance among the remaining three. He had the support of some elements of the party leadership, particularly of the national president Ulysses Guimarães, since Cardoso's candidacy on the *sublegenda* could attract to the MDB the electoral support of intellectuals, students and trade-unionists, thus covering some more ideological sectors for which apparently the candidacy of Franco Montoro had less appeal. The councillor Samir Achoa decided to give up on the eve of the convention and ensure for himself a place on the list for the Federal Chamber. Thus, only the three others went to contest the nomination at the convention. In the contest, Senator Franco Montoro obtained 62 per cent of the vote, Fernando Henrique Cardoso obtained 27 per cent which allowed him to be nominated as well, and João Paulo Arruda lost, since he obtained only 11 per cent of the vote at the convention.[20]

Apart from the meeting at the conventions and the period of electoral campaigns when there was more communication between the national, regional and local organizations, the functioning of the party structure, and the relationship between the different levels, was very limited. The participation and influence of the local organizations at the higher echelons were almost nonexistent. Even the influence of the higher organs on the lower echelons was restricted to the dispatch of instructions for the holding of the conventions, of material for electoral campaigns or information about some important resolution decided by the regional or national directorates.

In an authoritarian system, with all the problems faced by the opposition party – from repression to the difficulties of maintaining its organization at least formally established – it was obviously quite unlikely that the MDB could have had a dynamic and participatory mass organization. If we consider that even during the experience of the democratic regime (1945–64), the political parties were far from being considered mass organizations, it would be less probable that a political party which was created from above under a military-authoritarian regime would develop an active role at the grassroots.

Another factor which makes it difficult for party organization to function is the lack of financial resources. The two main funding sources of the party were: first, the monthly contribution provided by the party's members with a political mandate. These representatives were obliged to contribute 3 per cent of their fixed income from their political office. Of the contribution given by the federal parliamentarians, 40 per cent was allocated to the national directorate and 60 per cent sent to the regional directorate of the state from which the parliamentarian came. Second, there was the quota that the party received from the Special Fund of Financial Aid to Political Parties (*Fundo Partidário*). This fund, the revenue of which came basically from the money collected by fines on electors who had been penalized for not voting and an endowment from the national budget, was distributed quarterly by the Electoral Tribunal to the political parties. Ten per cent of this fund was shared equally among the political parties, and the remaining 90 per cent was distributed to the parties proportionately to the number of their representatives in the Federal Chamber. As the MDB had a minority in the Federal

Chamber, its quota was much lower than ARENA's. Thus the Party Fund did not contribute very much to cover the MDB's expenses. This was apart from the fact that this quota had to be shared by the national (20 per cent), the regional (80 per cent) and the local directorates (60 per cent of the share received by the regional directorate). Although in the party statute there was a clause which established that the municipal directorates could ask the affiliated members for the payment of an annual contribution to the party, this was a very rare practice. As we were told in interviews, it is very difficult to make the affiliated members pay a contribution to the party. First because they do not necessarily have the means to spare money for a political party, second, because in Brazil this has never been institutionalized as a natural practice: 'to contribute to the party funds in Brazil is considered like paying tax'.[21] Obviously, this reflects the lack of institutionalization of political parties as credible channels for representation and political participation. In any case, the fact that the MDB had precarious funds, made it quite hard to activate its organization. In such a large country even communications by post and by telephone represent heavy costs for a party without large financial resources.

During electoral campaigns the coverage of the expense was in fact left mainly to the candidates themselves who relied on their own financial resources or managed to raise some contributions from their supporters. Since the party did not have funds to help the individual campaigning of the candidates the consequence was that aspirants with meagre resources either did not think of contesting a mandate or entered in the contest under unequal conditions. This certainly diminished the possibility of opening the party to elements of lower socio-economic conditions.

The fact that the functioning of the structure of the MDB was quite limited, and the relationship between the several echelons of the organization very precarious, resulted in the party local organizations becoming quite autonomous. Sometimes the MDB local branches had little to do with the opposition role that the party tried to pursue on the national scene. On the other hand, this lack of inter-relationship between the party's hierarchical structures, made it possible for more ideologically oriented groups from the left to use the MDB local organizations to develop their political action without any interference from the party's higher echelons. The fact that all the left-wing organizations were outlawed (quite apart from the defeat of the experience of armed struggle), had left the left-wing groups and organizations without any means of political action. The MDB then ended up by providing a legal means of action for the left through the party's local organizations. Thus, militants from the Communist Parties, supporters of the several guerrilla organizations which had been dismantled by the regime, and all kinds of independent left-wingers, started to participate in the MDB at the local level in an attempt at developing grassroots work, particularly in the large cities. It is not possible to give an account of the number of directorates controlled by the several groupings from the left, nor to evaluate the effectiveness of their work. They were not predominant and not all of them managed to consolidate themselves and achieve grassroots participation; first, because their work was rather recent, that is, it started only after 1974 when most of the left discovered the MDB and when the country's political climate became less repressive; second, because grassroots' work with a population which had been politically demobilized for so many years or had never experienced political participation at all, was initially quite a hard enterprise. As several of the persons who were engaged in these activities told us, the first difficulty was to convince the residents of an area to join the MDB, since they could not see any particular reason to become members of a party. After that, the problem was to make the affiliated members come to a meeting of the party, or even make them read a pamphlet that the militants delivered door to door explaining the objectives of the party's work or dealing with the specific problems of the area. In fact, local organizations that succeeded in establishing a bridge with the population and attracting them to participate, were those which concentrated their activities on undertaking initiatives to help in the solution of specific problems affecting the everyday life of the population of an area. Particularly in the outskirts of the large cities where basic urban services are very precarious, some directorates set up by left-wing elements were quite effective in mobilizing the population or working with neighbourhood associations or religious communities, to demand a solution to their problems. Initiatives creating more active local organizations were also found in the cities of the interior of the states, although more ideologically committed opposition elements had some difficulty in penetrating the interior where traditional local politicians kept the party under their control.

The consolidation and increased rhythm of the MDB organization was a process which started to develop in the last years of the two-party system. This process has continued after the transformation of the MDB into PMDB. In spite of the fact that some steps in the direction of a more dynamic and consolidated organization have been achieved, the creation of a genuine mass party organization (by the PMDB or any one else) is still a long-term process which will depend on the improvement of political participation in a democratic regime.

GROUPS WITHIN THE MDB

The existence of groups and factions within a political party is encountered in almost a majority of political organizations which have been properly characterized as political parties.[22] In the case of the MDB which was above all an opposition front, the presence of elements and groups from a large ideological spectrum was certainly more pronounced than could normally be found in a political party which operates within a democratic system. The fact that the MDB was, aside from the government party, the only legal organization allowed to operate in the political system, made of the MDB the place for politicians from a wide range of political–ideological positions. If most of them were motivated by the intention of opposing the regime, there were also those who, moved by rivalries between local groups, had joined the MDB for no reason but to stay on the opposite side to their hated enemies who had rushed to join the ARENA. Thus, if one examines the ideological line of MDB members one would find a large range of positions: from conservative, liberal, social-democratic, reformist to several types of left-wing.

However, this large variety of ideological positions does not mean that distinct groups or factions based on this kind of cleavage were easily discernible within the party. The objectives of the MDB as a broad opposition front were essentially related to the political question of fighting for democracy. In spite of the fact that the MDB did not dispense with criticizing the government's socio-economic policies, these issues, which could give rise to properly ideological divergences, were secondary in the party's internal affairs. This was for the simple reason that the MDB did not have the immediate prospect of taking power and therefore implementing a government programme. Thus, conservatives and liberals coexisted with elements linked, for example, with the Brazilian Communist Party without grave dissensions emerging. It must be pointed out that the pro-Moscow Communist Party (PCB) was the only left-wing organization to have supported the MDB since its creation. The PCB had a policy which was in favour of strengthening a broad front of resistance against dictatorial rule. According to its policy, this front should be as wide as possible, including whoever wanted to join the MDB for whatever motive. Thus, over the period, the PCB supported the election of candidates from the MDB and even managed to have its own candidates elected for the legislative houses under the cover of the MDB label. Thus the PCB assumed a distinct strategy from that of the other left-wing organizations which took up armed struggle in the late 1960s and campaigned for spoiling ballot papers in the elections. PCB elements were not the only left-wingers who opted to work with the MDB in its early years. Several elements on the left, who did not properly belong to any of the organizations mentioned did join the MDB by running for a seat in the legislative houses from the 1966 elections onwards. Moreover, in the later period of the MDB, those left-wing organizations which had resorted to armed struggle changed their strategy after being defeated by the regime's repressive apparatus and when it became evident that the MDB was an effective means of opposition. Thus, after 1974, the pro-Albania Communist Party (*PC do B*), as well as the remnants of other organizations, started to work within the MDB. Some of the groups, such as the *PC do B*, managed to have some deputies elected in 1978, as a consequence of its influence on the grassroots movements.[23]

The left-wing organizations however did not have a base within the MDB's distinct factions. This was because they did not have a significant number of representatives to allow them to create a distinct group and influence MDB decision-making. Moreover, their support and participation in the MDB was not the result of a negotiation or an agreement between the PCB, for example, and the MDB leadership. They participated in the MDB because the party leadership, which was predominantly liberal, simply did not veto anybody who wanted to join the MDB, either from the left or from the right. As some of the MDB leaders told us, as long as the left-wing organizations followed the basic line defended by the MDB, that is, the fight for the re-establishment of democracy, the party was open to them. Moreover, as participation in elections was the major weapon of the MDB, it was important for the party to have the support of sectors of the left so as to attract the electoral support of those who were reluctant to accept the MDB as an opposition party.

In terms of groups within the MDB, the major cleavage dividing the party was actually related to the way in which the MDB should carry out its opposition role in the face of the regime. Thus, over the period in which the MDB existed as a single opposition party, two major groups were always apparent. On the one hand, there was the group which comprised those who defended and carried out a moderate opposition line. Called the moderate group and constituting the majority within the party, this group included experienced politicians who firmly believed that moderation was the correct strategy to face the regime's constraints, and those who were simply willing to be as close to the government as possible.[24] On the other hand, there were those who defended and carried out a more decisive opposition line against the regime and the government's policies. Called the radicals by the government, the parliamentarians who were identified with this line were, over the period of their emergence, given several names by the press: *grupo dos imaturos* (group of the immature politicians) in 1967, *grupo autentico* (authentic group) in 1971, and *grupo neo-autentico* (neo-authentic group) in 1975.

The moderate and radical groups were not however stable factions within the party, neither were they monolithic in their political–ideological line. Their differences and dissensions came out, as a rule, in the course of specific political events. Certainly, conservative and liberal politicians were in general those who defended a more moderate line, and left-wing parliamentarians were among those who assumed a more combative opposition role. However, there were several liberal or reformist politicians – such as some ex-PSD and ex-PTB figures – who sided with the more combative group. On the other hand, there were elements considered as left wingers, namely those linked with the PCB (pro-Moscow Communist Party) who always tended to support the moderate group's positions. According to the PCB's rationale – and pragmatism – the group that defended a more incisive opposition performance was a disaggregating force within the MDB, since by pressurizing the MDB to take more radical positions, the group produced dissensions which harmed the unity of the front.

In any case, the existence of these two major groups – moderates and 'radicals' – was quite beneficial for the MDB in so far as they were complementary to one another. Being the majority, and keeping under its control the party leadership, the moderate group maintained the party image for the regime as a trustworthy opposition party. On the other hand, the existence of a more incisive and militant opposition group of parliamentarians was important in so far as their discourse and active performance gave credibility to the MDB as a genuine opposition party towards the electorate, particularly towards the opposition sectors more ideologically committed. Being a minority and having no other means of legal political participation but the MDB, the 'radical' group used the political channel provided by the MDB, with the acquiescence of the moderate group which, in any case, not only controlled the party leadership but actually consisted of the founding members of the party. Since these major internal divisions in the MDB emerged in the course of the political process in which the MDB operated, their influence on the party's affairs and the dissensions between the factions will be looked at in the second part of this work, where the participation of the MDB in the political system is examined.

A final remark must be made regarding the politicians who belonged to the MDB. When we discussed the different ideological positions and differing ways MDB politicians had of performing the opposition role, we were referring to their positions and behaviour towards national politics. Another question is their relationship with their electoral base or constituency, that is, the extent to which the MDB representatives were accountable to their voter supporters and the basis on which politicians managed to gain electoral support. Without going through a deep examination of this question, two points must be noted. First, the representatives in the houses of the legislature had a precarious relationship with those they were supposed to represent, that is, their electoral base. This is partly due to the fact that an electoral system based on PR in such extensive constituencies (that is, the states of the Federation) means that the electoral support of a deputy is dispersed over a wide area, and as a consequence the link between the representatives and their supporters is diluted.[25] On the other hand, the legislative power has been so powerless that even the electorate does not expect very much from those for whom they voted for in terms of defending their interests through parliamentarian activity.[26] This leads us to a second point: ideological or interest group motivation versus clientelism. Certainly, there were ideologically committed opposition politicians whose electoral support resulted from the fact that they tried to be more accountable in their parliamentarian performance. And clientelistic practices as a means of capturing votes were not as widespread among MDB politicians as among the ARENA's, for the simple reason that the MDB did not hold positions of power, that is, they did not dispose of a government machine to distribute favours.[27] But this does not mean that clientelism was not a practice used by MDB politicians as well. Actually the idea that a deputy is somebody to whom one can appeal in order to solve a personal problem is still rooted in the population. Since the level of political participation and the means of organization in civil society were still precarious (aggravated by so many years of authoritarianism), and since the majority of the Brazilian population do not have their basic civil rights guaranteed, an ordinary citizen normally expects that somebody who has at least some influence – the deputy – can help him/her to, for example, obtain a place in a hospital to receive medical care through the inefficient Brazilian national health institute (INPS), a scholarship for his/her children, and so forth. It is not by chance that the deputy in São Paulo who received most votes for the Federal Chamber in 1978, is a traditional politician (Samir Achoa) who has an office in which he received thousands of people every day asking for help to solve a personal problem. In his work with the poor population, work to which he attends, he provides letters of recommendation for jobs, he draws petitions asking for electricity for an area and sends it to a government agency and so forth. When we asked him how he managed to develop his work being in the opposition party, he said:

> I do not depend on the government. But the government is obliged to respond positively when the claim is just, because, the government knows that if he does not solve the problem the political cost is for the government, not for me. Thus, when I make a claim for specific problems I manage to get a solution for at least some. But I never ask for a job in the public sector or any other favour which could make me dependent on the government. I consider myself completely independent to say whatever I want. . . . But it is important for me to be in the MDB. I believe that if I were from the government party, first I would not adapt there, second, I think that the people believed in my opposition position. The people from São Paulo in particular are an opposition people.[28]

The majority of the politicians resort to some extent, to this kind of practice – some on a very small scale, others on a very large, like Deputy Samir Achoa.[29] Several of the more ideological politicians whom we interviewed considered this a problem which will not change in the short term, since it implies the development and consolidation of grassroot work to increase political participation and institutionalize political parties as a vehicle through which interest-group representation can be expressed. Moreover, it implies the institutionalization of the legislature as a political arena where political parties can influence decision-making. As a politician told us in an interview, it is quite difficult for politicians to convince somebody that their role is not to distribute favours when they cannot affirm that they decisively have influence in Congress to defend aggregate or class interests.

THE MDB PROGRAMME

As a broad opposition front fighting for the re-establishment of democracy, the MDB could hardly be considered a party which had a clearly defined set of policies, expected to become a programme of government – particularly with respect to socio-economic issues. Although it seems a relatively formal exercise to discuss the MDB programme outlined in the party's constitution, a summary of the main points of this programme can give an idea of the MDB's position – at least at the level of political discourse.[30]

Apart from stating the essential principles defended by the party, the MDB programme presented a brief diagnosis of the country's socio-economic situation as well as the set of objectives of the party regarding political and socio-economic policies. As an opposition front against military–authoritarian rule, the basic aims of the MDB were defined as the fight for the establishment of representative democracy, of civil rights and freedom of organization for all sectors of civil society. The defence of an effective path of economic development which would tackle the problem of poverty, unemployment and inequality was also stated as one of the party's fundamental principles.

In its analysis of the country's socio-economic situation, the MDB document started by emphasizing that the position defended by the party was not against private initiative, nor was it against state intervention in the economy. Rather, it considered that the state and the private sector have complementary roles. Thus, the state must not only preserve the survival of free enterprise and ensure capital accumulation – 'without allowing, however, over-appropriation of the surplus' – but also fulfill the gaps in production and promote the development of natural resources. In sum the state must always intervene in all the tasks which can facilitate national development. The MDB programme then discusses the disfunctional and unequal character of the economic policy implemented by the government. Although this policy achieved a positive performance in terms of economic growth, it has led to a high concentration of income in a few hands which consequently has curtailed the expansion of the domestic market, given the lack of demand, notably in the poorest regions of the country. The expansion noticed in certain parts of the domestic market has been limited, to a large extent, to durable goods and has occurred only in the more prosperous regions. Given limited internal demand, the expansion of the global supply is sustained by export incentives through a privileged fiscal policy of export tax reduction. With regard to the industrial structure, the insufficiencies of large scale production, and technical and financial irrationalism have prevailed in most of the sectors, notably in the traditional sector. As long as barriers to the expansion of the domestic market and to the financial structure persist, this situation will not change, for these barriers have obstructed the development of the local sector in particular. In fact, the process of concentration into larger firms is even encouraged by government regulations. The document notes the contradictory character of the financial policy in so far as it is based, on the one hand, on a heavy overall taxation of the economy, and on the other, on preferential taxation rates for certain sectors so as to cope with cyclical problems. These problems range from the need to ensure the continuity of the production of a specific industrial sector, to the encouragement of regional or sectorial investments, to the resolution of financial problems in the production unit level, or to the stimulation of the capital market.

Showing concern with the social consequences of this economic policy, the MDB's diagnosis pointed out the unequal distribution of income and the aggravation of regional and sectoral disequilibria. It remarked that the country 'has been in a situation in which the bottom layer of the income pyramid has been widening' in terms of depressed real wages and the weakening of consumption capacity. The consequences have already been shown by the massive marginal population living in the large cities, in the poorer regions, and in particular rural areas even in the Centre–South region. Yet, the pattern of inequality is aggravated in the Northeast and in the rural areas where in addition to long rooted problems, others have emerged as a consequence of misdirected policies which were supposed to tackle the drastic situation in these areas.

In the final section of the MDB's document, the set of policies at the political and socio-economic levels defended by the party is presented. It can be summarized as follows:

the establishment of a democratic regime based on a representative system with elections for all political offices through universal, direct and secret suffrage;

autonomy for the legislative power and the re-establishment of parliamentary immunities;

autonomy for the judiciary with the re-establishment of constitutional safeguards for the magistrates, and the re-establishment of *habeas corpus*;

the defence of human rights, and consequently the condemnation of police repression, indiscriminate arrests and the practice of torture;

the freedom of press, expression, ideology, religion and organization;

revision of the federative principle so as to allow the strengthening of state and municipal autonomy.;

the repeal of the Institutional Act Number 5 and the other discretionary legislation decreed by the government;

general amnesty for all civilians and military officers purged after 1964;

the stabilization of domestic currency through: the revision of fiscal policy and the financial system; the improvement of the situation regarding the excessive public and private internal debt and foreign debt; the revision of the system of fiscal, regional and sectorial incentives; and the restructuring of the mechanisms for stimulating domestic savings;

an economic development policy which is directed to the correction of disequilibria, the increase of the efficiency index at the global and sectorial levels, the planning of investments, and a rational development of the primary, secondary and tertiary sectors;

raising the population's standard of living by increasing the real wages levels and consumption of basic goods;

the implementation of a land reform, including the abolition of the *latifundios* and *minifundios* which are non-economic forms of property; the establishment of cooperativism and social ownership; and the modernization and mechanization of agriculture;

a social policy for the labour sector by establishing: autonomy for trade-union organizations; job stability; individual and family wages increases in accordance with cost-of-living index; unemployment benefit; worker's participation in the profits and management of the enterprises; revision in the legislation about the right to strike and about work injury insurance;

the reformulation of the social welfare policy by increasing the efficiency of the national health system; raising the level of retirement pensions and by extending social benefits to all categories of workers;

the invigoration of local enterprises by improving the financial support to local enterprise and the rational protection of domestic production;

the reform of education: through the expansion of the education network and the literacy programme, the encouragement of technical and scientific development; freedom of teaching and autonomy for the universities;

a rational urban policy aiming at halting and decreasing concentration in the large populated areas, the elimination of slums and widening the opportunities for house ownership;

the reform of the administrative structure of the public sector in order to improve efficiency;

a foreign policy with a clear position regarding national independence, autonomy and security; and

the revision of the policy for development of the Northeast and the rational planning of a gradual settlement in the Amazon region as a means of defending Brazilian sovereignty over its territory.

Adding to this declaration of intent, the MDB programme stresses the party's nationalist principles which aim at: the nationalization and state monopoly over the prospection and production of all kinds of natural resources; local control of the production of energy, transportation, mining and infrastructural industries considered as a vital prioritary; state control over exports in economically and militarily strategic products, and over the commercialization of rubber; the exclusive right of navigation in coastal trade for Brazilian ships; the control and taxation of foreign profit outflows; the nationalization of foreign enterprises the activities of which are considered essential for economic development and national security; the policy of progressive replacement of foreign technology by domestic technology; the fight against the increasing participation of foreign capital in the economy; the fight against all forms of imperialism.

The MDB programme combined quite a wide range of issues emphasizing not only the defence of liberal democratic ideas, but also reformist policies to cope with the country's acute problems of social inequalities and development. It was also quite a nationalist view regarding economic development, in the implementation of which the state would play an important role. One can easily argue that the MDB programme was vague and sustained quite advanced positions for a party which was a broad opposition front, including a significant number of conservative politicians. Certainly its programme was no vaguer than is customary with party programmes in Brazil. On the other hand, the fact that the MDB was far from having chances of reaching power allowed it to assume the defence of principles and policies which if they were to be put into practice would certainly clash with the interest of several groups within the party.[31] In any case, if the MDB policies established in its programme had little possibility of implementation, at least they served as a guide for the party's opposition discourse and criticisms of the government's socio-economic policies.

3 Elections under the Two-Party System: Electoral Trends 1966–78

This chapter examines the main features of the performance of the MDB in the elections held during the period of the two-party system. The first section provides basic information about the electoral system under which elections were held. In the second the electoral data will be analysed in order to explain the main trends in the electoral process from 1966 to 1978.

THE BRAZILIAN ELECTORAL SYSTEM: PROPORTIONAL REPRESENTATION AND OTHER ELECTORAL REGULATIONS

In order to understand the influence of electoral regulations on the parties' electoral performance and therefore on political representation, two aspects deserve consideration. The first has to do with the nature of the regime under which the elections took place and refers to the restrictions imposed on electors' participation in the process. The second concerns the distorting character of the electoral system which actually is a legacy of the period prior to 1964.

Regarding the electors' exercise of their voting rights, during the period of military rule a process of increasing exclusion from participation in the electoral process took place.[1] First, after 1964, electors were prohibited from participating in the election of the President of the Republic, the appointment of which was made a formal prerogative of the Congress by the Institutional Act Number 2 of 1965 (AI-2). The establishment of 'indirect elections' for the Presidency was later incorporated into the 1967 and 1969 constitutions. These delegated the formal selection of the head of state to an electoral college composed of the members of the Congress and delegates of the State Assemblies. Needless to say the actual role of the electoral college was just to rubber-stamp previously appointed presidential successors chosen by the armed forces. Secondly, mayors of the city-capitals of the states and of cities considered 'areas of national security' or where hydromineral resources were located were appointed by the governor of their respective states.[2] Thirdly, after 1965, gubernatorial elections also ceased to be a voting right of the Brazilian electorate, becoming a prerogative of the State Assemblies which in fact merely had the power of ratifying candidates previously appointed by the central government.[3] Finally, the Constitutional Amendment Number 8 decreed by President Geisel in April 1977, also imposed 'indirect elections' for one-third of Senate seats. That amendment established that a third of the Senate – as well as state governors – were to be elected by an electoral college composed of the members of the State Assembly and delegates from the municipal councils.[4] With respect to the restrictions imposed by the military regime on the electoral process, the use of all kinds of intimidation against opposition candidates during electoral campaigns, particularly in the period from 1966 to 1973, and the establishment of the so called *Falcão Law (Lei Falcão)* which, introduced in 1976, considerably restricted the party's campaigning on radio and television, should also be mentioned. In addition to these restrictive measures, there were also the constraints under which parliamentarians exercised their functions, namely the constraints imposed by the Institutional Act Number 5 (AI–5) of 1968 which suppressed parliamentary immunities, placing elected representatives under permanent threat of being purged by the executive.

The liberalization of the regime after 1978, brought about the revocation of some of these restrictions. In 1979, the AI–5 ceased to be in effect and was replaced by less inflexible 'Safeguards of the State'; in 1980, direct elections for state governors were reestablished. The other restrictions were finally abolished after the inauguration of the civilian government in 1985. In any case, during the period with which we are dealing, elections were held only for the national, state and local legislatures, and for the municipal executive in those cities which were not state capitals, or areas of 'national security' and hydromineral resources.

The second aspect which deserves consideration is related to those aspects of the Brazilian electoral system which affect the representative character of the legislature. As we have said, these features were not a particular product of the regime established after 1964, since they had been in practice even during the 1945–64 democratic period. Firstly, only literate men and women over eighteen years old were enfranchised. This means that in Brazil, where the rate of illiteracy remains high, a significant part of the adult population was marginalized from the electoral process: in 1970 35 per cent of the population over 18 years old were illiterate, and taking the Northeast region alone, the rate of illiteracy represented about half adult population.[5] Although in the course of the 1970s, the illiteracy rate has decreased, in 1980 27 per cent of the country's adult population was still illiterate and, therefore, were not considered full citizens.[6] The franchise was finally extended to illiterates in 1985 with the return to civilian rule.

Although 65 per cent and 73 per cent of the adult population in 1970 and 1980 respectively, were entitled to vote, this proportion cannot be considered to be the proportion of the population who actually participated in the electoral process.[7] There remains a difference between the number of people enfranchised and the number of people who have got an electoral card (that is, the electorate) and, again, a difference with the number of people who actually participate in the elections. Nonetheless, the difference is not all that high: the Brazilian electorate represented 61 per cent of the adult population in 1970 and 69 per cent in 1978 – a difference of only 4 per cent with the percentages of the population who were enfranchised.[8] This is explained by the fact that in Brazil voting is compulsory.[9] The citizen's obligation to participate in elections certainly makes the rate of abstention lower than would be expected in a country which cannot be considered to have a highly politicized population. As can be seen from Table 3.1, the percentage of abstentions do not exceed 23 per cent. Although it is difficult to interpret the meaning of blank and spoiled (null) ballots, which must be due partly to deliberate protest action and partly to the voter's difficulty in filling out the ballot paper correctly, we can assert that the large number of, particularly, blank ballots were due to voters who possibly would have abstained from voting had participation in elections not been compulsory.

Second, the mechanisms of the electoral system itself which have contributed to distorting representation in the legislature, (in spite of the fact that the system of proportional representation has been adopted in Brazil) should be considered. Elections for the two national legislative houses – Senate and Federal Chamber – follow different procedures: the system of 'first past the post' is used in elections for the Senate while the system of proportional representation (PR) is used in elections for the Federal Chamber.[10] These different procedures and the fact that in elections for both houses the principle of representation by state is obeyed (that is, that constituencies

Table 3.1   Brazilian electorate, percentage of abstentions and blank and spoiled ballots

Year*	Electorate	Abstention (%)	Blank (%)		Null (%)
1960	15,543,332	19.0	2.8	(5.8)	3.0
1962	18,528,847	20.4		(14.1)	
1966	22,387,251	22.8	11.0	(16.3)	5.3
1970	28,966,114	22.5	16.2	(23.4)	7.2
1974	35,810,715	19.1	11.5	(17.2)	5.7
1978	45,962,601	18.1	10.9	(16.8)	5.9

* 1960 refers to the presidential elections. The other years refer to the elections for the Federal Chamber. The percentage in brackets are the ones grouping together blank and null ballots.
Source: Official data from the Electoral Tribunal (TSE).

coincide with state boundaries) have consequences for the electoral outcome, which will be discussed later. First, let us show how the system of proportional representation works.

The Brazilian PR system is based on electoral and party quotas in the distribution of seats among political parties, and on the 'highest average' system in the distribution of the remaining seats. The electoral quota is the result of the division of the number of valid votes (which include blank ballots) by the number of seats assigned to each constituency (that is, to each state in the federation). The party quota is determined by dividing the number of votes which each political party has obtained by electoral quota. The Electoral code also determines that unallocated remaining seats will be shared out *only* by those parties that filled the electoral quota, according to the following procedures: (a) the number of votes obtained by each party is divided by the number of seats which the party has obtained *plus one*, and the seat will be allocated to the party which has the highest average; (b) this operation will be repeated for the distribution of each of the remaining seats.[11]

The problem of this system is that it leads to a non-proportional result in so far as the seats which are allocated to parties are not necessarily proportional to the votes they have gained: there is a bias in favour of the larger parties and against the smaller. This is due to the fact that the smaller parties (those which have not reached the electoral quota) are excluded from the distribution of the remaining seats which are allocated by the 'highest average' method. This results in that the larger parties gain additional seats in spite of the fact that their average of votes per seat is lower than the number of votes received by the parties which have not gained any representation because they failed to reach the electoral quota.[12]

Nonetheless, the disproportionality of the Brazilian PR system is due less to this problem than to the criterion by which the seats are distributed among the States of the Federation. Since the principle of proportional representation is allegedly established, one might expect, taking as a criterion either the states' population or their electorate, that the number of representatives per state be proportional to the population or to the electorate. However, all the Brazilian constitutions since 1934 have established a great disproportionality in state representation in the Congress. With respect to the Senate, the federalist principle of equal representation for each state has prevailed, regardless of differences in population between states and apart from the fact that senators are elected by the plurality system. The system of proportional representation is thus used in the elections for the Federal Chamber, it being there where the principle of proportional representation per state is allegedly respected. However, the legislation on the representation of states has had a bias against the more densely populated states and in favour of the less populous. This is because the legislation establishes not only a minimum number of deputies per state, but also a limit beyond which the ratio of seats to inhabitants becomes higher. For example, the 1946 constitution established that each state would have one deputy for every 150000 inhabitants up to a maximum of twenty deputies; beyond this limit, the figure would be one for every 250000 inhabitants. It also established that no state could have less than seven deputies. Owing to this criterion, the state of São Paulo, which comprised 18 per cent of the Brazilian population, was allowed a 14 per cent share of the representation in the Federal Chamber in 1962. Minas Gerais State was also under-represented: comprising 14 per cent of the total population, the number of deputies from this state represented 12 per cent of the total number of seats on the Federal Chamber. On the other hand, the northern state of Acre which contained 0.2 per cent of the total population, had a 2 per cent share of the representation in that Chamber. The criteria for State representation have been altered several times since 1945, but the same bias against the more densely populated states – which are in fact the more urbanized and industrialized ones – continued to affect the representation of the states in the Federal Chamber.[13]

The disproportionate share of seats per state, in addition to the unequal proportion of the party's share of seats in the Federal Chamber as a consequence of the type of proportional representation system adopted in Brazil, means that party representation in Congress does not reflect the actual electoral support obtained by the political parties.

A final consideration must be made here, concerning the consequences of using different systems in the elections for the two National Chambers: the absolute majority system for the Senate and PR for the Federal Chamber. The use of these different systems has produced what could be considered peculiar results in the elections: in all legislative elections during the two-party experience (see Table 3.2 below), electoral support for the MDB was much larger in the election for the Senate than in the elections for the Federal Chamber and State Assemblies. Conversely, ARENA had a larger proportion of votes for the Federal Chamber and State Assemblies than for the Senate. In order to explain this we must firstly point out that according to the PR system used in Brazil the candidate's ranking in the party's list is not decided by the party. It is the electors who, by voting for an individual candidate, decide the candidate's ranking in the party's list. In other words, the number of votes obtained by each candidate determines the order in which he appears on the party's list.[14] If on the one hand this method has the advantage of giving the electors rather than the parties the right to choose the candidates who will gain the seats, it tends, on the other, to make the contest more individualized in terms of candidates competing with each other rather than a competition between political parties. Paul Singer, comparing the elections for the Federal Chamber based on the PR system, with the elections for the executive based on the majority system, suggested:

> It is quite true that the large number of candidates for the legislature, each one competing for votes on an individual or group basis, *depoliticizes* the election. The elector ends up voting for a candidate recommended by someone, who is generally, a canvasser (*cabo eleitoral*). In contrast, when the elector votes for the president (or for the governor of some important state), political questions strongly influence the decision of the elector who, in this case, does not resign himself to accept the orientation of the *cabo eleitoral*.[15]

In other words, the adoption of the PR by state constituency in the elections for the Federal Chamber and State Assemblies, making voters choose, one out of, in some cases, about 300 candidates, has the effect that the voter's choice is either casual due to a lack of information about the many candidates, or based on personal links with local political bosses whose clientelistic style remains a common device to capture votes. In elections to the Senate, in which only two or three candidates are contesting any seat, the voter's choice is more politically oriented; after 1964 when presidential and gubernatorial elections were prohibited, elections to the Senate became the most important. It is through their candidate for the Senate that the political parties carried out their electoral campaign, creating therefore a much closer identification between the candidate and the political issues defended by the party. For an electorate which has traditionally shown much more interest in the majority elections for executive rather than for legislative offices, the senatorial elections replaced, to a certain extent, the presidential and gubernatorial elections in importance. The voter may choose a candidate for deputy without considering his/her party (sometimes just to keep a promise to a political godfather, friend, or to exchange a favour). but in general the voter tends to take into account the parties' campaign platform in choosing a candidate for the Senate.

ELECTORAL TRENDS DURING THE TWO-PARTY SYSTEM, 1966–78[16]

An examination of the electoral data and surveys on electoral behaviour provides evidence of the existence of three major electoral trends during this period. First, the decline in the government party's electoral support and the strengthening of that of the opposition party, notably in the urban and industrialized areas of the country. This trend has emerged especially since the 1974 legislative elections. Second, the presence of a differentiation in socio-economic groups' party support, particularly evidenced by the strong electoral support for the MDB in the poorer districts of the large cities. Third, the emergence of a party identification among MDB voters.

The MDB and the Urban Vote

If we consider the total national votes in the legislative elections since 1966, it is clear that the government party has suffered a systematic decline.[17] In 1966 ARENA won 45 per cent of Senate votes; in 1970 this proportion fell slightly, it decreased to 35 per cent in 1974 and 1978 (see Table 3.2). A similar process has occurred in the case of elections for the Federal Chamber and State Assemblies. This was not, however, accompanied by a corresponding growth in support for the MDB. Having obtained 34 per cent of the votes for the Senate, 28 per cent for the Federal Chamber and 29 per cent for the State Assemblies in 1966, the MDB witnessed a sharp decline in its electoral base in 1970. This can be partly explained by the impressive number of blank and null (spoiled) ballot papers registered in the 1966 and 1970 elections. In 1970, the proportion of blank and null ballots reached 30 per cent in the elections for the Federal Chamber, overtaking the MDB's vote by 9 per cent. In 1974, however, the MDB's situation changed. The party triumphed over ARENA in the Senate, electing 16 senators out of 22 (see Table 3.3.), and although the MDB did not defeat ARENA in the elections to the Federal Chamber and State Assemblies, it did significantly increase its share of votes and seats. Table 3.3. shows the distribution of seats obtained by each party in elections from 1966 to 1978, and the percentages that these represent in terms of the total number of seats being contested. It is worth comparing the proportion of the party's representation with the proportion of the party's votes, presented in Table 3.2., so as to see the consequences of the electoral system on party representation in the legislature.

By analysing the electoral results for each region of the country the national tendencies become clearer. Table 3.4 shows – taking the election results for the Federal Chamber[18] – that even in those regions which can be considered the government's electoral strongholds, (North, Northeast and Centre-West regions), ARENA did not maintain the percentage of voter support which it had obtained in 1966. It is worth observing that in those regions, particularly the North and Northeast, where ARENA's proportion of votes reached over 60 per cent in 1966, a marked decline in its electoral support was experienced in 1970. This contrasts with the South and Southeast regions where ARENA suffered a sharp decline later, that is, in the 1974 elections. This earlier decline in ARENA's electoral support in the Northern regions is certainly related to the increase in the proportion of blank and null ballots between 1966 and 1970, in fact an increase much higher than that observed in the South and Southeast between 1966 to 1970.[19] It is also possible that

Table 3.2 National results for the legislative elections, 1966–78 (%)

Years	Senate				Federal Chamber				State Assemblies			
	ARENA	MDB	Blank & null	Total	ARENA	MDB	Blank & null	Total	ARENA	MDB	Blank & null	Total
1966	44.7	34.2	21.2	17,259,598	50.5	28.4	21.0	17,285,556	52.2	29.2	18.6	17,260,382
1970*	43.7	28.6	27.7	46,986,492	48.4	21.3	30.3	22,435,521	51.0	22.0	26.8	22,435,521
1974	34.7	50.0	15.1	28,981,110	40.9	37.8	21.3	28,981,015	42.1	38.8	18.9	28,922,618
1978	35.0	46.4	18.6	37,775,212	40.0	39.3	20.7	37,629,180	41.1	39.6	19.3	37,449,488

* In 1970 there was a renewal of two-thirds of the Senate. Thus the total is twice the number of voters.
Source: My own calculations based on official electoral figures from the Electoral Tribunal (TSE).

Table 3.3   Number and percentage of seats obtained by ARENA and the MDB
in the Senate and Federal Chamber, 1966–78

Years	Senate*				Federal Chamber			
	Seats		% Representation		Seats		% Representation	
	ARENA	MDB	ARENA	MDB	ARENA	MDB	ARENA	MDB
1966	18	4	81.8	18.2	277	132	67.7	32.2
1970	41	5	89.1	10.9	223	87	71.9	28.1
1974	6	16	27.3	72.7	204	160	56.0	44.0
1978	15	8	65.2	34.8	231	189	55.0	45.0

* The seats and percentage of representation refer just to those results from the elections in the specified year. As in the Senate the mandate lasts eight years and there are elections either for one-third or two-thirds of the seats, the number of seats presented in the table do not coincide with the actual total of seats in the Senate.
Source: Official electoral figures from the Electoral Tribunal (TSE).

specific factors related to localized electoral competition (for example a less active electoral campaign carried out by ARENA since its victory was overwhelmingly assured) must have influenced ARENA's loss of support in 1970. However, this is a supposition which would require specific research in these regions.

Aside from the observation that ARENA declined and the MDB grew stronger, the data for regions reveal that the MDBs electoral support increased notably in the South and Southeast, the most urbanized and industrialized regions of the country. More evidence for this assertion lies in the fact that the states of São Paulo, Rio de Janeiro (including the ex-state of Guanabara) and Rio Grande do Sul, which contained 42 per cent of Brazil's electorate in 1974, were responsible for 61 per cent of the total number of votes obtained by the MDB and only 33 per cent of ARENA's votes, in the 1974 elections for the Federal Chamber. Table 3.5 shows the evolution of results of elections to the Federal Chamber in those states. In the first election under the two-party system, the MDB defeated the ARENA in the ex-state of Guanabara, and in the states of Rio de Janeiro and Rio Grande do Sul, losing in São Paulo by a margin of only 5 per cent. In the ex-state of Guanabara, the MDB have always come out ahead of the ARENA in the subsequent elections; and in Rio de Janeiro and Rio Grande do Sul, the MDB was defeated by ARENA only in 1970, on account of the effect of blank and null votes. The initial strength of the MDB in those states can be attributed to the

Table 3.4   Election results for the Federal Chamber by region, 1966–78 (%)

Regions*	Years	ARENA	MDB	Blank and null	Total (100%)
North	1966	60.0	18.8	21.2	431,682
	1970	45.4	21.9	32.7	551,525
	1974	45.3	30.7	24.0	826,632
	1978	44.1	30.4	25.5	1,272,326
Northeast	1966	67.8	20.3	11.9	3,819,040
	1970	55.4	16.5	28.1	5,037,464
	1974	59.2	20.4	20.3	6,370,642
	1978	57.8	22.1	20.1	8,677,800
Centre-West	1966	54.0	27.6	18.4	675,094
	1970	49.9	22.4	27.7	913,841
	1974	50.3	27.9	21.8	1,284,454
	1978	46.2	34.2	19.6	1,819,817
Southeast	1966	40.8	31.7	27.5	8,977,985
	1970	44.4	21.4	34.2	11,389,252
	1974	32.8	44.4	22.8	14,638,221
	1978	29.7	47.9	22.4	18,662,465
South	1966	55.0	30.2	14.8	3,381,755
	1970	51.0	26.0	23.0	4,543,489
	1974	38.7	43.4	17.9	5,861,066
	1978	43.0	40.8	16.2	7,196,772

*   *North* region is composed of the states of Acre, Amazonas, Pará and the territories of Amapá, Roraima and Rondonia (the latter became a state on 1 January 1982).
   Northeast is composed of the states of Piaui, Maranhão, Ceará, Rio Grande do Norte, Paraiba, Pernambuco, Alagoas, Sergipe, Bahia and Territory of Fernando de Noronha.
   Centre-West is composed of Distrito Federal (Brasilia), Goiás, Mato Grosso, and Mato Grosso do Sul (the latter two states resulted from the division of the former state of Mato Grosso, in 1978).
   Southeast includes the states of Minas Gerais, Espirito Santo, Rio de Janeiro and São Paulo.
   South is composed of the states of Paraná, Santa Catarina and Rio Grande do Sul.
Source: My own calculations based on official data from the Electoral Tribunal (TSE).

organizational support derived from the remnants of the parties dissolved by the military in 1965. The affiliation to the MDB of politicians from the PTB (Brazilian Labour Party), much more significant in the states of ex-Guanabara, Rio de Janeiro and Rio

Grande do Sul,[20] certainly influenced these elections. This is particularly clear in the case of Rio Grande do Sul where the MDB counted on the support of the PTB which, in this state, was a strong political organization. By contrast, it is not the case in São Paulo where the position of the nationally dominant parties before 1964 was relatively weak.

Table 3.5   Election results for the Federal Chamber in four states, 1966–1978 (%)

States	Years	ARENA	MDB	Blank and null	Total (=100%)
Ex-Guanabara	1966	20.4	54.2	25.4	1,284,646
	1970	25.3	50.0	24.6	1,531,238
	1974	21.3	60.2	18.5	1,928,541
	1978*	–	–	–	–
Rio de Janeiro	1966	33.8	40.4	25.8	1,025,437
	1970	39.3	28.4	32.3	1,275,778
	1974	31.6	46.0	22.4	1,680,060
	1978	19.7	57.9	22.4	4,494,128
Rio Grande do Sul	1966	41.7	44.0	14.3	1,578,515
	1970	43.8	36.4	19.8	2,031,032
	1974	35.2	50.0	14.8	2,579,774
	1978	38.3	47.6	14.1	3,129,585
São Paulo	1966	34.7	30.0	35.4	4,079,811
	1970	48.6	16.7	34.6	5,400,903
	1974	28.5	48.0	23.5	7,117,868
	1978	25.6	51.6	22.8	9,095,452

* In 1978 the data for the ex-state of Guanabara is included in Rio de Janeiro state, since Guanabara was incorporated to the state of Rio de Janeiro in 1975.
Source: My own calculations based on official data from the Electoral Tribunal (TSE).

To assert that electoral support for the opposition party is particularly localized in the South and Southeast does not lead one to conclude that there simply exists a regional cleavage, upon which support for ARENA and the MDB is based. A cleavage certainly exists, but it is based on the level of urbanization – and possibly industrialization – which to a large extent influences voting behaviour. In other words, if the support for the MDB is more prominent in the South and Southeast given the fact that these are the most industrialized and urbanized regions of the country, it is also true that in the urbanized areas of the other regions the opposition has built a strong electoral base. Using the electoral results of the 1978 elections, we subdivided the regions according to the size of the population of their cities: (a) capitals of the states included in every region; (b) cities which 30 000 and more inhabitants, exclusive of the capitals; and (c) towns with a population under 30 000 inhabitants. We then calculated the proportion of votes obtained by the parties in each of the categories. The results which are shown in Table 3.6., provide remarkable evidence to demonstrate that the government party's strongholds are in towns of less than 30 000 inhabitants, which can largely be considered rural areas.[21] On the other hand, the opposition party has strong electoral support even in the urban areas of the North, Northeast and Centre-West. It is worth remarking that in these three regions, the MDB obtained a higher proportion of votes than ARENA in the two first categories – the capitals and cities over 30 000 inhabitants – in elections to the Senate and the Federal Chamber. One deviant case was registered in the results of the elections to the Federal Chamber in the Northeast within the category of over 30 000 inhabitants. As Fabio W. Reis properly remarked on this pattern of voting behaviour,

> The nucleus of nonconformity in the present Brazilian political picture is represented, above all, by the most dynamic and modern poles of Brazilian life. Those which correspond to the urbanized, industrialized and developing areas, in which a large contingent of the population is concentrated. Whereas, the patterns which have traditionally characterized the structure of our political life continue to operate in municipalities in the countryside and in the more backward regions, making them the major stronghold in which the mechanisms of propaganda and control at the regime's disposal have a possibility of working effectively.[22]

This pattern, which emerged during the experience of the two-party system, actually reproduces a tendency already in process under the multi-party system (1945–65). The weakening of the conservative parties, particularly the PSD and UDN, and the strengthening of the *trabalhistas* or reformist parties have been clearly demonstrated by Glaucio Soares at the national level, by Helgio Trindade for the state of Rio Grande do Sul and by Olavo B. Lima Jr for the case of Rio de Janeiro state.[23] As G. Soares argues, for the 1945–65 period, these trends were due, on the one hand, to the expansion of the organizational network of the reformist and

Table 3.6 Election results for the Senate and Federal Chamber, by region and according to three categories of city size, in percentage, 1978

	Senate (%)			Federal Chamber (%)				
Regions and city sizes	ARENA	MDB	Blank & null	ARENA	MDB	Blank & null	Total (=100%)	% Abstentions
North[a]								
State Capitals	29.3	46.3	24.4	29.8	40.8	29.4	499,513	21.5
Cities > 30 000 inhabitants[b]	29.9	43.9	26.2	33.2	43.2	23.6	39,693	32.5
Towns < 30 000 inhabitants	52.9	26.4	20.7	55.6	18.8	25.6	604,929	26.8
Northeast								
State Capitals	32.2	52.7	15.1	35.7	42.8	21.5	1,755,248	20.9
Cities > 30 000 inhabitants	39.9	45.2	14.9	46.6	30.2	23.2	1,088,778	26.1
Towns < 30 000 inhabitants	61.2	24.7	14.1	66.6	14.3	19.1	5,807,400	26.5
Centre-West								
State Capitals	39.7	46.7	13.6	36.1	45.2	18.7	311,729[d]	17.8
Cities > 30 000 inhabitants	34.5	49.0	16.5	36.6	42.0	21.4	157,992	28.7
Towns < 30 000 inhabitants	48.2	33.6	18.2	49.8	30.7	19.5	1,346,199[e]	28.0
Southeast								
State Capitals	16.6	61.5	21.9	17.8	61.8	20.4	6,392,180	11.6
Cities > 30 000 inhabitants	21.2	55.6	23.2	26.2	50.5	23.3	6,363,651	11.4
Towns < 30 000 inhabitants	34.8	42.0	23.2	46.5	29.9	23.6	5,887,013	16.9

South							
State Capitals	27.2	60.1	12.7	32.7	50.3	17.0	954,838	13.6
Cities > 30 000 inhabitants	32.3	55.7	12.0	37.1	47.4	15.5	1,806,169	16.5
Towns < 30 000 inhabitants	43.7	43.9	12.4	47.6	36.1	16.3	4,433,680	19.3
Total[c]							
State Capitals	21.9	58.5	19.6	23.6	55.7	20.7	9,913,508[f]	14.3
Cities > 30 000 inhabitants	25.7	54.3	20.0	30.9	47.3	21.8	9,456,283	14.8
Towns < 30 000 inhabitants	47.1	35.7	17.2	53.8	26.1	20.1	18,079,221[g]	22.0

Source: My own calculations based on official electoral data: (TSE). I would like to thank Celina R. Duarte who helped me to collect the data.

[a] It was not possible to include in the calculations for the Federal Chamber, the data for the three territories (Amapá, Roraima and Rondonia – the latter became state in 1982) which belong to the North Region. However their exclusion does not make significant difference since they together only represent about 7% of the electorate (1974) of this region. Each Territory has two representatives in the Federal Chamber, but they do not have representation in the Senate.

[b] This category excludes the capital-cities.

[c] Excluding the three territories mentioned in note a. Also, votes of people who, although living in Brasilia (DF) are allowed to participate in the federal legislative elections in their state of origin, were excluded.

[d] The total for the Senate is 368,007, because in the state of Mato Grosso (given the division of Mato Grosso in two states – Mato Grosso and Mato Grosso do Sul) two senatorial seats, rather than one, were in contest. Thus there was double vote in that state. In the second category (cities > 30 000 inhabitants) the total did not change since there is no other city of more than 30 000 inhabitants, apart from the capital.

[e] The total for the Senate is 1 563 619. See note d.

[f] The total for the Senate is 9 969 786. See note d.

[g] The total for the Senate is 18 296 621. See note d.

trabalhista parties – enabling them to penetrate the states and municipalities formerly dominated by the conservative parties – on the other, they reflected significant changes in the social structure as a result of urbanization and industrialization which increased the size of that part of the electorate more inclined to support reformist, populist and left-wing parties.[24] This process was interrupted by the dissolution of the multi-party system, but it is clear that the process of increasing urbanization and industrialization during the post-1964 period certainly reinforced that electoral trend. The MDB, created by *fiat* at the establishment of the two-party system, did not succeed (during the first years of its existence) in attracting the mass of electors inclined to vote for the opposition, owing to its lack of credibility as an opposition party. It was only by 1974 that the MDB was able to capitalize on the votes of the opposition-inclined masses, as well as those who withdrew their support from the ARENA and the government. For the party system created by the military government, the 1974 elections represented the political turning point. Ballots started to express general disapproval of the country's situation, assuming the much alluded to plebiscitarian character of 'yes' or 'no', that is, ARENA or MDB.

The MDB and its Social Base

The previous section attempted to illustrate the electoral experience of the two-party system, stressing above all the marked support for the MDB in the more urbanized and industrialized areas of the country. Nevertheless, to sustain the view that there are socio-economic cleavages which differentiate the electoral bases of the parties by using highly aggregated data in the analysis could be a risky generalization. Would it still prove true if we took into account more disaggregated units and a more precise set of socio-economic variables? On the other hand, if it can be verified that there has been a distinct base of support for the MDB, what does it consist of and what does it mean?

An affirmative answer for the first of these questions has been demonstrated through analysis of electoral data and surveys of electoral behaviour. Using a hierarchical classification of the districts of São Paulo city according to socio-economic criteria, Bolivar Lamounier examined the distribution of votes for ARENA and the MDB in the 1970, 1974 and 1978 elections.[25] Lamounier's results are of such importance that it is worthwhile reproducing his figures and summarizing his conclusions. Table 3.7 shows the ratios MDB to ARENA votes for each of the eight areas in which the city was divided. These areas were composed of districts which were grouped together according to a hierarchy based on living conditions and available basic urban services – for example, Area I is characterized as having the highest average income and as being best provided with basic urban services, and Area VIII the opposite.[26] As the Table 3.7 shows, for each of the elections in the three years, the lower the socio-economic conditions that characterize a given area, the likelier it was that electoral support would go to the MDB (all ratios increase from Area I to Area VIII). The Table also shows that this pattern had already taken shape before 1974. That is, even in the 1970 elections when the MDB was electorally weak, its votes came largely from the poorer districts. Another conclusion that Lamounier remarks on in his analysis concerns the voting pattern in the poor outlying districts of the city (namely Areas VII and VIII): the impressively high ratios in favour of the MDB in these areas with lower family average income are evidence for the emergence of what Lamounier called *voto de periferia*, that is, a distinct pattern of voting behaviour in the outlying districts of large cities.[27]

Table 3.7 Ratios MDB/ARENA for the eight areas of São Paulo city, elections for the Senate and Federal Chamber, 1970–8

	Senate			Federal Chamber		
Areas	*1970*	*1974*	*1978*	*1970*	*1974*	*1978*
I	0.74	1.88	3.99	0.29	1.20	1.93
II	0.85	2.33	4.78	0.34	1.47	2.24
III	0.89	2.71	5.14	0.35	1.67	2.41
IV	0.92	3.03	5.58	0.36	1.97	2.55
V	1.05	3.48	6.77	0.39	2.22	3.14
VI	1.40	5.78	9.36	0.52	3.76	4.14
VII	1.55	5.82	10.27	0.54	3.83	4.63
VIII	1.85	7.15	12.39	0.64	4.94	5.99

Source: B. Lamounier, 'O Voto em São Paulo, 1970–1978', in B. Lamounier (ed.) *Voto de Desconfiança*, p. 29.

A linear correlation is not always very clear in examinations of the relationship between an individual socio-economic position and his/her party preference. Surveys of electoral behaviour carried out in the cities of Belo Horizonte and São Paulo in 1974, and in Juiz de Fora in 1976, found a consistent correlation between party preference and socio-economic variables such as education, income and occupation. That is, people who have lower levels of schooling, lower incomes and lower occupational levels were those who were more inclined to support the MDB.[28] However, the electoral surveys carried out in the cities of Presidente Prudente and Niteroi in 1976, and in São Paulo in 1978 verified that this negative correlation between MDB preference and lower socio-economic position was not so clear and linear in these case-studies.[29] As Lamounier observed of the social basis of party preference in the case-study of São Paulo in 1978:

> people of *extremely* low socio-economic levels are not necessarily the most *emedebistas* (MDB sympathizers); and there is not a linear and consistent association between the distribution of party preferences and the usual indicators of socio-economic position (occupation, income and education). A situation of massive electoral realignment as it occurred in São Paulo between 1970 and 1974 puts in operation powerful homogenizing tendencies in electoral behaviour.[30]

However we can still assert that the majority of wage earners are more inclined to support the MDB than ARENA. This assertion finds ground in the results produced by the same survey carried out by Lamounier in 1978. Table 3.8., reproducing some figures from Lamounier's work, reveals that 84.1 per cent of the workers who declared their party preference, support the MDB, whereas only 15.9 per cent of them supported ARENA. And 82.5 per cent of the middle occupational category ranking from manual unskilled workers to lower non-manual workers stated their preference for the MDB.[31]

The MDB and Party Identification

These considerations raise another question: how can we explain that an opposition party which in its activities was subjected to the 'reins' of the regime, achieved a solid popular base and gained considerable stability?

Table 3.8   Party preference according to levels of education and occupation, São Paulo city, 1978 (%)

Education	MDB	ARENA	(N)
Illiterate	64.2	35.8	53
Primary schooling	76.0	24.0	221
Secondary schooling	81.0	19.0	143
High schooling	78.0	22.0	91
Under-graduate and graduate schooling	81.7	18.3	71
Occupational position			
Biscateiros (informal sector)	57.1	42.9	7
Employee	84.1	15.9	289
Self-employed	74.2	25.8	62
Employer	52.2	47.8	23
Jobless (including students and housewives)	71.4	28.4	189
Occupational ranking			
Low (servants, irregular jobs, street traders)	68.0	32.0	28
Middle (from unskilled manual workers to low non-manual employees)	82.5	17.5	320
High (management, administrative business, teaching)	69.6	30.4	46

Source: B. Lamounier, 'O voto em São Paulo, 1970–1978', in B. Lamounier (ed.), *Voto de Desconfiança*, p. 56.

The most common explanation for this phenomenon has been to point out the fact that the MDB had become a channel of protest against the deprived economic and political situation which the military regime aggravated and reinforced. Nevertheless, research on electoral behaviour has shown that this is only a partial explanation. Actually, a party identification among the MDB voters had been created, derived from an image of the MDB as the party of the *povo*, the poor people. In a case-study of an outlying district of São Paulo city during the period of the electoral campaign in 1978, Teresa Caldeira observed the presence of an MDB party identification which precedes and partially conditions the voters' choice of certain candidates. Furthermore, the fact that 26 per cent of the votes obtained by the MDB in that district were cast for the party label, rather than for specific candidates of the party, is indicative of the appeal that the initials MDB had.[32] Studies based on survey analysis have also reached similar conclusions. They have pointed out that, to a large extent, the support given to the MDB has resulted from an identification which is actually partisan. However, the meaning of this identification is not associated with informed opinions regarding the economic and political situation of the country. With the exception of those who possess higher education and more political information, for most of the MDB sympathizers to support the MDB means to be on the side of those who have suffered from a political and economic system, the characteristics of which they cannot clearly express.[33] Referring to the opinions of people who were interviewed in the surveys carried out in São Paulo in 1974 and 1978, Lamounier concludes:

It has been observed that the MDB followers are predominantly the *underdogs*: the least educated people, the wage earners of low income, those who work in manual occupations, and so on. More emphatically nonetheless, one can assert that the *emedebistas* are those who attributed to the MDB an *image* of the party of the poor people (*povo*), against the ARENA which is defined as the party of the elite, of the rich, of the government. The MDB is the party which tries to defend the weakest people and, because of that, it is also the weakest party, which is involved in an unequal struggle with a greater power. This power is the government, is the rich, those who do not want reform. In these images – one must remark – categories of class connotation such as *povo* (popular people) and *pobres* (the poor), are combined with categories of specific political connotation. Political images sometimes allude diffusely to a distant government which is opposed to the 'popular people', sometimes refer explicitly to the suppression of direct elections. In any of the cases, one realizes, without any difficulty, a dissatisfaction resulted from the techniques used by the military government in order to suppress 'populism'. These techniques consisted, on the one hand, in prohibiting direct elections for the main executive offices and, on the other hand, in a calculated distance which intended to stress the impersonal character of the government assumed directly by the Armed Forces.[34]

From the analysis developed in this chapter, based on electoral data and results of surveys of electoral behaviour during the two-party experience, one can assert that the MDB, in spite of the fact that it was artificially created, was transformed over time into a party which could claim some legitimacy as a genuine opposition party. It is also important to remark that between 1966 and 1978 the Brazilian electorate increased by 51 per cent (see Table 3.1.). This means that more than half of the electorate have never known parties other than ARENA and the MDB. This would certainly help the MDB to consolidate itself as a party after the political party reform which took place with the dissolution of the two-party system in 1979. The second part of this book will examine the role of the MDB itself in the process that led to it becoming a *de facto* opposition party. We will therefore focus on the MDB's performance in national politics during the military-authoritarian regime.

Part II
The MDB in the Brazilian Political System

INTRODUCTION

The second part of this book will deal with the dynamics of the political process between 1966 and 1979, focusing on the relationship between the MDB and the governments of the 'revolution'. We will analyse the MDB's conduct during the different phases of the regime and evaluate the role played by the party in the political system since 1966.

An examination of the MDB's behaviour necessarily requires clarification as to the nature of the political party in question. In this respect, two factors which help clarify the MDB's role and behaviour should be pointed out. Obviously, the first one has to do with the military-authoritarian character of the regime in which the MDB operates. It is important to remember that it was the architects of the regime who allowed the creation of a legal opposition party. This being the case, it was not the MDB but the government which defined the space for political action granted to the party.

The second factor constraining the MDB's behaviour is related to its character as a broad front or coalition. Although the MDB could be considered a political party in the sense that it had a formal organization and structure,[1] it was primarily an opposition front. Given that the regime's architects established a two-party system, one of which was to represent the opposition, the MDB gathered diversified political forces together under its umbrella. As has been discussed in Chapter 2, the MDB was composed of politicians who shared little more than the will to re-establish a democratic regime in the country, not to mention those who simply wanted to guarantee their political survival by having a seat in Congress. Therefore we are dealing with an opposition party which was primarily a front, comprising political forces of different colours and even divergent ways of conceiving party politics. Furthermore we shall look at a party which was born and developed under a political system controlled by the military whose proclaimed legitimacy lies in the 'revolutionary

77

power' of the so-called 1964 revolution. Given these conditions it is obvious that an evaluation of the MDB's behaviour cannot be based on an ideal-type of political party in opposition within a competitive political system. Although this assertion seems redundant since we are referring to a military-authoritarian regime, it is worth emphasizing it here in light of a common posture which permeates comments on and analyses of the MDB. Most of them have criticized the MDB's behaviour from the perspective of what they consider to be the ideal role that an opposition party should play. In trying to avoid this posture, one should assume that, given the constraints placed on the MDB, the decision taken and the directions followed by the party could not have been very different. More relevant than pointing out what the party should have done is to show and explain what the MDB did accomplish, taking into account the intervening factors referred to here and the circumstances of a specific political conjuncture.

The second aspect that we would like to discuss in this introduction concerns the line of argument that will be adopted in the following chapters. As we have already mentioned, the examination of the MDB's conduct will trace the different phases of the military-authoritarian regime. By discussing some of the events in which the MDB was involved, we will weigh the role played by the opposition party in a given political conjuncture. Certainly, the role played by the MDB was to have an impact on the political system in so far as the conduct of the party could threaten to surpass the limits circumscribed by the regime. These limits, however, were not laid down on a definite basis but varied in accordance with the pendular opening and closing movements of the Brazilian military regime. Thus we can identify the development of two inter-related processes affecting the political system. On one hand, there was the conflictual process of establishing the new regime that ended up by consolidating the military in power. On the other hand, there was a process undergone by the opposition party that – although subordinate to the former process – had an effect on it.

The regime established after 1964, that resulted in twenty-one years of military rule in Brazil, is characterized by a process of conflict, the dynamic of which does not allow us to define the regime in a static way. As has been mentioned in Chapter 1, although one can more readily accept that the political forces which came to power in 1964 had an economic project, it is not so easy to assess whether they had a clear political project on the lines of establishing a semi-permanent authoritarian regime. On the political level, the only agreement that existed among the different protagonists of the 1964 coup lay in the defence of a constitutional order seen as threatened by communist subversion, corruption and the economic disorder which was embodied in Goulart's government. It must be mentioned that none of the military Presidents since 1964 have, in their rhetoric, excluded the aim of returning to democracy;[2] even General Medici who came into power at a time the regime was undergoing its most closed and repressive phase. Whatever meaning was given to the promises expressed, the fact is that the rhetoric of democratization used by the regime was to produce effects in the political process affecting the political action of the opposition, particularly the MDB.

Marcus Figueiredo in his study on political coercion during the post–1964 period identifies three political cycles which the 1964 revolution has gone through.[3] Each of these cycles starts with a repressive and authoritarian wave. It is followed by a period of political decompression which then leads to a political crisis produced by conflict among factions of the Revolution and between these and the opposition. This crisis consequently leads to a new wave of repression and authoritarianism. Three Institutional Acts decreed in the name of the revolution marked the initiation of each cycle: the first, the Institutional Act which later was called 'Number 1', was decreed by the Supreme Command of the Revolution in April 1964; the second, the Institutional Act Number 2 was issued by the Castelo Branco government in October 1965 after a politico-military crisis; and the third, the Institutional Act Number 5, was decreed by the Costa e Silva government in December 1968, after the 1968 political and military crisis. Marcus Figueiredo points out that these cycles were the natural result of a conflicting process which involved internal and external forces of the 1964 Movement. The group which controlled the state apparatus would confront pressures not only from the opposition which was sidelined by the coup, but also from factions fighting for control of the revolutionary process. Also according to Figueiredo, the outcome of this conflicting process was the isolation and consolidation in power of the military elite.

Since M. Figueiredo's analysis does not cover the period after 1977, his conclusions certainly would need some alteration in light of the developments of the political opening undertaken by the military. Thus just as the Brazilian military was able to consolidate itself in power by the end of Medici's government, it was also the

military that formulated the policy of controlled political liberalization. And, in the course of this process of controlled liberalization
which began with the inauguration of the Geisel government in
1974, another crisis within the system emerged leading to another
clamp down although on a lesser scale than the previous ones. This
happened in 1977 when, after the opposition refused to support the
executive's Bill on Judicial Reform, Geisel imposed a temporary
recess on Congress and decreed a set of restrictive measures, the so
called *April Package.* The policy of controlled political relaxation,
however, was resumed from 1978 onwards with some liberalizing
measures implemented during the last year of General Geisel's
government. This policy continued under the next military government headed by General Figueiredo who would be the last general-
president of the period initiated in 1964.

In any case, the remarks made by Marcus Figueiredo provide
support for the points we wish to emphasize regarding the situation
in which the MDB would operate. The fact that the Brazilian
military-authoritarian regime was not established on the 1 April
1964, but was a contradictory process of repression and relaxation,
affected the way in which the legal opposition conducted itself. In
other words, every sign of political relaxation made by the government, whether simply rhetorical or not, created a wave of optimism
and hope among the opposition forcing it to make a difficult choice:
either behave quietly and moderately in order not to 'frighten the
lion' and not to give a reason for halting the political opening; or
assume a more active role taking advantage of the enlarged space of
the relaxation, thus trying to pressure the government to move
further in the direction of democratization. This dilemma, with
which the MDB was faced and which permeated the party's internal
divisions will be seen in the analysis of the period.

Our analysis of the MDB's conduct between 1966 and 1979 is
divided into four periods. The first (Chapter 4), starts at the beginning of the MDB's parliamentary activities in 1966 and ends when
the government decreed the Institutional Act Number 5 in 1968 and
put Congress into forced recess. The second period (Chapter 5)
includes the events following the decreeing of the AI-5, the period of
Medici's government and ends with the 'election' of General Geisel
in January 1974. The third period (Chapter 6) starts with Geisel's
policy of political relaxation – the significant event in this process
was the 1974 legislative election – and ends with the 1977 break in
the process of relaxation when Geisel put Congress into forced

recess and decreed a set of political measures intended to limit the opposition's chances of electoral success. The fourth and final period, from 1977 to 1979, includes the events following the decreeing of the 1977 April Package, the liberalizing political reforms implemented during Geisel's last year in power (Chapter 7) and finally the dissolution of the two-party system (Chapter 8). In an attempt to develop a more analytical approach rather than merely describe a sequence of events in which the MDB was involved, some important events for each period, will be discussed. This will help understand the way in which the MDB defined and implemented its strategies and how it coped with the several altered situations which emerged in the political process. In the introduction to each chapter, the main features of the political scene will be discussed thus illustrating the major changes undergone by the regime.

4 1966–8: Searching for Identity

As recounted in Chapter 1, the MDB started operating as a legal opposition party in early 1966, the fourth and final year of the legislature of parliamentarians elected in 1962. To get used to the new party framework under which the parliamentarians had to carry on their political activity was the MDB's main problem. This would affect the party's performance in its first year of existence, as we will show in the first section of this chapter where some events in which the MDB was engaged are examined. In 1967 a new legislature composed of parliamentarians elected for the first time on ARENA and the MDB tickets, was inaugurated. This legislative period up to the decreeing of the Institutional Act Number 5 in 1968 is also discussed in this chapter. Its second section will therefore focus in detail a particular event in which the MDB was involved, and that was the apparent cause of the political and military crisis of 1968: the Marcio Moreira Alves episode.

LEARNING TO PERFORM AS AN OPPOSITION: THE YEAR 1966

The Presidential Succession Issue

As established by the Institutional Act Number 2, the next President of the Republic was to be elected by Congress on 3 October 1966. At the beginning of 1966 there was already no doubt that the Minister of War, General Costa e Silva, was to replace Castelo Branco in the presidency, despite President Castelo Branco's wishes. In fact Castelo Branco, who favoured the idea of choosing himself a civilian or a military officer from his group in the armed forces, had been thwarted in his attempt to do so. The candidacy of Costa e Silva was imposed on President Castelo Branco as a consequence of the October 1965 military crisis.[1] The Minister of War had played a crucial role in the government's negotiations to secure a compromise with the rebel hard-line officers. By playing the role of mediator between the military group in power and the radical officers who had rebelled, Costa e Silva emerged from the crisis in a position strong enough to demand his nomination to the high command of the country and still retained the support of the radical group within the armed forces. Although Costa e Silva had guaranteed his position as the only general who could ensure military unity, his candidacy was not easily accepted by the different factions of the revolution. His selection as the government's official candidate provoked discontent among other aspirants to the office – generals and civilians.

It was against this background that the MDB was to define its strategy. Three tendencies soon emerged inside the party. The first favoured the nomination of a party candidate to run against Costa e Silva in the indirect election. Some of the advocates of this position felt the party should present a civilian candidate to oppose the government's military candidate, thus stressing the party's opposition to the military continuing in government. A larger number of those who supported the nomination of a candidate were nonetheless in favour of it being a military officer. The argument was that the party should take advantage of the discontent created among those who saw their aspirations frustrated by the irrevocable choice of Costa e Silva. By choosing as candidate one of the generals who had had his ambitions thwarted, it was hoped to bring about a split within the military, the consequences of which might possibly benefit the opposition. Some beginnings were made in this direction by MDB politicians who made contact with potential candidates and even tried to promote, through the press, the MDB's intention to select as its candidate either General Amaury Kruel, Marshal Cordeiro de Farias or General Mourão Filho. The attempts to attract one of these high ranking military officers to the opposition's side were in fact not very successful. Although they had complained of the choice of Costa e Silva, both General Mourão Filho and Marshall Cordeiro de Farias (the latter was in fact Minister of Interior), had been actively involved with the revolution. Thus they preferred to protest silently rather than to serve as candidate of the adversaries of the revolution. The only general who went further in opposing the government's decision on presidential succession was Amaury Kruel – São Paulo's army commander – who not only tried to reach some form of agreement with the opposition, but also launched a manifesto against the government. He was eventually dismissed from his post and isolated within the army.[2]

The second tendency formed inside the MDB advocated support for the candidacy of General Costa e Silva. The few who were in favour of voting for the Minister of War argued that he represented opposition to the government since he was not Castelo Branco's candidate but the one that the President was forced to accept. Therefore support for Costa e Silva might open the possibility of the creation of a national front pressing for democratization. This tendency nevertheless had little support among MDB members, although its advocate – Deputy Anisio Rocha[3] – did not abandon his intention to support Costa e Silva, being the only MDB congressman who did not obey the party's position and voted for the government candidate when elections took place in Congress.

The third tendency, which was later officially adopted by the party, advocated the MDB's abstention from voting in the election as a means of protesting against the way in which the new President was to be appointed. This line, according to its supporters, was the only coherent strategy, since direct elections for the Presidency were one of the main issues advocated in the party programme.

The disagreement on the line to adopt led to the party's postponing the decision taken officially only two months before the election. Although the MDB national executive committee had opted for abstention in a meeting in June, the national convention, where this position was officially adopted, took place only in August. By that time, no alternative was actually left to the party other than abstention, since in July the government decreed the Complementary Act Number 16 which prohibited 'crossing the floor' vote in the indirect elections in which the voting procedure would also be by open ballot. Thus the parliamentarians were either obliged to follow the parties' official line or suffer expulsion from their parties or even cancellation of their mandates. This mechanism, introduced in order to prevent dissension within the government party, eliminated any possibility of the opposition participating in the contest with a candidate of its own. It is worth mentioning that, actually this decree establishing party discipline was aimed particularly at solving problems which the government faced in some states over the gubernatorial indirect elections. Similarly in the case of the presidential succession, the governors in the states where elections were to be held in that year, were to be chosen by the State Assemblies. The fact that government candidates were appointed by the central government, more precisely by Castelo Branco, aroused discontent among sectors of ARENA in some states. In Rio Grande do Sul, for example, this provoked dissension among ARENA's politicians which the MDB was able to use to its advantage. The opposition tried to promote the candidacy of Cirne Lima, whose aspiration to office had been thwarted by the government, receiving a great deal of support from ARENA's deputies. Obviously this calculated move by the MDB failed. The government thwarted it, not only by establishing party discipline but also by purging the MDB with the cancellation of the mandate of some of its state deputies. This was aimed at enlarging ARENA's narrow majority, which was of only one deputy in the Rio Grande do Sul Assembly.

On 3 October 1966, Costa e Silva was elected President of the Republic in a quiet Congressional session. As expected, all the ARENA parliamentarians voted for the general, and the MDB abstained, with the exception of one deputy who voted for the government candidate. Apart from the symbolic protest of the MDB Deputy João Herculino who attended the Congressional session wearing black from head to foot in 'mourning for the death of democracy' in the country, the opposition party avoided any radical move which might have contributed to disturbing the normal climate during the meeting. The speech made by the MDB leader was moderate. He explained the position taken by the party, stressing the illegitimacy of the electoral process which had chosen the President of the Republic, and went on to restate the main issues advocated by the party in favour of the reestablishment of democracy. In fact, the cautious speech of the opposition leader reflected the climate of hope brought about by the prospect of a new government. A majority of politicians from both parties believed that the inauguration of a new presidential period would represent a definite step towards the democratic normalization of political life. The MDB's moderate behaviour showing that it did not wish to provoke the government, and also the speech of the Congress chairman, Senator Moura Andrade, advocating the fulfilment of the Revolution's commitment to democratization, were significant indication of the climate of optimism that marked the event.

The MDB's conduct with regard to the presidential succession issue clearly showed the party's difficulties in formulating an elaborate strategy to be followed by its representatives. On the one hand, the political action of the MDB depended on the regime's moves towards liberalization, which placed the party in the dilemma of how far it should go in its role as opposition in order to avoid creating any excuse for retrogression. This accounted for its indecisiveness. For most of the time the MDB would end up assuming strategies dictated by events that had taken place. This happened with the issue of presidential succession, when abstention proved to be the only alternative left to the party, once the government had decreed party discipline and isolated potential military candidates. The opposition's difficulty in following a clear line was also highlighted when the MDB adopted a policy of obstructing the progress of legislative work in the Federal Chamber.

The MDB's Obstructionist Movement

On 23 August 1966, the leader of the opposition in the Federal Chamber made a speech in which he announced the MDB's decision to use the mechanism of obstruction in every proceeding on the parliamentary agenda 'until the government decided to offer real guarantees for the opposition regarding participation in the next legislative elections'.[4] The opposition was protesting particularly against the recent government decree – Complementary Act Number 20 – which had re-established the individual ballot paper for the direct elections of 15 November, considered to be regressive in terms of electoral legislation.[5] The vehement speech, in which the party explained their decision to obstruct every bill gave the impression that the opposition had decided to take a radical line which demanded nothing less than everything. The manifesto stressed that, within the framework of legality this was the only valid instrument for the restoration of democracy, and the MDB refused to be a political organization whose role was merely to disguise a dictatorship. It went on to say:

> When trade unions are closed or silenced; when Brazilian youth is forced to seek protection in the temples, re-editing events of the Middle Age; when even the Church feels threatened if it does not bless the existing powers; when the Brazilian working class is reduced to virtual serfdom ... when government relies on submissive parliamentary majority, making the Parliament into a rubber-stamp chamber which justifies arbitratary rule and conceals the fact of dictatorship, the MDB believes that its only recourse, at this moment, is to make Parliament a great amphitheatre for denouncing the sham of democracy. Using it in the normal way would mean accepting the abnormal; carrying on

with normal legislative routine, would mean agreeing with sub-
mission . . . Instead we will vigorously use the chair as a trench.
Nevertheless, at the time of voting, we shall be absent. We refuse
to rubber-stamp the farce into which the Brazilian legislative
process has been transformed, wherein Congress works and
produces bills, only to be ignored by the President of the Republic
who instead decrees Institutional Acts, Complementary Acts and
Decree-Laws.[6]

The manifesto nonetheless pointed out the MDB's readiness to
partake in a 'constructive dialogue' as soon as the government
provided 'minimum conditions for democratic tolerance'.

In spite of the radical tone of the manifesto, the MDB's policy of
obstruction did not provoke any impact, even though the opposition
continued to absent itself from voting on any bill in the Federal
Chamber for almost a month. The failure of the MDB's move was
due, first of all, to a disagreement within the party about that
decision. Those who were against it complained that it had been
taken on the basis of a small majority in a caucus meeting attended
by the minimum number of deputies required. Moreover, in the
same parliamentary session in which the party's policy of obstruction was announced, one of the MDB deputies reached the tribune
to declare himself in opposition to the obstruction of every bill and
to affirm his intention of submitting a petition against that decision
to the party's national executive committee. Moreover the obstructionist movement did not have the support of the MDB's representatives in the Senate, the MDB leader of which made public that this
policy would not be followed by the MDB Senators. Even the party's
national president was opposed to total obstruction of the
parliamentary agenda. It is worth mentioning that the obstructionist
movement was originally proposed by Deputy Amaral Neto, a politician belonging to the Lacerda group and who joined the MDB after
Lacerda's breaking with Castelo Branco. Interestingly the deputy
who had proposed radicalization, later left the MDB and joined the
government party in June 1967.[7]

The disagreement within the opposition party over the policy of
obstruction therefore caused the movement to be ineffective and to
die slowly without its even having been terminated by a party
decision. On the other hand, the obstruction movement did not
provoke the impact on public opinion which its promoters had

hoped. The main objective of the protest had been to create a favourable attitude towards the MDB among the electorate, by trying to
show a clear difference between ARENA and the MDB aimed at the
legislative elections which were to take place in November. In fact
the MDB's protest passed unnoticed by the population, and the
small amount of space given to the episode by the press, was used
more to show the MDB's internal dissension over the decision rather
than the opposition's protest and its objectives. The newpaper *Jornal
da Tarde*, for example, commented in its editorial that the dissension
within the MDB caused by the decision to obstruct the work of the
legislature showed clearly the natural divisions of 'a heterogenous
and artificial party'.[8]

The comments in the press about the MDB's performance during
that half year of the party's existence – even by journalists sympathetic to the party – all stressed the MDB's inability to provide
opportune answers to political events, being evasive as a consequence of its 'permanent perplexity' in reacting to government
policies and in supporting protests when they occurred in society.[9]
This 'permanent perplexity' attributed to the MDB, reflected in fact
the short period of existence of the party, which had not then created
a minimum basis for internal consensus to readjust the diverse
groups within the party to a new political and party reality. It must be
remembered that the old party labels were still very much present,
and inside the MDB the dissensions particularly between the ex-
PTB (the Labour Party) and the ex-PSD (the Social Democratic
Party) contributed significantly to the party's paralysis. On the other
hand, very little could be expected from the MDB in terms of active
opposition during that period: the party had been created by
parliamentarians who had escaped from the 'revolutionary' purges,
thus it actually had few politicians who really were opposed to the
1964 movement; not to mention the fact that any audacious move
meant risking the loss of their mandates. The MDB's indecisiveness
was also the product of uncertainty over the party's future. Indicative
of this was the fact that even the party's president Oscar Passos, suggested in June 1966 the self-dissolution of the MDB, considering that
the conditions for the party to contest the next legislative elections
which were to take place in November did not exist. We should point
out that the theme of self-dissolution would surface on every
occasion when the MDB's freedom was restricted by the many and
successive decrees issued by the military. Nevertheless this proposi-
tion has never had more than verbal support, since to take this

decision would mean the end of the political career of people who by no means wanted to lose their seat in Congress. The Complementary Act Number 17 decreed by Castelo Branco in July 1966 provided for the automatic suspension of political rights for a period of ten years of any parliamentarian who might resign due to the party's self-dissolution. Furthermore, those who regarded the MDB as having a function considered that to keep the MDB alive would mean to keep at least the narrow space left to opposition activities open for as long as possible and thus nourish opposition sentiments against the regime.

The October Protest in the Federal Chamber

The third event that is worth discussing here is the crisis between the legislature and the executive that arose following the purge of six MDB deputies. The main protagonist of this protest was in fact the president of the Federal Chamber the ARENA Deputy Adauto Lucio Cardoso, who in a rebellious gesture against the measure taken by Castelo Branco, provoked a crisis which led to the police intervening to close down Congress.

Rumours that a new list of purges was meant to be implemented during the period of the electoral campaign, had been revealed in early October. The government intended to prohibit some opposition deputies 'disliked' by the Revolution from standing for re-election. Thus on 12 October 1966 Castelo Branco used the powers granted by the Institutional Act Number 2 to cancel the elected mandates and political rights of six MDB deputies, including one of the opposition's deputy-leaders, Deputy Doutel de Andrade. The Federal Chamber's president who was responsible for implementing the government's decision, refused to do so. Instead, he let the purged deputies remain in the House and continue to exercise their rights as deputy under his protection until such time as the House's plenary passed judgement on the legality of the Executive's action. This rebellious attitude by the president of the Federal Chamber was caused by his personal indignation towards Castelo Branco who had assured him that no more purges would be made in that House, a promise that the deputy had confidently restated in the press. Furthermore, Deputy Cardoso's support for the punished opposition deputies reflected his dissatisfaction with the path taken by the 1964 revolution. Cardoso, like other liberal ex-UDN politicians who had actively participated in the 1964 coup, had begun to assume a

more independent attitude in relation to the government, trying to
stress the legislature's authority and believing that the revolution
would not have valid future if it did not proceed towards the re-
establishment of democracy. Deputy Cardoso was however disregarding a government measure taken in the name of the
'revolutionary power' of the 1964 movement embodied in the
Institutional Act. In so doing, and although he justified his action on
the basis that that Revolution had been diverted from its legitimate
purposes, his attitude implied denying the legality of the
Institutional Act and hence the revolution. Cardoso's protest which
was also supported by the Senate's president – Senator Moura
Andrade – resulted in a crisis involving the legislature and the
executive. Under the orders of the Federal Chamber's president, the
House was kept in permanent session, attended by the six punished
deputies, the majority of the MDB representatives and a few from
ARENA. Most of the ARENA deputies preferred to stay on the
government's side and thus chose not to attend the sessions. Deputy
Cardoso did not show any sign of relenting and remained determined to have that government decision judged by the House's
plenary. Attempts were made by the ARENA leadership to convince
Cardoso to give up his protest, on the grounds that the legitimacy of
a 'revolutionary act' could only be judged by the revolution. As this
was the logic of the revolution, the upshot was to come soon. It came
in the early morning of 20 October when Congress was surrounded
by military troops empowered to remove the parliamentarians from
the House and put Congress in forced recess. As the Deputy Mario
Piva, vice-leader of the MDB, narrated after the events:

> it was precisely 4.55a.m. on 20 October 1966 ... At that moment,
> assembled at the office of this House's president we had been
> quietly analyzing all the facts and news of which we had become
> aware. Suddenly, surprisingly the lights went off, the telephone
> lines were cut and there was no water in the House. The House's
> president asked a civil servant to turn on our own generator. It
> was not possible, because it was already surrounded by military
> troops. Then, somebody suggested we try mediation with the
> notable Deputy Pedro Aleixo (future vice-president of the
> Republic), in order to get us officially informed about what was
> happening. Well, in the House's exit in the car-parking, jeeps
> fitted with machine-guns, boxes of dynamite, guns and more than
> one hundred men wearing camouflaged uniforms and carrying

modern guns, steel helmets and with little moral authority, surrounded this House in order to make a demonstration of strength, despotism and violence on behalf of the government which had decreed the recess of the National Congress. . . . We had defended the legislature with the guns of legality, guns quite different from the ones used by the executive power.[10]

After the military troops' occupation of Congress the deputies, following the House's president, left the place showing their identification to the military officers blocking the exit. The dialogue that took place between Deputy Adauto Cardoso and the Colonel Meira Matos (in the command of the operation) when the deputy refused to show his credentials was quite sharp:

Deputy Cardoso: Colonel, I would never expect to meet you as the executor not of a recess decree but of an operation of military occupation of a disarmed House.
Colonel Matos: And I, deputy, would never expect to see you in such a counter-revolutionary attitude.
Deputy Cardoso: Colonel, I am, above all, at the service of the *civil power*.
Colonel Matos: And I am at the service of the *military power*.[11]

The Congress was placed in recess for a month, which meant that the legislative elections took place while Congress was closed. From this episode it is interesting to make some observations about the MDB. As our description of the facts shows, the crisis was provoked by the government's purging of six MDB deputies, in an action which was certainly aimed not only at cleansing the revolutionary camp of 'subversive and corrupt' elements, but also at warning the more audacious opposition candidates to control their actions during the electoral campaign. Despite the opposition party being the detonator of the crisis, its main protagonist was not the MDB but the president of the House of Deputies. The MDB in fact was taken in tow in the protest led by the ARENA Deputy Adauto Cardoso. Three days after Cardoso decided to refuse to recognise the *cassações* (political purges), the MDB had not yet been able to gather the minimum number of deputies necessary to open the House of Deputies' session, in spite of the MDB leadership's appeals to deputies to come to Brasilia. It is clear that the government chose the right moment to undertake the purges, when the majority of the politicians were in their states campaigning for the elections. It is also true that, from the fourth day of the crisis, the majority of the MDB representatives in the House were attending the session declared permanent and participating in the development of the crisis. But indicative of the MDB's indecisiveness and paralysis was the fact that the party's executive committee gave only signs of its existence by issuing a manifesto on 17 October, three days after the protest movement had started and when even the Senate's president had already declared to the press his support for his colleagues in the Lower House.

In spite of the fact that the MDB did not play the main role in this episode, it suffered all the consequences of the crisis. The Chamber of Deputies' president was not punished: Deputy Çardoso later resigned his position but ended up being granted a seat in the Federal Supreme Court in January 1967. His nomination for that important judicial office was made directly by President Castelo Branco who wanted to show that he did not intend to dispense with revolutionary civilians. On the other hand, the MDB had been deprived not only of those six deputies but also others who were purged in the states and municipalities during the period of electoral campaign.[12] Under these conditions it is clear that the MDB's electoral campaign could not be carried out freely and the outcome in that first election that the MDB contested, could not be other than a crushing defeat in most of the states. The large number of blank and spoiled ballots registered in that election was the natural outcome of a surrealistic situation in which elections were taking place to elect representatives for a Congress that was under imposed recess. The feeling of indifference and discredit towards the opposition party among the electorate was well depicted by the words of the political commentator Carlos Castello Branco, about the MDB's defeat:

> MDB's great adversary . . . was, undoubtedly, the blank ballot to which was added on a large scale the spoiled ballot. The latter, according to authentic witnesses, was characterized by an irritated manifestation of graphic art or scatological comments from the voters, in a protest which was addressed mainly to the government but which also involved highly negative attitudes towards the opposition party.[13]

It must be mentioned that the electorate's discredit of and indifference to the elections and particularly to the MDB was also a consequence of the campaign developed against the party. In this respect, the opposition had to face direct government interference in the development of the campaign, including the prohibition of public rallies such as occurred in São Paulo where the political police (DOPS) did not allow the rally in the main city square (Praça da Sé) which had been scheduled by the MDB. ARENA's candidates on the other hand, warned the electorate against the MDB, stressing in their campaign, that the opposition candidates were subversive, that a vote for the MDB meant to waste their vote since the opposition deputies would be purged later, and that if the opposition won in the town nothing good would come from the government. In *São Paulo* the MDB faced another strong adversary in its electoral campaign: the powerful newspaper *Estado de São Paulo*, a protagonist and strong defender of the 1964 revolution. This newspaper, the largest in the country, in its sharp criticism to the MDB, which continued at least up to 1969,[14] defined the party as a grouping of 'men who, yesterday, were the raw material for the *comuno-janguista* conspiracy',[15] and pointed out the 'Revolution's mistake in giving free hand to, and sometimes even encouraging, people of such a dark past and yet darker intentions'.[16] In its criticism of the heterogenous nature of the two parties recently created, the newspaper editorial referred to the MDB in the following manner:

> ... if its members come indifferently, like the ARENA's ones, from the four cardinal points of politics, the MDB members have at least this in common: they openly aspire to the return of the subversion. A fact which makes the MDB triply dangerous, for being subversive, for knowing what it wants and for being thus, more cohesive and therefore more powerful.[17]

Given their view of the MDB as the communist-populist danger, it is obvious that during the elections the newspaper would campaign against the party, and would moreover exploit the dissension and incoherence within the MDB, thus contributing to create a negative image of the opposition among the electorate. In the 1966 electoral campaign the *Jornal da Tarde*, the afternoon newspaper owned by the same press company, ironically described the MDB candidates as: 'Being by principle a party of the workers, one of its candidates is Mr Salvio de Almeida Prado, president of the Brazilian Rural Society and highly reactionary. ... Its senator's candidates are the revolutionary Priest Calazans and the counter-revolutionary *janista* Araripe Serpa. ... '[18] The comments continued in the same vein. No doubt, the MDB's list of candidates in São Paulo as in most of the states, was with rare exceptions, far from politically attractive. But the newspaper's comments were clearly propaganda against a party they regarded as being a nest of 'counter-revolutionaries'.

After the election results, discouragement spread through the MDB's ranks to such an extent that the party's national president Senator Oscar Passos, stated that the MDB was on the verge of being dissolved since it could not possibly fulfil the legal requirements needed to get permanent political party status and he did not see any special reason which would justify an effort to work for this. Senator Passos made his point on the basis of the artificiality of the new parties. The election as he viewed it, had been a contest dominated by the former traditional parties – PSD, UDN and PTB – which had retained their electoral base, and renewed their representation in the Congress. The observation of the MDB leader was quite correct, for in the few states where the MDB had made significant electoral gains it did so because the party could count on politicians from the main ex-parties.[19]

Added to the discouragement of the MDB politicians was its impotence in the face of a government which controlled everything. All opposition activity was ultimately determined by the government in so far as it was the President who decided on those who was allowed to participate in the country's political life. The number of purges under the Institutional Acts Numbers 1 and 2 had reached, by the end of Castelo Branco's administration 2794 cases involving several kinds of punishment: cancellation of political mandates, suspension of political rights, compulsory retirement from civil or military office, firing, involuntary transfer and so forth. Considering the cases of cancellation of electoral mandates and suspension of political rights alone, 624 civilians had been eliminated from political activity.[20]

The executive also controlled every sphere of policy-making, leaving Congress only with the function of rubber-stamping projects and decree-laws issued by the central executive. The numerical weakness of the MDB in Congress made it incapable of defeating any government bill unless the opposition could count on the support of ARENA's dissenting elements. Added to that was the mechanism of automatic approval of any government bill or decree-law that was not put to a vote in thirty days.[21] The opposition's resistance to government bills was reduced to attempts to obstruct the progress of legislative work and abstentions from voting leaving the responsibility of having a government bill ratified to ARENA. The last months of the Castelo Branco administration confirmed the opposition's impotence. The President's intention to leave the office to his successor under a political order drawn on 'revolutionary ideals', led him to use all his extensive power to accomplish this task. By the end of Castelo Branco's administration, three Institutional Acts and thirty-seven Complementary Acts had been decreed, and more than three hundred decree-laws had been sent to the Congress for ratification. In addition a new Constitution (1967), a Press Law and a National Security Law were all ratified by Congress during the special session of the Congress summoned during the Summer.

By the end of Castelo Branco's term – also the end of the legislature which had witnessed the change of the Brazilian political regime – the desolation and impotence of the opposition party which seemed bound to lose in the elections (thus placing in jeopardy the future of the party) and to witness the building of a regime that was gradually consolidating a military and authoritarian form, were quite evident. However, aside from this climate of desolation there also existed the expectations that the change of administration created. Hopes were being revived among politicians from both the MDB and ARENA, about the prospects of redemocratization because of comments about democracy made by the future general-president. The impression at the time was that along with the end of Castelo Branco's government military authoritarianism itself could end and the country would start to tread the path towards institutional normalization. It is interesting to note how the hybrid character of the Brazilian regime – one which, on the one side, an authoritarian framework to consolidate the revolution was being built, and on the other, the return to democracy was being promised – produced a false perception among civilian politicians about the military character of the regime. By being used to military intervention in the course of Brazilian political history, politicians – not to mention everybody else – seemed not to realize that, contrary to old times, a general-president was to be replaced by another general-president; that the central executive had not been taken over by a general-president but by a military institution and that a change of government would not mean the withdrawal of that institution. Yet the change of the guard had taken place in such a manner that a general whose accession was supported not by the legalist group in the army, but by the hard line military elements, was to take over the presidential office. The contradictory situation was that a general was leaving power, one who despite being a representative of the legalist faction in the army, had built an authoritarian system which controlled almost every area of political and economic decision making; and another general was to take office, one who promised democracy while acceding to power with the support of the more radical authoritarian faction within the military institution. Thus the Costa e Silva administration was inaugurated on the basis of contradictory expectations. On the one hand, politicians from both government and opposition were given a vote of confidence as to the democratic intentions of the new president. On the other hand, the hard line group inside the armed forces which had supported his candidacy was expecting to be in power at once. It is within this framework that the political-military crisis which was to start in the first year of the Costa e Silva government originated. It was aggravated in 1968 leading to the 'white coup' of December 1968 and inaugurating a new cycle of the Revolution, actually the darkest period of the Brazilian military-authoritarian regime. The last straw for the new period of repression was to be the so-called Marcio Moreira Alves case, an episode which involved an MDB deputy being prosecuted for criticizing the armed forces.

THE MDB IN THE LEGISLATURE 1967–8: THE MARCIO MOREIRA ALVES' EPISODE

On 13 September 1968 the Armed Forces ministers demanded the prosecution of two MDB deputies – Marcio Moreira Alves and Hermano Alves – for having offended the military. The first deputy was accused on the basis of a speech he had made in the Federal Chamber on 3 September. In that speech the deputy had vehemently criticized repression in the 30 August police invasion of the University of Brasilia and called for the boycott of the military parade in the celebration of Independence Day.[22] The second, Deputy Hermano Alves, was accused because of articles published by him in the newspaper *Correio da Manhã*, considered also to be defamatory statements against the armed forces.

Since the Institutional Act Number 2 which gave powers to the President to proscribe politicians had expired in March 1967, the military ministers resorted to the Article 51 of the 1967 constitution, in its request for punishment of these parliamentarians. This article allowed the prosecution of any citizen who had made any attempt against 'the democratic order' or practised corruption, the sentence being a suspension of political rights for a period of between two to ten years. Nonetheless, in the case of elected mandates, the prosecution would be conditional on the permission of the legislative house to which the parliamentarian belonged, a decision which had to be supported by two-thirds of its members in a secret ballot. The same constitution also guaranteed, according to Article 34, parliamentary immunity which entitled a deputy to state whatever he wanted in the house's tribune. Therefore, although the military was resorting to legal procedures to have the deputies punished, it seemed that it was merely to maintain a facade of legality, since the constitutional clause would not apply (particularly in the case of Marcio Moreira Alves, whose statement was made inside the House of Deputies).[23] It should come as no surprise that as soon as the petition was put forward it faced opposition even from government politicians, and was bound to lead to a confrontation between the executive and the legislature.

Certainly, both MDB deputies had been demonstrating aggressive opposition for too long to be easily ignored by the regime. Nonetheless, they were not alone in this and, during the same period 'there were even more impassioned speeches against the military than Marcio's one', as a reliable witness of the episode told us.[24] Moreover, Moreira Alves's speech was hardly noticed in the Federal Chamber since the deputy had talked in the short-speech session of the Chamber's agenda, one which actually had a small audience. As Mario Covas (then leader of the opposition in the Federal Chamber) said: 'I must say that I was the party's leader and only heard about Marcio's speech ... when the petition for prosecuting him arrived in the House. As for the majority of us! The majority no! All of us only heard about the speech at that moment'.[25]

The military's request for the punishment of the two deputies was merely a pretext to put pressure on the government to take hard action against the growing radicalization and political polarization that took place in 1968. Marcio Moreira Alves was to be made the scapegoat of a political-military crisis, the roots of which are found in the first year of the Costa e Silva administration. This crisis was produced, on the one hand, by the radicalization of the opposition movement which emerged not only at a parliamentary level but also in civil society. Aside from the more aggressive posture taken by the opposition party, the period from late 1967 to late 1968 was to witness growing opposition to the regime highlighted by the *Frente Ampla*'s (Broad Front) attempt at political mobilization, student strikes and demonstrations, the Church voicing its criticism of the regime, workers' strikes and the emergence of urban guerrilla activity. On the other hand, this crisis was also a product of disillusionment and discontent in light of the expectations created with regard to the Costa e Silva government. We are referring to the dissatisfaction of hard line military officers who felt thwarted in their power and influence given the soft line the President was following; the discontent of large part of ARENA's politicians who realized again and again their role as minor partners with the sole subservient task of accepting decisions taken by the central executive; and even the disillusionment of moderate opposition politicians who had believed in the democratic intentions of Costa e Silva.

It is not our intention here to probe deeply into the political crisis brought in 1968, a quite complex period which has even been compared to the eve of Goulart's deposition in so far as the grade of polarization and radicalization is concerned. Our intention is above all to look closely at events in which the MDB was involved as the party for the first time had gone beyond the limits of its Congressional role and had begun to support and participate actively in the opposition movement growing in civil society. In this respect, the group of new MDB deputies elected in 1966, the *Frente Ampla* movement led by Carlos Lacerda, and the student movement are key factors to be discussed.

The Renewal of the MDB

The new legislature, inaugurated in 1967, would bring a group of MDB deputies, to Congress, which would be known as *grupo dos imaturos* (group of imature politicians) given their novelty – basically young deputies elected for the first time and using radical rhetoric. The conduct of this group, which, although small in number was active and aggressive in its criticisms of the regime,[26] had an important impact on the revival of the MDB which was debilitated by its inactivity and inexpression. The two deputies who would later become the target of the 1968 crisis were leading figures of this group.

Already in early 1967 when the climate of optimism regarding the prospect of democratization promised by the new President was still alive, one of the new deputies claimed that it was in the MDB's political interest 'to promote permanent crisis'.[27] Another one, Deputy Marcio Moreira Alves, published a book whose title and content – *Tortura e Torturados*, referring to tortures suffered by political prisoners arrested after 1964 – caused a reaction by military officers which led to prosecution and the subsequent seizure of the book. The group's radical rhetoric was not grounded in disbelief in the new government's intentions to put forward a process of democratization. In fact, the MDB's more radical group also shared the optimism prevalent during the first months of the Costa e Silva administration; they actually saw good intentions in the President when he promised institutional normalization and lent a nationalist tone to his rhetoric by mentioning support for national industry and the need for an independent foreign policy. In this respect, Senator Mario Martins' comment about Costa e Silva administration is very indicative: 'it is essential to free Costa e Silva from the reactionary military scheme which impedes him from governing according to his thinking'.[28] We could presume, therefore, that the more radical strategy of the *grupo dos imaturos* was based on the reasoning that stronger pressures on the government would assure the accomplishment of Costa e Silva's democratic objectives. This would later prove to be a misinterpretation.

The regime and the government were not to be the sole targets of the radical parliamentarians' vehement criticisms. The group would also direct its criticism at the MDB leadership, which was accused of omission, of collaborating with the revolution and forming an oligarchic caste which blocked the access of the novice parliamentarians onto the party's directive board. They also complained about the party's lack of a clear programmatic line and the non-existence of a statute to regulate the party's internal organization. As Deputy Hermano Alves pointed out, 'if we can concretely do nothing in order to promote the modification of the party directorship, at least the MDB leadership cannot either punish us, simply because there is not even a statute'.[29]

Already, by early 1967 two groups were therefore dividing the opposition party. On the one side, the *grupo dos moderados* (moderate group) formed by the majority of traditional politicians who regarded the other group as young rebel politicians lacking experience in politics. On the other, the *grupo dos imaturos* or radicals which would be strengthened by the support or sympathy of some of the old politicians such as the *petebistas* Deputy Oswaldo Lima Filho and Senator Josafá Marinho and the *pessedista*[30] Deputy Martins Rodrigues; the latter was general-secretary of the party. The division of the party into two groups, to which should be added the earlier divisions related to the former parties, did not lead nonetheless to permanent dissensions. Although initially the moderate group assumed an intransigent posture of resisting the relaxation of its total domination of the directive board, they soon recognized that it was the more combative line of the *grupo dos imaturos* which was a source of credibility for the opposition, and thus agreed to accept most of the group's demands. In the party's National Convention in June 1967 not only a new programme and statute were approved but also the party's command was opened to the new parliamentarians who acquired representation on the national and regional directive boards. In that party meeting a committee of 'Popular Mobilization' was also created, whose aim was to establish more permanent contact with the electorate so as to enlarge the party's popular base.[31] The 1967 national convention was the first step in the course of the party's reorientation towards a stronger opposition, changing from a posture of mere acceptance or complacency with respect to the radicals who acted on their own, to a near identification with the radical line. This change in the party's behaviour was not caused by the radical's pressures on the top leadership alone. It was also a consequence of the disillusionment and discontent of the moderate group inside the party about the prospects for the redemocratization of the country. Already in the middle of 1967 there were signs of Costa e Silva's inaction and his inability to deal with political issues. The promises of institutional normalization were kept at the level of rhetoric. It should be mentioned that the disillusionment regarding the prospects of political opening was also shared by elements of the government party, a factor which would provoke rebellious moves in Congress around the approval of government's bills.

Also influential in the MDB's reformulation of its opposition line was the emergence of another opposition movement which would go beyond the legal party system thus threatening the MDB's position as the sole channel of political opposition: the *Frente Ampla*. The development of this movement, its role played in the radicalization of the opposition movement and the MDB's participation in it will now be examined.

The *Frente Ampla* and the MDB

The *Frente Ampla* was a movement organised under the leadership of Carlos Lacerda in alliance with the ex-president Juscelino

Kubitschek and the ousted president João Goulart. Although it was created in the last year of Castelo Branco's government (1966) it had a very strong presence only during the period between late 1967 and early 1968. Fundamental to the understanding of this opposition movement is the role played by its leader, Carlos Lacerda. A skilful politician from the UDN, he distinguished himself throughout his political career by his aggressive rhetoric in opposition to Vargas and against communism and corruption, and for having played the role of detonator in almost every political crisis since 1945. Carlos Lacerda, as mentioned in Chapter 1, was the governor of the state of Guanabara when the 1964 coup took place and he certainly was one of the main civilian conspirators involved in Goulart's overthrow. His support for the 1964 revolution nevertheless did not last very long. As soon as his ambitions of becoming President of the Republic had been thwarted he broke with the group which took power. After the unsuccessful coup attempt against Castelo Branco by the hard line military officers with which Lacerda allied himself, and the subsequent measures decreed by the President dissolving the political parties and establishing indirect elections for the Presidency, Lacerda's chances of becoming Castelo Branco's successor were definitely buried. Since he could no longer count on his military allies – the hard line group, which had been appeased, by the hard measures decreed by Castelo Branco – Carlos Lacerda sought new allies and tried another strategy against the group in power. Thus he resorted to his old adversaries – namely the *pessedista* and *petebista* politicians in the MDB – and sought to create an opposition movement with the support of wide sectors of civil society.

In November 1966 Lacerda met Juscelino Kubitschek in Lisbon and formalized the alliance between them – the Pact of Lisbon. They agreed to form a movement and work together for the re-establishment of democracy, in particular, for the restoration of direct elections for the Presidency of the Republic. Nonetheless, the *Frente Ampla*'s presence on the political scene became more active only in September 1967. A meeting in Belo Horizonte (Minas Gerais' capital) formally established the opposition movement, intended to mobilize public opinion to join the fight for the return of democracy and the resumption of economic development. In late September Lacerda went to meet João Goulart in Montevidéo thus establishing publicly Lacerda's alliance with the ex-president who he had actively helped to oust. The Pact of Montivideo – as the meeting of the two politicians would be called – was a significant event in so far as it would help to promote acceptance of the *Frente Ampla* among those *petebista* and left-wing sectors which had still resisted joining the movement led by Lacerda. The support of Goulart and his followers for the *Frente* not only enlarged the bases of the movement but also made Lacerda incorporate in this rhetoric themes such as political amnesty and support for the salaried workers hit by government economic policy.

It was also in late September 1967 that the MDB finally made clear its official position with respect to the *Frente Ampla*, after almost a year of indecisiveness about what the party line should be. It must be pointed out that the MDB politicians had been participating in Lacerda's movement since its origin. Obviously the *Frente* would have not been created if the initial alliance established between Lacerda and the MDB politicians, followers of Kubitschek and Goulart, had not been carried out. But the participation of MDB politicians in the *Frente Ampla* were individual initiatives of those who considered the organization of that movement either to play a complementary opposition role beside the MDB, or to be the only instrument capable of making the country return to democracy since the MDB was imprisoned by its condition as a legal and congressional party. Most of the MDB politicians who adhered to the *Frente* claimed that the party should become integrated into the movement, probably in order to lend legal support to the *Frente*'s activities. However, there was strong resistance to MDB adhesion to the *Frente Ampla*: mainly among politicians from the moderate group represented particularly by the party's president, Senator Oscar Passos. The argument against the *Frente* varied from personal aversion to Lacerda to the fear that the movement might unleash a military reaction which would end up suppressing democracy in the country definitively, not to mention concerns about the MDB's future in so far as the *Frente* could replace it. Nonetheless the moderate group was not able to take any measure to prevent party members from joining the *Frente*, since a prohibition to participate in it could only be effective if it was accompanied by a repressive measure such as expulsion from the party. This would not be feasible since a large number of the MDB's politicians, and even part of its leadership such as the general-secretary Deputy Martins Rodrigues and the leader in the Federal Chamber, Deputy Mario Covas, were already integrated into the movement. Finally, in September, the party's directive board reached a compromise solution, in fact the only alternative that could be assumed to be the official position of the party: the MDB's official statement pointed out that the party as an organization would not participate in the movement although it would not place restrictions on its members from adhering to the *Frente* since the MDB acknowledged that both the opposition party and the *Frente Ampla* were fighting for the same objective of bringing democracy back to the country. The MDB's official position with respect to the *Frente Ampla* seems to have been based on the same rationale which had guided the party compromise between radicals and moderates within the party, that is, that the moderates would not themselves assume more radical positions but they would not prevent those who wanted to from doing so. In fact this was quite convenient for the moderates since they would benefit from a more opposition image of the party created by the radicals, without taking much risk themselves. Only when the political crisis was aggravated in mid-1968 would the moderates agree to the party assuming a stronger opposition posture, as a consequence of the radicalization of the political process.

Despite the *Frente Ampla*'s gathering of support from the majority of the opposition sectors,[32] its activities were in fact very limited. The *Frente*'s presence on the political scene was evident basically in Lacerda's statements in the press and speeches in meetings of a select audience in which the leader addressed his criticism of the regime and advocated the theses of the movement: direct elections for the Presidency, redemocratization, amnesty and resumption of economic development. With respect to the mobilization of public opinion which the *Frente* apparently intended to promote, the movement did not go very far. Mainly, this was because the *Frente* did not manage to create an organizational structure in society. The limited mobilization by the *Frente* is evidenced by the fact that only in the end of March 1968 was a public rally of some importance promoted – the one which took place in São Caetano do Sul, a city with a large working class population located in Greater São Paulo.

Lacerda actually offered some resistance to the implementation of popular mobilization as a policy which the *Frente*'s organizers wanted to promote. Lacerda's cautious attitude was probably caused by his fear of losing control of the movement, opening the way to the left's domination of the *Frente*. This was not a concern to be taken lightly given the messages sent by Goulart from Montevideo asking for the active participation in the *Frente* of all *trabalhista* and left wing groups in order to counterbalance the excessive presence of Lacerda at the helm of the movement. On the other hand Lacerda, skilful politician as he was, knew that popular mobilization would certainly be followed by a government reaction.

Actually, since Lacerda's agreement with the ousted president Goulart, the government had shown signs of restlessness with regard to the *Frente*. The alliance with Goulart not only closed off any possibility for Lacerda to seek the support of his old allies in the army – the hard line officers – but also placed the *Frente Ampla* beyond the limits of opposition action tolerated by the regime. Warning signals were issued in the presidential speech of December 1967, in which the President characterized the activities of his adversaries as subversive. Other reactions came from the armed forces, such as the hard-line General Albuquerque Lima who, in reply to Lacerda's criticism of the military character of the regime, denounced the *Frente Ampla* as being a focus of agitation and demanded the government act against it. Certainly it was not part of Lacerda's strategy to intensify the radicalization of an opposition movement which could not count on the support of a military group to assure its effectiveness. Whatever Lacerda's intention was, the fact is that less than fifteen days after the São Caetano public rally, the Minister of Justice[33] decreed the prohibition of *Frente Ampla* activities (5 April 1968).[34]

The intensification of the crisis

The *Frente Ampla* therefore died in April 1968. But the movement of opposition to the regime that the *Frente* helped intensify did not die with it. On the contrary, the opposition to the regime was to be aggravated and radicalized, and the main focus of this was to be the student movement. On 28 March 1968, a student was killed by the police during a student protest in Rio de Janeiro. His body was taken to the State Assembly and was mourned through the night. The nationwide commotion provoked by the killing of the student was a sign that from then on the process of radicalization on both sides – government–opposition, left–right – would sharply aggravate.

The prohibition of the *Frente Ampla* a week after the death of the student was the first step towards a clamp down by the regime, but also indicated the President's reluctance to act more drastically against the opposition despite pressures for this sort of action. The journalist Carlos Castello Branco reported in April 1968, after the measure against the *Frente Ampla*:

Military sources revealed that the prohibition was decided before the events which shook the country during the last two weeks. Before the crisis, the government felt already trapped by Lacerda's aggressions. After the crisis, nonetheless, large sectors of the Army consider that the measure now adopted is somewhat or completely out of focus, as it does not provide the government with the instruments to restrain the opposition deputies who were named as inciting subversive actions. Mr Lacerda had been involved in a political campaign, but there are deputies who make subversive exhortations. Mr Lacerda was punished, and the others were not.[35]

The year 1968 had already begun with a political and military crisis which was being aggravated every day as a result of the discontent of the more radical sectors of the right in face of the soft and immobile President's attitude towards the opposition which had intensified its actions not only in Congress but also in society at large. The wide spread opposition to the regime was forecast in C.C. Branco's comments of 4 February, 1968:

The process of radicalization proposed by the *Frente* ... has already reached important sectors of the MDB in the Congress. It can be presumed that from now on the opposition parliamentary group will grow politically aggressive in proportion to the decreasing chance of the opposition to influence and recover a position of prestige in the institutional picture. Not having power in sight ... the opposition will try to break the barrier with the weapons which it holds, namely verbal intimidation. The MDB and the *Frente Ampla* will have, in this task, as an auxiliary force, thwarted groups from the ARENA, which, cautious in tribune speeches, tend to become more audacious in voting. The defeat of three presidential decree-laws has to do with this informal alliance ...[36]

The restlessness of Congress was made evident not only by the opposition speeches and attempts at obstructing government bills, but also by the emergence of a dissident group among ARENA which led to the defeat of other government decree-laws. This restlessness would characterize the period. With the outburst of the student protests which followed the killing of the student in March, the stage for the parliamentarians' opposition would reach through the opposition solidarity with the student movement, beyond the door of Congress to society. An amnesty bill proposed by an MDB deputy demanding the freeing of students and strikers arrested during the demonstrations which followed the student's killing was actively debated in Congress, and although it was not approved, no less than thirty-five ARENA's deputies voted in favour of the bill. The direct involvement of MDB parliamentarians – namely those from the *grupo dos imaturos* – in support of the student protest was indicative of the legal opposition's transgression of the limits set by the regime. By April the press was reporting frequent statements of military dissatisfaction with the behaviour of politicians in general, who were seen as protecting student rebellion against authority. Military officers blamed particularly some MDB politicians of whom it was said: 'besides protecting the agitators, they stimulate agitation and aggravate it with clear incitement to subversion'.[37] ARENA was also accused of complacency by behaving in Congress as a silent and passive voice. The frequency of political statements from military officers criticizing the opposition for radicalization and the government for not reacting properly, indicated not only the growing discontent among military sectors but also that Costa e Silva's authority had been eroded and he was losing control of the situation in every sphere. To complete the 1968 crisis picture, on 22 April, about seven thousand metal workers went on strike in Contagem (Minas Gerais); in July it was the turn of the metal workers in Osasco (São Paulo); in September there were also attempts at strikes in Minas Gerais and Rio de Janeiro. Adding to the wide social unrest, the country began to witness terrorist bombing put in action by both left and right-wing groups. As R. Schneider pointed out, 'terrorist bombings, which had peaked in May before dropping to four incidents in June and only three in July, had risen to nine in August'.[38]

The radicalization and polarization of the political system had reached such an intensity that even the moderate sectors of the MDB started assuming a much stronger oppositional line. In August the party's national executive committee officially defined a more audacious policy by adopting measures to intensify the party's protection of people reached by the repressive apparatus such as: visits of solidarity to the political prisoners, legal assistance for the trials, an examination of adequate means to publicize authority's responsibilities for abuse of power.

If by August the political temperature was already very high, it reached the maximum on 30 August when the police invaded the University of Brasilia using such brutal means of repression that even MDB parliamentarians who rushed to the campus to try to negotiate with the police left wounded. A parliamentarian commission of enquiry to investigate responsibility for the violence against the university's students and teachers was created, and a statement – also signed by most of ARENA's parliamentarians – was issued protesting against the military invasion and expressing solidarity with the students and teachers who had been hit by police violence. This episode was the theme of Marcio Moreira Alves's speech in the Chamber of Deputies in the 3 September 1968 session. His vehement protest against the military invasion of the university finally gave the military hard-line sectors a pretext for action against the opposition movement.

The 'legal' proceedings of the request to prosecute Marcio Moreira Alves remained almost two months in the Judiciary before reaching the House of Deputies. Worrying about the international repercussions of the deputy's trial, the government was certainly waiting for the departure of the United Kingdom's Queen Elizabeth who was on official visit to Brazil in early November. When the petition arrived in the Federal Chamber on 19 November, it was already clear that the government would encounter strong resistance to it even from its own party. The prediction that the Justice Committee of the Federal Chamber would vote against the measure caused the replacement of nine members of the committee so that the vote would be favourable to the government. This government's request, implemented by its loyal leadership, provoked the protest and resignation of the Justice Committee's chairman, ARENA deputy Djalma Marinho. His speech announcing his resignation brought strength to the growing group of ARENA's deputies who were refusing to back the government in a measure that was, by and large, against the legislative institution.

The MDB used obstruction of the voting procedure as a strategy to delay the decision so that the case would be postponed until the next year, since the Congress's work term was to end in early December. The MDB leadership expected that during the long parliamentary summer recess, there would be enough time to calm the overheated climate reached by the crisis and so a negotiation possibly could be reached. Nevertheless, given growing pressures from the hard line military sectors, Costa e Silva summoned Congress to meet in special session in order to vote on the action against Marcio Moreira Alves. By then, nothing more could be done. Deputy Mario Covas, opposition leader, narrates:

It was worthless to continue with obstruction. We ended up voting on the petition on 12 December. In that day Congress rejected the petition to punish Marcio Moreira Alves. It rejected it by an expressive majority: 270 votes. It is evident that we had to count on the people from the other side, as we had only 127 votes. At that time Congress acted as an institution. It was a moment of the reconciliation of Congress with popular sentiment. For those as myself who were present there, when the vote representing the defeat of the petition was obtained, somebody, from the public gallery of the House which was completely full, started to sing the National anthem... it was a moment that we will never forget.[39]

On the day after, however, Institutional Act Number 5 (AI–5) was decreed, which gave almost unlimited power to the President.[40] As Carlos Castello Branco wrote on 14 December 1968:

The Institutional Act decreed yesterday will not be followed by any other. It is complete and it did not leave anything aside in the matter of expressed discretionary power.... The measure stopped all sources of political resistance to the government, not leaving any exit valve. There will not exist the minimum possibility of producing opposition, unless, and while it lasts, press freedom is respected. Anyhow the politicians are so restricted that their access to the press would surely mean risking themselves.... The House of Deputies, in the end, has had the sole consolation of falling fighting, manifesting itself in the plenitude of its sovereignty. The Congress celebration however did not last more than 24 hours.[41]

Twenty-four hours later this journalist was also arrested, together with other journalists, politicians, and other professionals.

The new instrument of power, by which discretionary power was institutionalized, did not have a pre-fixed expiry date, as the Institutional Acts issued earlier had. Using AI–5, the President decreed the indefinite recess of Congress and the state Assemblies of Guanabara, Rio de Janeiro, São Paulo, Pernambuco and Sergipe.[42] On 30 December 1968 the wave of purges started, when Marcio Moreira Alves, Hermano Alves, Carlos Lacerda and nine more federal deputies lost their political rights. These *cassacções* were followed by many others in the ensuing months, reaching, by April 1969, the total of 92 federal deputies and four senators. The MDB in

Congress alone lost 45 per cent of its parliamentarians, not to mention the large purges suffered by the party at state and municipal levels.[43] Five judges from the Supreme Court and one from the Supreme Military Court were forced to retire. About five hundred professionals who retained socially and politically important positions in the country – university professors, journalists, military officers, judges and diplomats – lost their jobs and their political rights. Censorship was established over every means of communications and over cultural activities.[44] The military regime had moved into the darkest period of the country's political history. The opposition movement had gone too far in a political regime in formation which at least initially seemed to be reluctant to establish a military dictatorship – the government's reluctance to decree the Institutional Act No 5 was evidence for that. It ended up by consolidating the military institution in power, at least while the regime did not need to search for legitimization in society.

5 1969-74: From Retreat to Rebuilding

THE INSTITUTIONAL ACT NUMBER 5 AND THE REGIME'S MOVE TOWARDS REPRESSIVE AUTHORITARIANISM

The promulgation of Institutional Act Number 5 inaugurated the third political cycle of the '1964 revolution'. It started a period in which the resort to repression in all its dimensions and the exercise of arbitrary powers would reach the highest level ever seen in Brazilian political history. In contrast to earlier Institutional Acts issued by the regime to block and purge the 'adverse forces of the revolution', the new Act indicated (by the absence of an expiry date) that the so-called 'Revolution' had become permanent. If the AI-1 decreed in 1964 and the AI-2 of 1966 limited the President's exercise of arbitrary power to a definite period of time, the AI-5 meant that exceptional powers were to be used, not only as a corrective measure but also as a preventive instrument to retain the 'revolutionary process' along its course. Thus the AI-5 provided clear indications that from then on the power of the 'revolution' was to last until the revolutionary command decided that the country was prepared for a return to democracy. The 'ideals of the revolution' would again be recalled to justify repression. As the prologue of the AI-5 restated, the 'revolutionary process' aimed at

> giving the country a regime which, taking into consideration the requirements of a juridical and political system, would assure an *authentic democratic order* based on freedom, on the respect for human dignity, on the *fight against subversion and ideologies contrary to the traditions of our people*, on the fight against corruption, thereby searching for the indispensable means for the economic, financial, political and moral reconstruction of Brazil.[1]

Therefore, in defence of the 'democratic order', 'it becomes imperative to adopt measures to prevent the thwarting of the superior ideals of the revolution, preserving order, security, tranquility, economic and cultural development and the country's political and social

110

harmony which has been jeopardized by a process of subversion and revolutionary warfare'.[2] Moreover, the new Institutional Act also signed the death of the 1967 constitution – the authoritarian charter promulgated by Castelo Branco in his attempt to institutionalize the revolution. The preamble of the AI–5 asserted that: 'Clear subversive actions, originating from diverse political and cultural sectors, confirmed that *the juridical instruments that the triumphant Revolution granted the Nation*, for its defense and the development and welfare of its people, *are serving as the means to combat and destroy it*'.[3]

The Institutional Act Number 5, therefore, was to be not only the basis for far-reaching and recurring political purges, but also the potential instrument to be used whenever and against whomever was regarded as a threat to the revolution and the regime established by it. Moreover, having been used to impose an indefinite recess of Congress, the AI–5 granted the executive power the role of being the sole legislator for the country, thereby depriving politicians from having even that minimal influence on decision-making to which they were entitled in virtue of being members of the National Congress. During the long period of imposed parliamentary recess – from December 1968 to October 1969 – President Costa e Silva and the military Junta who took over when the President fell ill, decreed thirteen Institutional Acts, forty Complementary Acts, and twenty Decree-laws dealing strictly with economic, political and national security policies. All these measures 'would consolidate the authoritarian principles of political organization that had been put into force during the earlier revolutionary cycles'.[4]

Despite the closed nature of the political system that the new wave of political repression had brought about, there were also signs that the military once again appeared unwilling to deprive civilian politicians altogether from playing a role in the political system. The Congress, together with some State Assemblies and Municipal Chambers had not been closed down, giving rise to the hope that they would be able to function again. As an ARENA politician replied when he was asked about the prospects of reopening Congress: 'it will be opened. This is the government's answer, at least the answer which was implicit in the government's decision to put Congress in recess instead of closing it down'.[5] Another indication that the regime would not dispense with formal mechanisms of parliamentarian politics was the fact that the political parties as organizations were not punished. Although the President resorted widely to AI–5 to purge opposition politicians and even parliamentarians from the government party, he did not decree the dissolution of the two parties which, according to the regime, had failed to 'serve the revolution'. The behaviour of important figures of ARENA, refusing to support the government's request to prosecute Deputy Marcio Moreira Alves, sharply increased the military's dissatisfaction with their civilian allies in the Congress. But the ARENA's 'bad behaviour' – not to mention the MDB's – seemed not to be a sufficiently strong motive to justify the outright banning of all parties, even though this proposal had some supporters. In fact, during the long period of imposed parliamentary recess, ARENA and the MDB were to be involved in the task of reconstructing their organizations in accordance with the requirements demanded by the Party Organization Law. And the government, willing to preserve the two parties, issued two Complementary Acts in order to relax the law's requirements in face of the difficulties encountered by the parties (particularly the MDB) in carrying out the task of reorganization. Certainly, parliamentary politics from then on would be defined on a much more restricted basis. Nonetheless, the fact that the regime had not closed all the doors produced hopes that at some time the government would bring back political normalization. In this respect, it is interesting to follow the daily political comments of the journalist C. C. Branco who from 1969 onwards had to use a more cautious approach in dealing with the unfavourable political conditions at the time, but did not avoid touching on relevant problems of the political conjuncture. We have observed through following his daily comments, that the prospects of reopening Congress was never in doubt. The question always raised was when this would happen. In January it was expected that the government would reconvene Congress in March; then, the hopes were postponed to June, and then to August.[6]

The long wait for the suspension of the parliamentary recess which was postponed every month, showed that parliamentary politics would be re-established only when the 'revolutionary camp' had completed its 'cleansing' process and had established a new set of political rules. Actually, Costa e Silva soon announced his intention of promoting a revision of the 1967 constitution in order to adapt it to the new order. As the constitution granted by the former general-president Castelo Branco had proved ineffective, it was considered necessary to reform the legal framework of the regime. Certainly, that constitutional revision intended only to provide a façade of legality for the new order established with the AI–5. Nonetheless Costa e Silva's decision to give the task of elaborating the con- stitutional reform to the civilian Vice-President Pedro Aleixo gave rise to the hope that the President had good intentions regarding his promises of reestablishing normality. A significant interpretation of Costa e Silva's commitment to the reestablishment of democratic order is given by ex-Senator and ex-Minister Jarbas Passarinho, himself a military officer, who went into politics and had taken important positions in the military governments.[7] According to Passarinho, in 1968,

> the revolutionary process was diverted from its course because of left wingers' irresponsible armed actions . . . There were specific examples of this radical left orientation seeking to disrupt the status quo. The examples included mass demonstrations, student protest etc. We could have returned to a democratic order easily after 1967 if there had not been this kind of activity. I witnessed the suffering of the President when signing the AI–5. He did not want to. He was horrified by the idea of dictatorship. He carried out the purges, including both military and civilians, and then, in August 1969 he called me and said: 'You will go back to the Senate to be the government's leader and help me to restore a democratic order with a Constitution which we have been preparing with the help of Dr Pedro Aleixo. I will have the courage to promulgate the new Constitution. On the 7th of September this Constitution will be promulgated; I will then revoke the recess of the Congress and eliminate the AI–5'. Yes, he said that. He really intended to do it. He had strength to accomplish it; he dominated even the military sector opposing him, which believed he had changed. Costa e Silva, who had come to power with the support of the hard liners, was then facing their resistance as well, for they blamed him for becoming soft, for following the same path as Castelo Branco's government. Costa e Silva intended to re-establish a democratic order. Unfortunately, however, he became ill, was removed from office and then died. He could not implement his plans. Thus I defend this thesis of the deviation from the original course of the Revolution. That is, the deviation was a response to the subversive threat which lasted until 1973.[8]

It is not our intention to question Jarbas Passarinho's interpreta- tion of the events, one in fact which expressed the regime's point of view. There is no doubt that Costa e Silva was carrying on, albeit slowly, a process towards a kind of political normalization. The press at the time reported every step followed by the government's elaboration of the Constitutional revision and the prospects of reopening Congress. But by way of the political comments in the press we can also see that the political normalization promised by Costa e Silva would be very limited indeed in terms of resembling democratic features. The pessimistic remarks made by C. C. Branco on 31 July 1969 are a good example:

> If official sources' forecasts are confirmed, we are a few days away from the Constitutional reform. Nevertheless we are still very far from democratic normalization, since the rules of the state of exception ... will be incorporated into the revised Charter.... Rights and guarantees will continue to be suspended without definite prospect of when these restrictions will be lifted. We will continue in a state of exception, and under an indefinite exception, as we are today ... The President of the Republic, according to some indications, has not yet been in a position to carry out his commitment to re-establish the political process. On the one hand, the definition of an expiry date for the AI-5 was considered inconvenient. On the other, perplexity remains regarding Congress' reopening which should occur following the reform's decree but it became known that this would not happen.... With or without the reform, the Constitution will continue to be suspended, thus deprived from being ... an instrument which sets rights and duties. Mr Pedro Aleixo and his colleagues at the summit will have worked, then, on an academic construction of no practical effect'.[9]

Two factors must be pointed out in order to understand the state of uncertainty regarding the destiny of the political process after the promulgation of the AI-5. The first has to do with the meaning of the expression 're-establishment of democratic normalization' so often used by the military. 'Democratic order' for the military seems to denote something very far from what is traditionally considered to be representative democracy. The military officers, irrespective of whether they are legalists or hardliners, were agreed on the values of discipline. These, they claimed, were essential to preserve national security, and were to be the basis of a 'democratic order'. The small amount a latitude allowed for conflict, and the scant respect for political negotiation through democratic mechanisms as a means of defusing political dissent, are certainly not characteristic of the military alone. The particularity of the military group lies in the characteristics of the military institution, which is based on hierarchy and discipline. In Brazil it became commonplace to stress the armed forces' commitment to democracy: this either emanated from civilians wishing to keep alive an optimistic view of the future, or derived from political commentators who seemed to stress the military's democratic commitment as a means of exerting pressure for political relaxation, or it came from the military institution itself. The remarks of the military-politician Jarbas Passarinho when asked about the meaning of democracy for the military are noteworthy:

> The Brazilian Army's vocation for democracy is one to which I can testify. I was a leader in the Military School, I was president of the *Sociedade Academica Militar*. I went to the *Escola de Aperfeiçoamento* and finally to the *Escola do Estado Maior*. In short, I have been in every school in the Army. The Army vocation was entirely democratic. The military are socialist without knowing it, are they not? Because they get used to sharing the food. The military are underpaid, have bad salaries. Anyone of us, here, as a senator, earns much more than a four-star general with 45 years of service. If you want to touch the military's sensitivity, you talk about corruption, above all, or about communism. . . . So, *the democratic conception of the Armed Forces is a democratic idea of austerity, of dedication to the country's superior interests and not of the interest of the individual. This idea is viscerally democratic in so far as it is not authoritarian. But force (Armed Forces) by itself is authoritarian, for it is based on hierarchy, as is the Church.* So, when we exchange the military life for the political life – as was the case with me – we feel the difference enormously! Because we are accustomed to knowing that the regiment never changes, it is today the same as it has always been. In *my Senate* for example, a senator asks to speak and, as a leader, he has 20 minutes. Because of my formation, I think that after this 20 minutes, he should stop speaking. But he speaks for 20 minutes, 10 minutes more, 15 minutes more, another 20 minutes and I cannot turn him out of his chair or the Tribune. Here then, is a clash of values'.[10]

It is this 'military style' of dealing with politics that C. C. Branco referred to in his evaluation of Costa e Silva's behaviour in the 1968 political crisis:

His relationship with the Congress and the government party were typical: he expected that both would accomplish their missions, in the certainty that, as in the barracks, it is enough that one has a mission to feel obliged to accomplish it.[11]

In 1972 the journalist Fernando Pedreira well expressed the feeling of exhaustion from the long wait for the so promised return to democracy:

> For us ... democracy is a kind of prize for good behaviour. It supposes the previous agreement on the minimization or even suppression of deeper dissensions.... We live in an exceptional state which has already lasted some time. Well, the stated (and generally accepted) condition for the eventual return to the so-called democratic plenitude, is to level political and social differences; is the disappearance of forces capable of effectively opposing the government's policy and the regime's stability. In other words: we agree that return to democracy can only occur with certainty when everybody conforms to the permanence of a recognizably anti-democratic regime. Curious country! This is enough to prove that the problem of democracy among us, rather than political, is semantic; rather than military, is ideological.... For us, democracy is a kind of bread made only of crust, without crumb.... Nonetheless, although unprepared for democracy, Brazil does not rid itself of this deep democratic nostalgia which even today is reflected even in the statements of our more illustrous military chiefs.[12]

The second point that we should mention regarding the political picture after the promulgation of the AI–5 has to do with the implementation of the political relaxation which Costa e Silva wanted to promote. The dissensions within the military institution did not cease after the promulgation of the AI–5. However restricted was the constitutional revision that Costa e Silva was trying to promote, the fact remains that there were indications that the President was facing resistance within the armed forces to implementing some measures of political relaxation with the consequent reopening of Congress. Among the military sectors there were those who wanted to maintain the arbitrary powers embodied in the AI–5 for a much longer period. As Jarbas Passarinho defined, 'the "missionary group" considered that the Armed Forces had a mission and only after that mission had been accomplished should we return to democratic normality'.[13] In addition, the intensification of the urban guerilla movement towards 1969 strengthened the hardliner's argument against political normalization. As Schneider pointed out:

Urban violence and terrorism . . . assumed dramatic proportions in the mid-year, just in time to undercut moves toward reconstitutionalization by strengthening the hands of the most security-minded regime elements. On July 16, extremists destroyed a São Paulo television transmitter located a few short blocks from the state-house, bringing to three the total of such dramatic destructions of mass communications facilities in a period of a week.[14]

However, the resistance to political relaxation did not come only from military sectors. It also had supporters among the government technocracy who could put into practice, through decree, the government's economic policy without any kind of interference. In several articles the journalist C. C. Branco stressed this point as one of the serious obstacles to the reopening of the Congress. On 4 March 1969 he wrote:

In 1968 the index of economic growth was 6.5. . . . In 1969, this index must still rise and inflation will by December be 15%. The government technical experts do not hide the conviction that those results became possible thanks to the elimination of the obstacles represented by the functioning of Congress, which always creates barriers to the adoption of measures in the economic-finance and administrative areas. The parliamentary recess freed the planning agencies to accomplish adjustments which would be extremely difficult in a period of institutional normalcy. From their point of view . . . the regime of the AI–5 produced beneficial results. . . . Although the economic-finance legislation had been concluded, several measures in the administrative instance . . . will still be taken, according to some sources. This makes the technocrats expect the parliamentary recess to last for a period long enough to allow them to touch a politically sensitive sector, that is, the public administration.[15]

In August 1969 again the journalist blamed the technocrats for the difficulties faced by Costa e Silva in his attempt to implement political normalization:

Many of the difficulties that he faces stem from the military's worries about questions of internal security. But these questions were neither the overall problem nor, possibly, the most active and present. Among the civilian highest echelon of the public administration there are the saviours and reformers who pretend to replace permanent institutions in order to break down History's door.[16]

The journalist's remarks indicated clearly the convenience for the technocrats and the dominant class coalition whose interests the former were expressing, to maintain an authoritarian order so as to implement their economic development policy.[17] The problems involving Costa e Silva's intentions to re-establish constitutional order (whichever form the political order would assume) cannot therefore be reduced to a military–civilian split. However, it certainly resulted in the strengthening of the military control over the political system. Reasons of 'economic development' for the technocrat-civilian sectors and reasons of 'national security' and military unity for the Armed Forces, would lead to the marginalization of the civilian politicians in August 1969. The military Junta's take-over when Costa e Silva fell ill, barring the civilian Vice-President from assuming office, was the turning point in the process of consolidation of military control over the political system.

On 31 August 1969, the Armed Forces Ministers – General Lira Tavares, Admiral Augusto Rademaker and Air Marshall Marcio de Souza Melo – decreed the Institutional Act Number 12 by which they informed the Nation of Costa e Silva's illness, and his inability to carry out his state functions. This military move indicated that civilian politicians could not under any circumstances assume the highest political office, for reasons of 'national security'. It is not coincidental that the two subsequent Vice-Presidents would also be military officers. Nonetheless, the marginalization of the politicians from the Presidency did not mean that the military would discard them. In fact the military Junta's take-over and the events which followed it, defined more clearly than ever before the place and role destined to the politicians: the place, Congress; and the role, the function of legitimizing the military power, not only in relation to society but primarily in relation to the military institution itself. Internal military dissension (which had in fact been growing before Costa e Silva's illness) intensified during the Junta's government.

Problems of 'national security' which were aggravated by the intensification of urban guerilla activity, particularly with the kidnapping
of the US Ambassador,[18] and the power struggle when it became
known that Costa e Silva was incapable of returning to his office,
were threatening the military unity. The nomination of General
Medici, after a month-long search to find a general who could be
widely accepted by the several groups within the Armed Forces, was
the compromise solution for the military crisis following Costa e
Silva's illness.[19] Then the role of politicians was to appear: to give
Congress's rubber-stamp to the appointment of General Emilio
Garrastazu Medici and Admiral Augusto Rademaker as President
and Vice-President for the next four years. Given the military's
internal conflict, it appears that Congress' formal endorsement was a
means of guaranteeing that the presidential nomination made by the
high Command of the Armed Forces would be accepted and respected,
thereby preventing the fomenting of rebellion within the military
corps.

Before the suspension of the Congressional recess, the Junta
resorted extensively to the AI–5, not only by purging more
politicians, but also by decreeing measures for curbing the radical
opposition. Examples are the Institutional Act Number 13 which
provided for the banishment of those who were considered as a
threat to national security, and the Institutional Act Number 14
which established the death penalty for cases of acts of
'revolutionary or subversive war'. In addition, a constitutional
revision (amendment Number 1 of the 1967 constitution) was
decreed, substantially modifying the already authoritarian 1967
Charter and retaining all the Institutional Acts decreed since
1968.

Under this restricted political order, Congress was summoned to
meet after more than ten months of imposed recess. On 25 October
1969 the Congress which had been reduced from 475 to 380 members
as a consequence of the political purges, 'elected' the new head of
state, with the votes of ARENA's 293 parliamentarians and 76
abstentions from the MDB's representatives. On the occasion,
General Medici promised to re-establish democracy and to promote
economic and social development. He stated as the task of his
government: 'to complete the 1964 Movement, by transforming it
into an authentic revolution of democracy and development.... This reform of the economic, social and political

institutions will not be achieved simply through corrective or repressive measures adopted at the whim of events. It actually demands a revolution.'[20] The inauguration of Medici's government began a new period of 'parliamentary politics' in which hopes would be mixed with discredit and fears about the future of the country's political life. This would bring back to the scene a tamed opposition party which would have to conform in order to survive.

THE PERIOD OF DISILLUSIONMENT: THE MDB FROM 1969 TO THE 1970 ELECTORAL DEFEAT

As we pointed out in the introduction to Part II, the MDB's space of action in the political system would depend on limits set by the regime. That space could vary according to the process of repression and relaxation of the military-authoritarian regime. We also mentioned that the MDB would go through a process of change in its behaviour which, although subordinated to the pendular opening and closing movements of the regime, would affect the political process as a whole. We can suppose the possibility that a political organization such as the MDB, which operated within a political system whose rules of the game were not well defined, could have its space enlarged according to the party's ability to exert pressure on the system in such a way as not to threaten the system as a whole. Thus the opposition party was always facing the problem of defining a strategy within the range from moderation to radicalization. The changes in the MDB's behaviour on the basis of that range, were not only a response to the regime's moves, but also the product of the ability of the different factions within the party to enforce their political orientation so as to become accepted as the party's official line. We have seen that, up to the end of 1968, the MDB tended towards radicalization.[21] In 1969 and 1970, we shall see that the party moved in the opposite direction, that is, towards moderation. If this was possibly the only feasible strategy to cope with a restrictive and repressive situation, it was also the product of the predominance of the moderate group in the party. The problem of adopting a too-moderate line would affect the party's electoral performance. If the MDB depended on the regime for its survival, it also depended on the electorate. Unlike the government party, the opposition could not have at its disposal the government machine to resort to patronage politics. Thus for the MDB the only means of getting electoral support was by building a credible image which differentiated it from ARENA, so as to attract the votes of those who did not support the government or the regime. We shall see later that one of the causes of the MDB's overwhelming defeat in the 1970 legislative elections was its inability to express the oppositional feelings of those who did not support the government party.

As we have said in the first section of this chapter, the military-authoritarian regime began a period of severe repression after 1968. Although there were signs that this repressive period would last much longer than similar situations in the past, there were also signs that the doors would not be completely closed, thus creating hopes for a future political relaxation. Based on these hopes the MDB adopted a policy of 'good behaviour' expecting that this would help to return the country to democracy.

The MDB returned to the scene after the 1968 crisis in such a quiet manner that it seemed that the opposition party had finally agreed to play the role the regime had originally intended for it when the two-party system was created. With its representation in the Federal Chamber reduced by half as a consequence of the political purges, and with the threat of the AI–5 over its parliamentarians' heads, the party quietly accepted the very restricted conditions to which it would have to conform. In fact, the MDB very soon had its role defined by the regime. In February 1969 a government spokesman announced that the government would expect a 'patriotic action from the opposition', meaning that 'constructive criticisms of the government and its administration will be welcome, but the opposition shall not abuse its role to the point of defying the Constitution and the regime'.[22] The government's warnings on its intolerance of opposition to the revolution and the regime, considered as a synonym for subversion, would be reiterated several times in the course of 1969. The borderline between what was considered acceptable opposition to the government and defiance of the regime was ill-defined, thus aggravating the MDB's difficulties in articulating an effective line of opposition. Moreover, the more militant elements of the party had been purged. As a consequence, the position of those who advocated a more moderate line became predominant within the party. If most of the MDB politicians who still could carry on their political career were moderate by nature, it is understandable that in such a repressive situation, the tendency was to assume a much more prudent stance.

During the long period of imposed Congressional recess the MDB remained involved with the problems of its reorganization in accordance with the requirements of the law on political parties. The government had issued a complementary act establishing a deadline for the parties to structure their organizations across the country as defined by that law which had, in fact, been promulgated four years before but had not yet been enforced. The law established that, in order to acquire permanent status, the political parties had to establish their organization in half the country's states. These regional organizations could only be created if the party had local organizations in at least a quarter of the state's number of municipalities. In short, ARENA and the MDB had to carry out the work of affiliating members to the party in a large number of municipalities in order to establish their organization over the country. It is obvious that in such adverse conditions this task would not be easy, particularly for the MDB. The political purges which affected the MDB at the federal level as well as at the state and local levels caused the disruption of the MDB's already weak organizational network. Moreover, local politicians and the electorate were reluctant to affiliate to a party which could be identified with subversion. Under such adverse conditions the argument for self-dissolution would be raised again. This tendency would have triumphed had it not been the government's intention to keep the opposition party alive. In any case, the fact that the party's self-dissolution would imply the cancellation of the mandates of the MDB politicians precluded this option.[23] The MDB opted to transfer its problem of survival to the government. It claimed that if the government intended to preserve the opposition party, it would have to provide minimal conditions to enable the opposition to operate, otherwise the regime would have to face the reality of a one-party system, which was a clear feature of non-democratic regimes.[24] Since it was in the regime's interest to maintain the façade of democracy, the government promptly responded to the MDB's demands by relaxing the law's procedures for the creation of municipal directorates. In addition, the Minister of Justice announced to the press the assurance that people were allowed to affiliate to the MDB, and that there was no danger attached to belonging to the opposition party. He nevertheless concluded that the government would not tolerate defiance, agitation and subversion to the regime.[25]

During the period of compulsory parliamentary recess, little was heard about the MDB apart from those problems related to the organization of the party. The party's leadership even avoided summoning the national directorate as had been demanded by the Rio Grande do Sul MDB's section which wanted to discuss the party's problems and future. A meeting of the national directorate was also necessary for the nomination of a new general-secretary since that position became vacant due to the *cassação* of the party's secretary, Deputy Martins Rodrigues. The MDB president Oscar Passos preferred, however, to nominate the substitute himself, and chose the moderate and ex-UDN Deputy Adolfo de Oliveira. By avoiding a party meeting the MDB leadership possibly wanted to prevent a situation in which protests against the government's constant purges could have arisen, for fear of further weakening of the position of the party. The national directorate was only summoned when the government announced the suspension of the recess of Congress and the MDB needed to define its position with regard to the 'election' of General Medici. The MDB's national directorate eventually decided to attend the Congress meeting which was to 'elect' General Medici, but the opposition would abstain from voting. This position received the support of the majority of the Directorate's members with the exception of Senator Josafá Marinho and the deputies Franco Montoro and João Borges who argued that the MDB should absent itself from that Congressional session so as to stress its rejection of the 'indirect election'.

The speech that the MDB's president (Oscar Passos) addressed to the Congress on the occasion of Medici's 'election' was cautious. The MDB leader nonetheless did not avoid making criticisms of the new order established with the AI–5 and the 1969 constitutional amendment. Nor did he forget to pay tribute to the purged parliamentarians who were not allowed to come back to Congress. Senator Passos reiterated the MDB's fight for democracy, amnesty and national economic development, within the use of legal means, and announced the party's intention to 'give credit to the promised normalization of the national life', thus hoping that the new President would promote the re-establishment of the rule of law.[26] Senator Passos's speech seemed to indicate that the party would resolutely intend to function as an effective opposition, albeit cautioned by prudence.

In the subsequent parliamentary meetings the MDB's leaders in both legislative houses also criticized the AI–5 and the arbitrary legislation decreed by the government, remarking on the opposition's disappointment about the often-announced reopening of the political process. Nonetheless, the opposition party would soon show that it preferred to be prudent and moderate before anything else. The new line of the party became explicit in the leadership's statements emphasizing that the MDB was not to oppose the revolution but to accept the rules so as to become a trustworthy party able to compete for power. As the general-secretary Adolfo de Oliveira announced, the MDB's main task was to prepare itself for the next elections by which the party could enlarge its influence and become a political force whose access to power could be seen as an acceptable alternative in the eyes of the Armed Forces. He considered that the MDB should not criticize the restricted situation to which the party had to conform, rather it should re-establish its image as a legal party so as to be trusted by the regime.[27] In short, the MDB's general-secretary was advocating just the line of 'good behaviour' and collaboration with the government that the regime expected from the MDB. As a journalist later commented on the position defended by the MDB's general-secretary, 'the deputy Adolfo de Oliveira cannot be an ardent revolutionary, but he is much closer to this attitude than to an opposition line. The circumstance of his having been appointed as MDB's secretary just demonstrates the extreme level of alienation reached by the party after the devastation which the AI–5 produced in its ranks.[28]

The criticisms addressed to the party in the press were a clear indication that the strategy advocated by the MDB's general-secretary had been indeed put into practice. The political commentator C. C. Branco constantly remarked on the MDB's conformist and submissive attitude in Congress during the course of 1970. In his criticism he defined as excessively prudent the MDB's performance in Congress where its presence had been reduced to vague statements about the problems of the political situation. He added that in Congress 'there is a fear that a sole voice or the action of a small group, could jeopardize the entire political class'.[29] The deputy Pedroso Horta, for example, was several times restrained by the MDB leadership who feared that his vehement speeches would jeopardize the survival of Congress. On one occasion, he was persuaded by his colleagues to refrain from making a speech in which he was going to denounce cases of torture against political prisoners. The journalist C. C. Branco also remarked that the MDB was adhering too strictly to the regime's slogan of permitting opposition to the government but not to the regime. By doing so while serving the purpose of the regime, the MDB would discredit itself among the opposition public opinion. On 19 April 1970 C. C. Branco wrote:

> The opposition does not give any sign that its resistance is legitimate, thus disregarding the fact that its deputies and

senators exercise a popular mandate originating in direct elections. The role of the opposition is to express, through its criticism, its non-conformity, its combat, that part of public opinion dissatisfied with the present conduct of the state. The MDB does not have the right to nullify itself on the pretext that it must not indulge in those practices which the government set beyond its limits of tolerance. . . . The MDB must contest the borderlines. . . By defining its tactics of excessive prudence, the MDB leadership will have only identified a reality to which they provisionally conform. We think however that an authentic opposition party needs a dose of quixotism which is the sign of idealism inherent in every real opposition.[30]

Possibly the journalist was expecting too much of the MDB in such adverse conditions. The fact that the MDB was constantly suffering the consequences of the punitive sword of the regime,[31] did not, nonetheless, justify the adoption of a collaborationist attitude, as witnessed by the MDB's attempt to enter into negotiations with the government on political reforms by offering suggestions to the Minister of Justice. To quote C. C. Branco's comments again: 'perhaps the country has never had, at any time, an opposition so inclined to visit government's offices and so remiss in its Congressional functions'.[32]

The MDB's excessively conformist behaviour was certainly one of the factors which contributed to the party's overwhelming defeat in the 1970 elections. In that election the MDB's representation in Congress was drastically reduced. Only 5 of the 46 senatorial seats contested and 28 per cent of the Federal Chamber's seats were captured by the MDB. Moreover, most of the MDB leaders running for re-election were defeated: the party's national president Senator Oscar Passos; the treasurer Senator Ermirio de Moraes; the party's leader in the Senate, Senator Aurelio Vianna; the leader in the Federal Chamber, Deputy Humberto Lucena who ran for a senatorial seat; the party's president in São Paulo, Senator Lino de Mattos; and also the senators Josafá Marinho and Argemiro de Figueiredo. The fact that the MDB had not shown any sign of genuine opposition in 1970, combined with its cautious electoral campaign, contributed to the discrediting of the opposition party's image among the electorate. As the newspaper *Jornal da Tarde* reported the comments about the MDB defeat: 'By having accommodated itself to the situation, the MDB did not differentiate from ARENA, leaving the electorate without any valid option: either voting for an openly government party, or voting for a false opposition party, or leaving the ballot paper blank as so many did.'[33]

We must point out that the themes officially defined by the MDB in July as the basis for its electoral campaign were not very different from the ones that the party would use later, in 1974: return to democracy – that is, revocation of the Institutional Acts, re-establishment of direct elections, *habeas corpus*, defence of human rights – and attention to socio-economic issues such as wage policy, agrarian reform, education, and defence of the economy against foreign capital. The problem in 1970 was that very few candidates actually stressed these themes during the electoral campaign. In fact, the MDB politicians who had assumed a more combative opposition attitude in Congress and emphasized those issues in the electoral campaign, obtained considerable electoral support. This was particularly the case of Oscar Pedroso Horta, São Paulo's federal deputy who received more votes than any MDB's candidate for the chamber in that state. It was also the case of Deputy Franco Montoro who won one of the two seats for São Paulo in the Senate, while the other MDB candidate for the Senate, Senator Lino de Mattos was not re-elected.[34]

However, the cause of the MDB defeat cannot be attributable only to the party's moderate performance. This factor certainly contributed to the increase in the number of blank and null ballots, which was stimulated by the campaign staged by the left in support of the spoiled ballot. There are other factors which decisively interfered in the election. The government's control exerted over the electoral process was perhaps the greatest ever seen in Brazil. The government machine, from federal to local level, was extensively used to get votes for ARENA by means of traditional patronage politics. This made even the MDB protest against the State governor's interference in the electoral campaign, regarded by the opposition as a means of pressure and instrument of corruption and violence towards the electorate.[35] We must point out that resort to clientelism is a feature present in the electoral process throughout Brazilian history. What is characteristic of the post-1964 period is that, since the opposition was barred from getting power in the central and state governments, the use of government machine as a means of gathering electoral support became a monopoly of the political forces which supported the regime.[36]

Another means of control exerted by the government was through censorship of the press, radio and television in the electoral campaign and through police repression. The government intimidated the opposition not only by threatening it with the possibility of 'closing everything' in case that the campaign was used as means of political agitation against the regime,[37] but also by resorting to police repression. On 4 November – ten days before the elections – the political police apparatus launched a wave of massive arrests across the country on the pretext of searching for terrorists. The wide police operation arrested indiscriminately whoever was considered 'suspicious', from writers, artists, lawyers, to MDB politicians.[38]

To counter-balance the repressive measures against the opposition, the regime showed the electorate the high rates of economic growth produced by the so-called 'Brazilian miracle'. Government propaganda massively intensified during the election campaign through the use of radio and television, showed the Revolution's achievements and presented an image of President Medici as the great entrepreneur who would make Brazil a future Great Power. Examples of the government's search for electoral support were the promulgation, in September, of the Programme for Social Integration (PIS) – the regime's version of workers' sharing in productivity[39] – and the announcement in October of the government's *Plano de Metas* which, among other things, would promote the so-called *projetos-impacto* (impact projects) such as the building of the Trans-Amazon highway aiming at integrating the distant and poor North region to development. All this propaganda would add optimism to the existing widespread atmosphere of euphoria produced by Brazil's winning of its third Football World Cup. In July ARENA had already announced that its electoral campaign would be based not only on the 'revolutionary government's accomplishments' but also on Brazilian successes in sports: football, basketball, volleyball, tennis and horse racing.[40] Democracy would also be mentioned in ARENA's campaign, but as an aim to be achieved in the future. As Senator Mem de Sá stated in his campaign for re-election, 'if we still do not have an ideal democracy, at least we have a formal democracy, with Congress and free elections (sic). Only developed countries can afford to have a perfect democracy. And this is exactly what President Medici intends: to leave the government with Brazil under complete democratic freedom.'[41]

Under such unfavourable circumstances for the opposition party, the MDB faced problems in recruiting candidates to contest an uncompetitive election for unattractive legislative mandates. In fact, to challenge for a legislative mandate had become so unattractive that even the government party experienced problems in filling the lists of candidates for the Federal Chamber. Obviously for the MDB the difficulty would be much greater as evidenced by the fact that in 14 out of 22 States, the party did not manage to recruit enough candidates to fill the State's list for the Federal Chamber. In Bahia State, for example, the MDB ran only 6 candidates for that State's 22 seats in the Federal Chamber, and in Minas Gerais the party had only 19 candidates for the 35 seats.[42] Also, in 11 States the MDB put up only one candidate to contest the senatorial elections, when in every State two senatorial seats were being contested. These all reduced MDB's possibility of getting a larger representation in Congress.

The crushing defeat of the MDB – much greater than in the 1966 legislative elections – astonished not only the opposition party but also the government, for whom an excessively weak opposition was not convenient. As the *Jornal da Tarde* pointed out in its comment on the election results: 'ARENA had surely expected to win the elections. What it had not predicted was to massacre the MDB. . . . The massacre does not serve government's interest. After all, it is essential for the regime to have an opposition which is numerically strong enough to be noticed and weak enough not to create problems.'[43] ARENA's just-elected Senator Tarso Dutra expressed his concern about the MDB's defeat, stating that if the government had known this would occur to such an extent it would have taken some precautions to avoid the disaster. He considered that the MDB's merely symbolic representation in Congress might produce an image abroad of the country being under a one-party regime.[44] Although ARENA had obtained a large majority in Congress, the government could not disregard the fact that ARENA's victory was in fact based on weak electoral support, given the large amount of blank and spoiled ballots, which for the Federal Chamber reached 30 per cent of the total. This certainly also produced government concern albeit unacknowledged.

There was no doubt that the MDB had good reasons to blame the government for its electoral defeat. Nonetheless the electoral results had also clearly shown the consequences of the MDB's submissive behaviour as an opposition party. The MDB which had been punished by the regime for having assumed a more radical stance in the 1968 political crisis, was punished by the electorate in 1970 for having moved too far along the path of moderation.

THE 1971–3 PERIOD: THE PRELUDE TO THE 1974 ELECTORAL VICTORY

The MDB's electoral defeat in the 1970 elections produced great discouragement among the party's ranks but also brought out the feeling that something should be done if the party was not to disappear. Predictably, the position advocating the party's self-dissolution emerged once more; although, as happened previously, it was more a manifestation of MDB impotence than a position which could command support within the party. But if the party's self-dissolution had on several occasions proved infeasible and unwanted, as we explained before, the opposition party still had to do something more than complain about its unfortunate situation. Among the MDB leadership it became accepted that although the control exerted by the regime over the 1970 election was the main cause for the electoral defeat, the party itself had to bear the blame for failing to be a credible alternative for the electorate. We shall see that, in the period from 1971 to 1974, the MDB underwent a process of change in its orientation so as to build a more favourable image of the opposition party towards the electorate. Contrary to current assertions which recognize a change of the MDB's strategy only in the 1974 electoral campaign, we shall see that the opposition party had actually gone through a process of change after 1971 as a response to the 1970 electoral defeat.

The first sign of change has to do with the party's leadership. Those MDB leaders who were defeated in that election resigned from their positions in the party's national executive committee. As a consequence the MDB's national presidency was transferred to its then vice-president Deputy Ulysses Guimarães, an ex-PSD politician from São Paulo whose political ability would later prove to be an important factor in the revitalization of the MDB. Perhaps more important was the nomination of the Deputy Pedroso Horta as the opposition leader in the Federal Chamber – a clear indication of the party's recognition of the failure of its excessively moderate line, since this deputy was one of the few MDB parliamentarians who had vigorously criticized the regime in 1970. In fact the nomination of Pedroso Horta would be a very important step in the MDB's process of change. The deputy from São Paulo, reinforced by the significant number of votes received in his re-election, would keep his firm opposition attitude and would also contribute to the renewal of the party by nominating eight deputies of first mandate as vice-leaders in the Federal Chamber (thus half the 17 positions in the vice-leadership). This, as we shall see later, would contribute to the creation of the so-called *grupo autentico*.

As early as February 1971 Pedrosa Horta gave a press interview in which he not only called for the revocation of the AI–5 and the re-establishment of democracy, but also touched a very sensitive point for the regime: he denounced the use of torture on political prisoners, mentioning specific cases such as the murder by poisoning of a trade-union leader in São Paulo's Military Hospital, and the disappearance of the ex-deputy Rubem Paiva, who had been arrested in Rio de Janeiro. He continued the interview saying that 'up to now our regime has been a dictatorship. We are waiting, however, for the solemn promises made by President Medici for the country's redemocratization.'[45] When he was asked about the government's achievements in its economic policy he replied: 'I would rather quote President Medici who said: "the country is getting richer and richer and the people poorer and poorer".[46] Although Pedroso Horta had earlier made similar statements, at this time he was addressing criticism in his capacity as leader of the party in the Federal Chamber, thus as a party's official spokesman. In this respect, his statements in this interview can be seen as the first sign of the MDB's willingness to adopt a more combative opposition stance. By asserting this we do not mean to suggest that the MDB's leadership had already agreed on the adoption of a more aggressive opposition line, but just to point it out as an indication of some receptivity among the leadership towards a revision of the MDB's strategies. In fact, Pedroso Horta's interview provoked a strong reaction by the general-secretary Adolfo de Oliveira who considered the interview a manifestation of radicalism which was harmful to the party. The reaction of the MDB's general-secretary was an indication that the revision of the MDB's line would be a long process. It would involve internal dissension which would sometimes undermine the party's possibility of effective action. In any case, among the party leadership there were elements who recognized the convenience of adopting a more aggressive stance. These elements would react more receptively to the pressures which would come from those groups within the party demanding changes.

From 1971 onwards there were indeed indications that the MDB was more determined to become a dynamic and forceful party and occupy the small space for legal opposition allowed by the regime. In

Congress the party started to show its presence more effectively, scheduling its parliamentarians to speak about specific political and economic issues. Criticisms of the increasing foreign investments in the economy, of the government's gigantic project of the Trans-Amazon highway, of the death penalty decree, press censorship and so on were raised by the MDB parliamentarians. After being so inactive in 1970, the inauguration of the new legislative term with an opposition assuming more initiative, took ARENA so much by surprise that the opposition began to lead the debate in Congress. According to an ARENA parliamentarian the opposition was using the weapons it had got: 'initiative and sensationalism'. The first, he explained, gave the opposition an advantage over ARENA, since the MDB parliamentarians spent days and days preparing their speeches, while ARENA had to improvise its replies; and the second – 'sensationalism' – opened the pages of the press to the opposition.[47]

The MDB also appeared to be more dynamic in working through its organization across the country. As a means of publicizing the party's activities in Congress as well as providing elements for the defence of the party's official orientation by its representatives in the State Assemblies, the MDB national leadership started to send copies of the main speeches made in the Congress to the regional directorates and state deputies. Also, a series of regional meetings were promoted with the aim of revitilizing the party. The first was held in Porto Alegre (Rio Grande do Sul), in April 1971, gathering about 1500 party members whose objective was to study and debate the country's socio-economic and political situation. At that meeting a manifesto was drawn up – the *Declaração de Porto Alegre* – stating twenty principles to be advocated by the party. Besides calling for amnesty and democracy, the manifesto advocated voting rights for illiterates, effective agrarian reform, a just wage policy, rational control over foreign capital borrowings and control over foreign investments in the economy.[48]

In July, in Recife (Pernambuco), another meeting was organized by the party. On this occasion, a group of new parliamentarians who would later be known as the *grupo autentico*, marked its presence for the first time by calling for a national constituent assembly. This in fact provoked a sharp debate on the relative merits of the party's adoption of an issue considered radical for the time. Those who were against it argued that the party should accept the 1964 revolution as an irreversible fact, and fight instead, for the return of the less authoritarian 1967 constitution. The advocates of the constituent assembly, refusing to recognize any constitutional framework produced by the post 1964-regime, argued that the fight for the summoning of a national constituent assembly and the drawing up of a democratic constitution, was a fundamental step for the country's democratization. The proponents of this position won the debate, managing to have it included in that meeting's manifesto – the *Carta de Recife* (Letter from Recife). Nonetheless the slogan of the national constituent assembly was hardly remembered after its announcement in that manifesto.[49] In fact, the outcome of the Recife meeting, rather than indicating the party's adoption of a more radical position, opened a long period of internal dissensions within the MDB.

Pressure Groups within the MDB

A decisive factor which would influence the revision of the MDB's attitude after 1970, was the criticism of and pressure on the leadership from groups within the party. We can identify at least two groups which would exert pressure on the leadership over the question of changing the party's line. The first came from a group of politicians from São Paulo state led by the Mayor of Campinas, Orestes Quércia. In February 1971, at a party meeting in Campinas with the presence of several national leaders, Quércia made sharp criticisms of the MDB leadership and called for a revision of the party's election strategy. He blamed the party's leaders for being too attached to the past and not listening to the people's aspirations. He claimed: 'We are not interested in the past. . . . In Campinas, as in the rest of Brazil, we are a generation of politicians who did not participate in that past, nor in the dissensions and fights which occured then.'[50] He was referring to the period prior to 1964 and advocating that the MDB should accept the 1964 revolution as a fact.[51] Also, Quércia demanded a revision of the MDB's strategies in electoral campaigns. He maintained that the party should not restrict its electoral appeal on political issues, but that it should instead incorporate themes related to the government's economic policies. He stated:

> When we make an effort at seeking the re-establishment of *habeas corpus*, the revocation of the AI–5 and the defence of the democratic freedom, we indeed carry out our primordial duty and

devote ourselves to just and noble causes.... But, it is also important for the MDB to go along with the national problems, with the
issues related to development.... Apart from direct elections,
democratic freedom, there are questions which vitally interest the
nation and deserve the people's thoughtful attention.... Our task
is to listen to the people's aspirations, to interpret them and
condense them in a programme of immediate action.[52]

Aiming at increasing the electoral support of the MDB he advocated
a pragmatic line to 'avoid radicalization which would obstruct any
possibility of the party becoming the government in the future'.[53]
However pragmatic the position defended by Quercia, he was at
least right in pointing out the MDB's necessity of changing its electoral appeal so as to express the social and economic problems of the
population. The fight for democracy alone, which had been the
main slogan of the MDB in electoral campaigns, seemed to evoke
little response from an electorate quite disillusioned with the electoral process. Quercia's group nonetheless would be more concerned
with enlarging its influence on the São Paulo section of the MDB.
His actions to exert control over the party's organization in that state
and carry out his ambitions to be the MDB's candidate for the governorship in 1974, [54] made him implement the building of the MDB
organization in the interior São Paulo. The work developed by
Quercia was actually very decisive in his eventual nomination for
the MDB's candidacy for the Senate in 1974. If Quercia's group
limited its actions basically to the state of São Paulo, at national level
another pressure group over the national leadership emerged, one
that became known as the *grupo autentico*.

The *grupo autentico* (authentic group), as the press named a group of
deputies whose presence in Congress became very active, resembled
in some way the former *grupo dos imaturos* which, as we showed in
the previous chapter, had been so militant in the MDB during 1967
and 1968. The 1970 elections brought to the Federal Chamber a
group of new deputies willing to make the MDB a forceful voice of
opposition to the regime. Obviously, they faced far more restrictive
conditions than the ones which the former *grupo dos imaturos*
encountered but, as the latter, they would not only assume a more
aggressive performance but also pressurise the party's leadership for
the adoption of a more determined opposition line. The group consisted basically of first time deputies and represented about 25 per

cent of the MDB's parliamentarians in the Federal Chamber. Talking about the creation of the group, the Deputy Fernando Lyra narrated:

In 1970 I was elected MDB deputy from Pernambuco. When I arrived here (in the Federal Chamber), by a curious coincidence several colleagues who immediately identified themselves with our line also arrived. Among them I would mention Francisco Pinto and Alencar Furtado, and with them I had the first talks about the necessity of our adopting a vanguard role. But I could name about 20 colleagues who shared more or less this position ... Colleagues coming from different places, one or two from each state, met here in 1971.... Some of them were here before, such as Deputy Paes de Andrade, Santilli Sobrinho ... who joined our struggle. Paes de Andrade is an ex-PSD politician from Ceará, and was nominated the Chamber's second-secretary; and it was at the second-secretariat's office that we used to meet, discuss and prepare our strategy.... But I must say that we had very important help from Deputy Pedroso Horta. He was the party's leader in the House and a very conscious and convinced liberal. He nominated almost all of us for the positions of vice-leaders: myself, Alencar Furtado, Marcos Freire, Nadir Rossetti, Alceu Collares ... Through Pedroso Horta, because of his liberal convictions and obstinacy in the fight for democracy, we had the opportunity to act.... Despite strict press censorship we managed to break into the news and our speeches, made with a lot of difficulty, started to be publicized. We denounced the tortures, all the violation of human rights, we called for a Constitutional Assembly and the extinction of the AI-5. We were considered to be the group of *contestação* against the *sistema*.... In fact we had to carry out two kinds of struggle: we had to fight within the MDB in order to bring the party over to our position; and we had to fight against the system.[55]

The *grupo autentico* cannot be characterized as having a clearly defined idealogical orientation which would distinguish it from the moderate sectors of the party. As the Deputy João Gilberto quite properly characterized it, 'courage rather than ideology, was the mark of the *autenticos*'.[56] A similar account of this group was given by Ulysses Guimarães, the MDB national president:

The dissensions between *autenticos* and *moderados* were rather a

problem of generation: the *autenticos* were young parliamentarians. Second, they wanted positions in the party. They wanted
even the party's presidency, the leadership, which traditional
figures had been holding. It was not a struggle of an ideological
nature; because everybody was in the opposition. It was rather a
different style of opposition. They were younger and perhaps
more militant...I used to say that they just wanted to
use organizational instruments – the leadership, the executive
committee – to put into practice their ideas. But it was not a
conflict based on ideological reasons. Anyhow I think that the
autenticos brought into the party much energy, much life, because
they were very active, they occupied space in the press -something
very important. The press naturally publicized the disagreements
as a conflict within the party between *autenticos* and *moderados*,
anyhow this was publicity for the party, we appeared in the
press.[57]

The *grupo autentico* wanted the party to take a more aggressive
attitude in its opposition performance. The *autenticos*, therefore, not
only had an active presence in Congress but also fought for control
of the party's leadership. The struggle for the leadership would
become, from 1972 onwards, one of the main issues involving the
party's internal divisions between *autenticos* and *moderados*. In
February 1972 the *autenticos* sent a letter of demands to the party's
national executive committee requesting not only a revision of the
party's statute and programme but also the key position of either the
national presidency or the general-secretary for a representative of
the group. In this letter they criticized the leadership for not having
yet defined a clear line compatible with a spirit of opposition. The
deputy Alencar Furtado explained the group's position: 'the MDB
leadership had forgotten the demands of the people, the situation of
the workers. The MDB has not studied the government's development plan, as a consequence, it has not been pointing out the
government's mistakes and failures.'[58] The group therefore wanted
key positions in the party's executive committee so as to exert more
influence on the definition of the MDB's line and performance.

The *grupo autentico*'s pressure for the participation in the party's
command had in fact emerged since the replacement of the party's
leader in the Federal Chamber. The leader Pedroso Horta – a supporter of the group – fell ill and was replaced by the moderate
Deputy Jairo Brum. This caused discontent among the *autenticos*

who, failing in their attempt to elect a representative of the group for that position, saw their influence diminish. The dissension between *autenticos* and *moderados* would be sharpened in April 1972 when the election for the party's national directorate took place. After unsuccessful attempts at negotiations between the two groups in order to work out a distribution of the places in the party's executive committee, the *autenticos* decided to present a dissident list to contest all the places in the executive committee. In the election which was held during the national convention, the *autenticos'* dissident list received 96 votes, while Ulysses Guimarães, heading the official list, was re-elected as the party president with 200 votes. Despite having been defeated, the *autenticos* obtained fourteen places (out of forty-nine) in the national directorate, since the political party law guaranteed representation proportionally to the votes obtained by each list. At that national convention the party programme was also revised, as demanded by the *autenticos*, to include a diagnosis of the Brazilian socio-economic situation.[59]

The *grupo autentico* made a valuable contribution to the revitalization of the MDB. The more militant deputies who raised criticisms which put in question the government's policies and the nature of the regime, contributed to improving the image of the opposition party.[60] Moreover, their pressures on the leadership had a positive effect regarding the revision of the party's strategies. Nonetheless the internal dispute between *autenticos* and *moderados* over positions in the leadership, occupied a lot of the party's energy and hampered the MDB's ability to function as a party in a more structured and coordinated way. The MDB's performance in Congress in 1972 for example, received widespread criticism in the press for having been ineffective because of the party's preoccupation with its internal disputes. This was pointed out by the press as the main cause of the poor results obtained by the opposition party in the 1972 municipal elections.[61] Certainly, the MDB's performance in Congress was dependent on individual initiatives, particularly of the more militant deputies, rather than on concerted action based on a strategy defined by the party.[62] The lack of an organized strategy by the MDB in Congress, caused the individual initiatives of the militant elements to be lost for lack of continuity in the party's actions. But the Congress itself had become so powerless and the MDB's representation was so numerically weak, that even if the opposition party had dedicated most of its effort to legislative matters, the outcome would probably not have been very different.

Regarding the 1972 municipal elections, it would be unfair to stress the party's shortcomings as the cause of its electoral defeat, as most political commentators and some groups within the party had claimed. In fact, in the 1972 municipal elections the MDB did try to co-ordinate a more appealing electoral campaign. Aimed at giving a nationwide orientation to the party's campaign, the national directorate produced a manual (guidelines for the candidates) which not only raised the problems of the municipalities but also pointed out their links to the government's national policies and their social implications.[63] Nonetheless the meagre results obtained by the MDB in those elections showed that this attempt had little effect in terms of increasing the electoral support of the party. One of the main reasons certainly lies in the nature of those elections. They were municipal elections to choose mayors and local councillors, thus making it difficult to introduce themes of national scope in a dispute dominated by local politics. The situation of dependence of municipal governments on the state governments – so long rooted in Brazilian political system and aggravated after 1964 – makes opposition politics at a local level difficult.[64] This situation was aggravated by the fact that the MDB had not established a strong organization. In those elections the MDB was not able to present candidates in more than half the municipalities where elections were held because the party had not created local organizations. Apart from these problems faced by the opposition party, the repressive political climate which existed in the 1970 elections was repeated in 1972. In August 1972, a deputy leader of ARENA denounced in the Federal Chamber an alleged involvement of the MDB with the Brazilian Communist Party (PCB). Presenting a document provided by the National Security Information Agency (SNI) he claimed to have uncovered negotiations between MDB candidates and PCB elements. Aside from the attempt at intimidation, arrests were carried out again during the electoral campaign, including an MDB councillor in São Paulo and several MDB local politicians in Goias.[65] Therefore, the tight political situation still at its high point and the nature of the 1972 elections, made it difficult for the MDB to obtain any fruit from that election when the party had just started a process of change. We must say that in fact the electoral support that the MDB would later obtain (in 1974) was not a product of its conduct in Congress but a result of the implementation of a strategy to reach the electorate by slowly building the image of an opposition party through electoral campaigns. Notwithstanding the other factors that influenced the 1974 legislative elections, which will be discussed in the next chapter, it must be underlined that the MDB gradually developed an effective strategy which would help the creation of a more favourable party image among the electorate. In this respect, the campaign of the 'anti-candidate' for the Presidency of the Republic in 1973, was an important contribution.

The 'Anti-candidacy' for the Presidency of the Republic

The *autenticos* proposed in early 1973 that the MDB should contest the indirect election for the Presidency scheduled to take place on 15 January 1974. Nobody had any doubt on the 'marked cards' of that election which would only reconfirm the previously chosen successor to Medici: General Ernesto Geisel. The purpose of the MDB's participation in that electoral game was to use the opportunity for launching a nationwide opposition campaign. This campaign would not only serve to denounce the false process by which the President of the Republic was selected, but it would also provide a way of reaching the electorate, thereby planting the seeds which could bear fruit in the campaign for the legislative elections in the following year. This strategy, suggested by the *autenticos*, received the support of the moderates who controlled the party leadership, although they considered that this issue should be discussed only after the government had defined the rules for the composition of the Electoral College. Nevertheless disagreement about the procedures to implement it soon started to provoke dissensions between the two groups. The first problem arose about the choice of the MDB candidates. The *autenticos* were not very keen on accepting the name of Ulysses Guimarães, the MDB national president, since they considered that a 'national name', not linked to the MDB, might be more capable of obtaining support from all opposition sectors in the country.

Despite the opposition of the *autenticos*, on 5 September 1973 the national directorate approved unanimously the names of Ulysses Guimarães and the journalist Barbosa Lima Sobrinho as the MDB candidates for President and Vice-President. On 22 September, the MDB candidates received the approval of the party's national convention in a meeting which was regarded by the press as 'the most important political manifestation of the opposition since 1968'. As the commentator continued, 'if ARENA will have the advantage of having the certainty of its imposed candidate being elected for the Presidency, the MDB at least had the right to choose its candidate who will be defeated'.[66] The Convention had its high point when the candidate Ulysses Guimarães made a brilliant and vehement speech which received the approval even of the more radical elements within the party. In his speech in which he named the MDB's campaign an anti-candidate campaign for the Presidency, he started by saying:

A paradox is the hallmark of the present Brazilian presidential succession. For the government, the announced candidate is already the President, who is not waiting for his election but only to take office. Neither is there a candidate for the opposition, since there cannot be a candidate for a position which has been filled beforehand.... The lack of viability of the opposition candidate testifies to the nation and to the world that the current system is not democratic.... It is not an MDB candidate who will travel throughout the country. It is an anti-candidate, who will denounce the anti-election imposed by the anti-constitution which the AI–5 expounds, submitting the legislature and judiciary to executive power, allowing arrests without the safeguard of *habeas corpus* and condemnations without defence; violating the privacy of homes and offices with clandestine listening devices, rendering dissenting voices inaudible through censorship over the press, the radio, television, theatre and cinema.[67]

Stressing the MDB's commitment to freedom and social justice as preconditions for development, he criticized the so-called Brazilian economic miracle by stating:

We must emphasize that development is not a monumental and inhuman silo built to store and exhibit the mythology or folklore of the gross domestic product, an inaccessible treasure in the deep sea, unattainable to the people. It is intolerable to mystify a nation on the pretext of developing it, to reduce the nation to a store of wealth having as its privileged or even exclusive clientele, the government which finances pharoah-like enterprises and the economic might, individual or entrepreneurial, particularly foreign, *denationalizing* our industry and withdrawing from the country undeserved profits.[68]

The MDB's candidate also made reference to the future president, claiming that history had granted General Geisel perhaps the last opportunity for the re-establishment in Brazil 'through evolution, of a government of order with liberty, of development with social justice, of people as the origin and finality of power.... [69] He concluded his speech calling for political amnesty and, paraphrasing the Portuguese writer Fernando Pessoa in his verse 'Navegar é preciso. Viver não é preciso', Ulysses Guimarães compared the MDB campaign to the departure of a sailboat from the harbour aiming at liberty: 'Posto hoje no alto da gávea, espero em Deus que em breve possa gritar ao povo brasileiro: Alvissaras, meu capitão. Terra à vista! Sem sombra, medo e pesadelo, à vista a terra limpa e abençoada da liberdade'.[70]

Commentating on the speech of the MDB's candidate, the journalist Carlos Chagas wrote on the day after the convention:

> In a climate of arbitrarity ... suffocated by a system which forbids the opposition the simple right of communication with the people, Ulysses Guimarães's words had the same effect as a thunderbolt in the dark night. With extreme simplicity, his words revealed the dark clouds, showing them all in their immensity.... Transfigured into a Quixote who did not lack the company of Sancho Panza in the figure of Barbosa Lima Sobrinho, the MDB's chairman summarized in 20 minutes a picture which took ten years to be crystallized in the unexpected form that we see today. He did not contest it, but showed it. He did not subvert but denounced. He did not complain but showed paths.... The voice of the MDB chairman united and projected the party as never before. It is possible to predict that if the opposition campaign can be carried out, it will represent one of the high points in this difficult period of Brazilian current politics.[71]

Despite the indication in the MDB national convention that the candidates were really committed to the implementation of an effective campaign capable of uniting *autenticos* and *moderados* in a common aim, dissensions between the two groups would emerge again. This time it would be about how the campaign should progress in case the party were denied access to radio and TV broadcasting. It was the MDB's intention to develop its campaign not only through the promotion of public rallies and party meetings across the country, but also through the use of the mass media. According to the electoral law, parties were granted free access to radio and television in the sixty days before an election. As the law was not explicit regarding the nature of the elections (that is, direct or occasion, the *autenticos*, who had sent a signed statement to the Electoral College's chairman, declared their vote by saying: 'I refuse to vote as stated in the manifesto which was handed to the House's chairman and which was prohibited from receiving publicity in the press.'[73] In the manifesto which carried the signature of twenty-one federal deputies, they stated:

> We give our right to vote back to the great absentees: the Brazilian people, whose wish, which was withdrawn from the process, should be the source of all power. . . . Faithful to the party's programme which condemns indirect elections, we had admitted the party's candidacy only as a means of enlarging the precarious ribbon of communication, thus trying to re-establish the dialogue with the Brazilian people. At no time did we acknowledge that the anti-candidates should be converted to candidates. . . . Therefore our refusal to vote in this rubber-stamp College is an expression of dissent of those who do not vote, of those who do not choose, of those who do not decide and even cannot speak.[74]

Undoubtedly the *autenticos* had a strong argument in refusing to participate in that election which certainly gave a façade of legitimacy to the appointment of Geisel who had actually been already elected by another more restricted 'electoral college', that is, the so-called military system. Nevertheless we should also regard the attitude taken by the group as an indication of low esteem for democratic procedure, since they ignored a decision approved by the party's national convention which was supposed to be the party's sovereign body.[75] In any case, it seems to be quite unrealistic to expect that the MDB, whose majority was moderate, would opt for the position assumed by the *autenticos*. Certainly the position taken by the MDB of playing the game according to the regime's rules covered the appointment of the new President with a façade of legitimacy. But we must also point out that under the restricted political situation that existed at the time, the moderate leadership had advanced considerably since the party's period of retirement after the 1968 crisis. It is undeniable that the party leadership, although moderate, had the capacity to revise its position and to mount an effective presidential campaign. Moreover, the 'anti-candidate' campaign served as a barometer for the MDB leadership to measure a latent climate of dissatisfaction among the population, thus making it realize the MDB's potential to become the vehicle for the expression of that discontent. The perception of the MDB's main issue which would provoke a heated debate, at the convention, was around the participation of the opposition candidates in the election at the Electoral College. The *autenticos* put forward a motion which accepted the continuation of the campaign but advocated the resignation of the MDB's candidates before the election day so that they would not be submitted to the vote. The argument defended by the *autenticos* was that if the MDB voted for its candidates in the Electoral College this would legitimize Geisel's appointment and even the current political regime. Arguing against this position, Barbosa Lima Sobrinho – the MDB's vice-presidential candidate – pointed out: 'Some sectors within the party think that the participation in the indirect elections on the 15 of January would, in fact, endorse them. But, following this logic, the presence of MDB parliamentarians in the legislative house would also imply an endorsement of the regime.'[72]

At the national convention the opinion of the moderate majority prevailed in approving the continuation of the campaign and the participation of the MDB candidates in the contest at the Electoral College. As some political commentators underlined, it would be too bold a defiance of the regime if the MDB refused to contest the presidential elections after the promotion of a nationwide campaign. Certainly it was not the intention of the moderate majority in the party to challenge the rules of the game so openly that it could close any future prospect of a political relaxation; a relaxation about which the future President had already given rise to hope. Although defeated in the convention, the *autenticos* refused to accept the decision approved by the party, thus they were resolute in carrying out their position of refusing to vote for the MDB candidates in the Electoral College.

On 15 January, the Electoral College composed of the senators, federal and state deputies, met in Congress to elect the future President of the Republic. On the occasion, the MDB candidate was given the right to address the meeting in a twenty-minute speech. Ulysses Guimarães, more cautiously than in previous speeches during the campaign, restated the position of the party in participating in that event. As expected, the outcome of the election was the ratification of General Ernesto Geisel and General Adalberto Pereira dos Santos (respectively President and Vice-President) who received 400 votes against the 76 votes obtained by Ulysses Guimarães and Barbosa Lima Sobrinho. Twenty-one votes were registered as blank ballots, that is, the ones which came from the MDB's dissident group. On the indirect suffrage), the MDB put forward a petition to the Tribunal of Electoral Justice claiming its right to use the means of communications in its presidential campaign. It was very unlikely that this could be granted, since the government had already shown signs that it would not let the opposition go too far in this move. The government's subtle prohibition of TV broadcasting of the MDB national convention had been a good indication. In that event, the government acted cleverly to avoid mass media coverage of the MDB convention, despite all the MDB's attempts to ensure the same right as ARENA had had in its convention. The government gave permission to the opposition for television coverage, but it sent a message to all TV companies warning them that they would have to assume the responsibility of the decision to broadcast the MDB convention. This meant that the MDB ended up not having television coverage of its meeting. Given the dependence of television companies on the government's permission to work, they preferred to avoid any future problem with the government. This episode was an indication that the regime would certainly not allow the opposition to carry out a free campaign. If the government had shown sympathy to the MDB's initiative to participate in the presidential contest in so far as this granted Geisel's appointment some kind of legitimacy, it certainly would not permit a free opposition campaign of which criticisms of the government and the regime would be the main feature.

Despite the likelihood that the MDB would suffer restrictions in its strategic move, the *autenticos* strongly defended their position that the campaign should only be carried out if the candidates could have access to the radio and television networks. This issue had been put forward by the *autenticos* in the national convention which selected the candidates. Although they did not manage to have their motion passed, another was passed postponing a decision on the matter until after the reply of the Electoral Tribunal. That is, in the case of the refusal of the MDB's access to the mass media, another convention would have to be summoned to decide about the continuation of the campaign. As expected, the Electoral Tribunal's reply was negative. As a consequence, on 28 November the national convention met again to decide about the future of the campaign. In fact, the *autenticos* had already revised their position in face of the popular support that the MDB's anti-candidates had been receiving in their travels across the country. As it was widely accepted that it would be unwise to stop a campaign which had already proven successful, the possibilities of being this channel of opposition were clearly revealed in the first rally promoting the party's anti-candidate campaign. In that event which took place in Blumenau (Santa Catarina state) in September 1973, the MDB candidates received enthusiastic applause when they addressed criticisms to the government's policy of holding down wages and to the high cost of living. The favourable reception to the MDB campaign was well depicted in this comment of the newspaper *Estado de São Paulo*:

> The manifestation sent to the party by the regional directorates asking for the promotion of rallies in their party bases, will certainly be reason enough for the continuation of the campaign and even its extension beyond 15 January, aiming at the legislative elections. The results already achieved in terms of communication and mobilization of the electorate have been considered more than satisfactory. The themes chosen for the campaign have obtained wide coverage in the press and the effects, as has been the case with the denouncing of the high cost of living and inflation – which touches the common voter directly – are undeniable.... The campaign ... has taken the MDB out of the uncomfortable and abrasive defensive position in which the party had practically been maintained since its creation.[76]

The anti-candidates were telling the population what everybody wanted to hear or express, thus opening up a means of communication with public opinion. Certainly that rate of communication was still very narrow since the candidates were not allowed to campaign on the radio and television and faced a lot of difficulty in promoting public meetings.[77] Besides, the public rallies promoted by the party during the candidates' travels across the country were far from mass meetings. But they certainly were the first significant contacts that the MDB had with the electorate, thus helping to create a more positive image of the opposition party. The 1974 legislative elections would show the fruits of the changes in the MDB.

6   1974-7:   Attempting to Consolidate Legal Opposition Politics

The inauguration of Geisel's presidential term in 1974 and the announcement of his project of 'gradual and secure' political relaxation marked the start of a new period of military-authoritarian rule. The President's statements signalling the prospects of political changes seemed to be more meaningful and forceful than the frequent promises of a return to democracy made by his predecessors. In fact, the appointment of Ernesto Geisel – a general who was not in active service in the army, but who was, at the time, holding the important position of president of the state oil company, Petrobrás – was in itself a significant event. As most political analysts pointed out, it represented the return to power of the *castelistas* – the military group linked to the *Escola Superior de Guerra* (the War School), which, gathered around Castelo Branco, had controlled the government during the first years of the regime.[1]

In contrast to his predecessors, Geisel did not promise democratization, but rather a 'gradual and secure democratic improvement' which aimed at accomplishing the institutionalization of 'revolutionary principles'. In his speech made at the first ministerial meeting of March 1974, he stated:

> We will direct our sincere efforts towards a gradual, but safe, democratic improvement by promoting an honest and mutually respectful dialogue and by stimulating more participation by the responsible elite and the people in general, leading to the creation of an edifying climate of consensus and the definitive institutionalization of the principles of the 1964 Revolution. With respect to the exceptional instruments that the government has retained for the preservation of a climate of security and order – essential for the country's economic and social development without interruptions and dangerous reversals – I would wish to see them, less as permanent instruments to be used frequently, and more as potential resource of repressive action and drastic restraint. These will prevail until they are eventually superseded

145

by the product of a more creative political imagination capable of establishing effective safeguards within a constitutional framework.[2]

If the period of Geisel's administration was to witness the start of a process of political relaxation, it would also witness the end of the Brazilian 'economic miracle' and the beginning of a prolonged economic crisis which, together with an enduring political crisis, would constitute the major problem confronting the military – authoritarian regime. The tripling of oil prices and the world economic recession would have drastic repercussions on the Brazilian economic model which was heavily dependent on imports and on the foreign financial system and export market. The cycle of economic expansion from 1967 to 1973 was over when the gross domestic product started to decelerate: from 14 per cent in 1973, it fell to 9.8 per cent in 1974, and to 5.6 per cent in the following year. The deficit on the current account jumped from US $ 1.7 billion in 1973 to 7.1 billion in 1974, while the foreign debt grew from US $ 6.2 billion in 1973, then to US $ 11.9 billion in 1974, to reach 56.3 billion in 1981.[3]

It is in the light of this new political and economic picture that we shall examine the role of the MDB in the political system from 1974 to 1977. The most important event affecting the opposition party during this period was undoubtedly the 1974 legislative elections when, for the first time, the MDB's electoral performance had an important impact on the political framework established after the 1964 coup.

THE MDB IN THE 1974 LEGISLATIVE ELECTIONS

As discussed in the last chapter, the MDB's 'anti-candidate campaign' for the 'indirect presidential elections' in late 1973 had at least the merit of paving the way for the party's electoral performance in the 1974 elections. The contact with the population during the 'anti-candidate campaign' made the MDB leadership realize the possibilities open to the party, given the growing dissatisfaction of the population regarding the socio-economic situation in the country. It was then realized that if the MDB could express this discontent in its electoral appeal, the party might eventually have better chances in the coming elections. The MDB's optimism also seemed to be grounded on revived hopes of political relaxation following the inauguration of Geisel's administration. Geisel's first statements announcing his policy of 'gradual and secure' political relaxation proclaimed that its implementation would depend upon the collaboration of the 'political class', exhorted to make use of 'its creative political imagination'. This revived the optimism of politicians from both parties.[4] The new President also seemed to have included the MDB in his allusion to the 'political class' when he referred to them as the 'constructive opposition' which should accomplish its role of pointing out the government's mistakes and offering suggestions.[5] There were also indications that the new President was willing to make the coming elections an important event designed to be not only a step in the process of political relaxation but also a means of obtaining some legitimacy for the regime. Therefore, the MDB's perception of better prospects for the opposition in the elections would make the party spare no effort to prepare and carry out its electoral campaign. Attempting to set up a nation-wide campaign, a manual designed to serve as the basic guide for the candidates was drawn up. This manual contained the party's electoral platform and provided the candidates with strong arguments to support their criticisms of the government's socio-economic policies. In fact, the MDB leadership asked for the collaboration of specialists to help in the drafting of its electoral platform. Referring to the participation of intellectuals from CEBRAP (The Brazilian Centre of Analysis and Planning) in this undertaking, the sociologist and currently Senator Fernando Henrique Cardoso stated:

> In fact it was Ulysses Guimarães and Pacheco Chaves who called on Paul Singer at his house, because the MDB leaders had read both his and my articles in the newspaper *Opinião*. Then Paul Singer arranged a meeting of the MDB leaders with us at CEBRAP. The MDB leaders wanted our help in defining a platform for the electoral campaign. Ulysses Guimarães ... had carried out the 'anti-candidate' campaign and he was convinced that there was a rising tide in favour of the MDB. None of us were sure of that. We had not had any contact with the MDB before, or with any other party. . . . We, from CEBRAP, had decided not to participate as CEBRAP in any party, even the MDB – a policy that we have maintained until now. But, as we told Ulysses, some of us were prepared, as individuals to meet the MDB leadership and see if it was worth helping them. I remember, at that meeting,

apart from Paul Singer and myself, there was also Weffort, Chico
de Oliveira, Werneck, . . . so we decided to help, but we wanted to
have prior discussions with the party's top leadership. Then we
wrote a draft outlining the ideas which we thought should be
included in the MDB platform. In fact, there was no great disagreement between what we were defending and what the party
wanted. The main idea was to make the connection between
socio-economic issues and the political question. In short, democracy with wages, income distribution, trade union organizations,
participation of women, blacks and so on. This was the
idea . . . We went to Brasilia for a meeting with the top leadership,
and they approved the ideas. Then, we wrote the manual for the
electoral campaign. But I must say that we did not invent these
ideas; we did not introduce them to the MDB. In fact they were
already in the MDB programme. We just developed them and put
more emphasis on socio-economic issues, such as trade-
unionism, wage policy, social movements and so forth (. . .) That
manual was very useful, since it was read everywhere in the
country.[6]

Copies of the MDB manual as well as a quantity of material with
additional information and statistics were distributed at the
meetings with the candidates during the organization of the electoral
campaign. The candidates were also instructed to follow the party's
strategy of emphasizing the problems related to the government's
social, economic and financial policies. Thus, themes such as the
high cost of living, the disparities in income distribution, the tight
wage policy implemented by the government, the increasing incur-
sions of foreign capital into the Brazilian industrial sector, the huge
external debt, and the excessive centralization at the federal government level of economic and political decision making, were the major
issues to be emphasized in the MDB's electoral campaign.

The opposition party was to pay particular attention to the
organization of its campaign on radio and television. As the electoral law allowed the political parties to have free radio and television coverage during the two months preceding the elections, the
MDB tried to use these means of mass communication with the electorate as effectively as possible. It should be said that, in general,
electoral broadcasts had little impact on the population. The population's indifference to the messages shown by the candidates who,
most of the time, used to appear on the television screen to make

boring and uninteresting speeches which stressed their personal 'qualities', had made it very hard to increase the audience for electoral broadcasts.[7] In order to cope with this problem the MDB tried to change the conventional format of party broadcasting. The organizers of the electoral campaign instructed the candidates to make short speeches in which criticisms of the government's economic and social policies should be stressed rather than the individual characteristics of the candidates. In addition, short films were prepared, showing the party symbol (MDB) accompanied by didactic messages focusing on specific themes of the campaign. In Pernambuco state, for example, television channels showed the MDB symbol followed by clips of workers cutting sugar-cane and the message: 'a working day in the *zona da mata* (area of sugar-cane plantation) is worth eight cruzeiros; a kilo of charque (dried meat) costs 26 cruzeiros, that is, the equivalent of more than three working days'.[8] In São Paulo state, advertising executives were hired to work in the organization of the electoral campaign, and in particular, to help to popularize the image of the little known MDB candidate for the Senate, Orestes Quercia. The organizers of the campaign in that state managed to negotiate with ARENA a way of using more effectively the evening period of electoral broadcast reserved for the parties. According to the electoral law, the political parties were granted one hour of broadcasting in the evening, but the channels had the right to allocate it at any time between 8 and 11 pm. This meant that the channels would conveniently leave the transmission of electoral propaganda to the later hour thus avoiding interference with their prime time programmes. The MDB, in agreement with ARENA, managed to strike a deal with the TV channels. The parties agreed to give up twenty minutes of electoral broadcast in the evening in exchange for the broadcast of 20 short 30 second films to be shown at regular intervals during prime television time.[9] As the organizers of the MDB's electoral campaign explained, 'the TV viewers who deliberately watch electoral broadcasts have already formed their opinion. The people we want to reach through these intermittent messages are the new voters'.[10] Thus the MDB candidate for the Senate, Orestes Quercia, appeared on the screen in short films in which, for example, he was shown walking through crowds of people in the streets of São Paulo or, as an ordinary citizen, struggling to hail a taxi.

Certainly, the MDB's promotion through the media of its candidate for the Senate in São Paulo was particularly effective, since

Orestes Quercia, who was virtually unknown when the campaign started, managed to defeat the well known ARENA candidate, Senator Carvalho Pinto, by a landslide of about three million votes.[11] An equally remarkable result of the MDB's well organized electoral campaign was the number of votes received by the party list for the Federal Chamber elections. As pointed out in Chapter 3, the PR system adopted in Brazil is not based on party lists of candidates ranked in advance. It is the number of votes each candidate obtains that determines the order in which he appears in the party list. Thus the electors are instructed to give their vote for a particular candidate although they are also allowed to vote just for the party should they have no preference for any candidate. As a consequence of this system, the candidates need to develop their own campaign in order to guarantee a good place in the party list. In turn, votes cast just for the party (without specification of a candidate) tend to be insignificant. In the 1974 elections, however, the number of votes obtained by the MDB label was quite impressive, probably due to the party's attempt to promote its platform in the campaign. Thus, while only 3.5 per cent of ARENA votes in the Federal Chamber were cast for its party label, 12.6 per cent of the MDB votes had been cast for its label. In São Paulo, the MDB's proportion reached 28 per cent.[12]

There is little doubt that the MDB managed to assume a leading position in the 1974 legislative elections through its effective and carefully planned electoral campaign. ARENA's loss of control over the campaign in the face of the much more convincing appeal of the opposition is clearly revealed in the comment made by the president of the Senate, Paulo Torres. This ARENA Senator, who failed in his bid to be re-elected, showed his astonishment by saying:

> I presented graphs and statistics on TV showing that there were so many illiterates in 1963 and that now there were only so many. I talked about the achievements of the Revolution, particularly about the Rio-Niteroi bridge. But they (the MDB candidates) would then come out and say that 'so many working hours are needed to buy a kilo of meat' and that the bridge did not fill up anybody's stomach!'[13]

The MDB's victory in November 1974 in which it won 16 out of the 22 seats in the Senate, increased its representation in the Federal Chamber from 87 to 160 and obtained majorities in six State Assemblies,[14] did not only astonish the government party alone. Even the MDB was surprised by its victory which the party president, Ulysses

Guimarães, described thus: 'more than a flood it was a tidal wave which took us by surprise: we had elected 16 senators, an extraordinary victory'.[15] At this point we should remember that if anybody had been optimistic about the opposition's chances in the elections, it had been the MDB itself. In May 1974, for example, the party's general-secretary had predicted that the MDB would get more than 130 seats in the Federal Chamber.[16] More cautiously, the party president claimed in September that the opposition would obtain 100 seats in the Federal Chamber and 5 seats in the Senate.[17] Even these underestimated figures were discredited in the press which considered them to be merely part of the electoral game. In fact, during 1974 and even in the final months of the electoral campaign there was not a single comment in the press suggesting that the MDB might have better chances in these elections. On the contrary, all their comments clearly assumed an ARENA victory to be a *fait accompli*. In July, the *Estado de São Paulo* commented:

> 'Despite the MDB leaders' euphoria which they are of course obliged to show, the party will be extremely hard pressed to maintain its present representation of seven senators. Even the ARENA president, Petronio Portella, has already expressed his concern, since the weakening of the opposition in the Senate would be, according to him, harmful for the overall political picture.[18]

In October, the magazine *Veja's* comments clearly indicated the climate of certainty regarding an ARENA victory, albeit acknowledging the MDB's efforts in the electoral campaign:

> For ARENA – strong, organized, well connected with all the government offices where decisions are taken – are reserved all the best tickets for the Senate, the Federal Chamber and the State Assemblies. . . . It is clear that not even the more optimistic opposition militant believes in an overflow of victories for the MDB in the contest for the Senate. With three senators, of the MDB's seven representatives, running for re-election, the MDB will be pleased if it manages at least to retain them. . . . Therefore, nobody must either expect or anticipate large wins by the MDB, in spite of the fact that the party has made good use of the provisional truce conceded to the MDB to conduct its campaign.[19]

Surprisingly, it was in the Senate that the MDB obtained an overwhelming victory, increasing its representation from seven to twenty senators. Certainly the most surprised were the government and ARENA when the results of the polls were released. In fact, Geisel's project of political relaxation, of which the first step was to carry out elections under freer conditions,[20] was based on the premise of the unquestionable dominance of ARENA at the polls. It was important for the regime to get some legitimacy through the electoral process and for that it was necessary to allow the opposition to contest under less unequal conditions, thus avoiding a repetition of the 1970 elections when the blank and spoiled votes functioned as the government's major opponent. The government's confidence in ARENA's success was only questioned when opinion polls started to indicate that the MDB was increasing its support in the course of the electoral campaign. Although this provoked some concern in government circles, the tendencies shown by opinion polls were taken as particular cases localized in a few states, considered to be no reason for hampering ARENA's prospects of success. In fact, two weeks before the elections, the ARENA's president Petronio Portella went to the government palace to report on the situation of the party in every state and to assure President Geisel that the government party would not suffer any crucial defeat in the elections. It should be said that one of the failures of ARENA was perhaps its excessive optimism and certainty that the party would continue its history of success at the poll since its creation in 1966.

Two other factors that contributed to the ARENA's poor electoral performance and the same time increased the MDB's chances of winning should also be remarked. The first factor has to do with the lack of appeal of the ARENA's campaign. Accustomed to being in the government's shadow, ARENA's electoral platform was nothing but a defence of vague statements of social and economic principles, and the reiteration that its programme was the government's programme and that ARENA was the party of the 'Revolution'. The party's conviction of the power of the government's achievements to attract votes was so strong that one finds comments such as this vehement statement made by a local politician: 'not to believe in the Brazilian miracle would be as much a blasphemy as to say that one does not believe in God'.[21] Without any appeal or argument to counter-attack the MDB's criticisms of government policies, the ARENA resorted to its usual technique of intimidation, accusing the opposition of extremism and blaming it for attempting to jeopardize the process of political relaxation. Reporting on the ARENA's electoral broadcasts in São Paulo, a journalist commented:

The unattractiveness of the ARENA's TV broadcasts is such that they might have been produced by MDB agents. Cantidio Sampaio, for example, introduced himself as a defender of the government and of the Revolution and took on the role of mordant critic of the opposition, thus repeating the name of the opposition several times. . . . He spoke so much about Quercia, he spoke so much about the MDB that, in the end, these words prevailed in his message much more than the words ARENA and Carvalho Pinto.[22]

The government – at both state and federal levels – spared no efforts during the electoral campaign to help ARENA's candidates in the face of the more active and aggressive electoral campaign waged by the opposition. In an attempt to boost popularity so as to attract voters to ARENA, the federal government decreed in late October an emergency wage bonus for the workers and expanded credit facilities for the agricultural sector. These measures nonetheless seemed to have come too late to produce a favourable response for the government party at the polls.

The second factor that influenced the electoral results in 1974 has to do with dissension within the government party. In contrast to the MDB, which managed to overcome its internal problems and went to the electoral campaign united,[23] the ARENA leadership was unable to resolve the problems caused by the process of nominating state governors and selecting candidates for the Senate. A party that comprised divergent factions based mostly on traditional oligarchies, would necessarily face difficulties in pleasing all groups, when selection for positions was a decision taken only by the restricted top government circle. The discontent provoked by the selection of governors and candidates for the senatorial contest led the aggrieved factions to distance themselves from the electoral campaign. In Ceará state, for example, Senator Virgilio Távora – ARENA's main figure in that state – went to Japan so as to avoid participating in the electoral campaign, since the candidate appointed to run for the Senate was from a rival faction. Similar problems were faced by ARENA in most of the states as a consequence of dissensions amongst the party's leading figures. It was reported in the press that in several places, ARENA candidates for the Federal Chamber and State Assemblies had carried out their campaigns without any mention of the party's candidate for the Senate, so as to disassociate themselves from a candidate whom they did not support.

Thus, ARENA's internal dissensions must have also contributed to the party's poor electoral performance, consequently benefitting the MDB. This is worth underlining since most interpretations of the 1974 elections seem to have forgotten to mention ARENA's role in these elections. We are referring particularly to those interpretations that suggest that the growth of the MDB vote was merely the result of the changing nature of popular protest: before 1974 the voters used to protest by spoiling their ballot papers; in 1974 they decided instead to vote for the MDB. C. E. Martins's analysis gives us a good example of this line of interpretation in his article on the 1974 electoral campaign in São Paulo.[24] In his explanation of the MDB's success, he remarks on the efficacy of the MDB in creating a new channel of protest which had emerged following the party's 'anti-candidate campaign' for the 'indirect presidential elections'. He asserts that:

> The quixotic audacity of the MDB served, above all, to institute a new modality of political behaviour: the protest against the rules of the game through the strict observance of those rules of the game. The MDB's candidacy of protest was, therefore, an inspired move which opened the way for the voter's protest. . . . By inventing a politically useful meaning for a juridically useless election, the MDB managed to destroy the main argument in favour of the spoiled ballot. Those who had insisted on the null vote had always alleged the vote's inefficacy as an instrument of power, but they could not deny the vote's efficacy as an instrument of expression. In fact, the MDB managed to create a new political language by demonstrating that there were two ways of saying 'no': the old fashioned way was to say 'no' by spoiling the ballot; the modern way was to say 'no' by voting for the MDB'.[25]

This interpretation, with which in general we do not disagree, was also shared by the MDB's chairman who, in his first statement after hearing of the electoral results, explained the MDB's victory by saying: 'In previous elections the opposition was divided into two groups: the MDB voters and the supporters of blank and spoiled votes. We managed to attract the latter to vote for the MDB by presenting a message, a programme'.[26] Although this kind of interpretation is correct in the sense that the voters who protested by spoiling their ballots in previous elections almost certainly supported the MDB in 1974, it does not explain the fact that the government party vote actually decreased proportionately to former elections. In other words, even if we assume that all the blank and spoiled votes cast in 1970 elections were protest votes (something difficult to prove),[27] the increase in the MDB vote was much higher than the decrease in the blank and spoiled vote, as we can see from the figures shown in Table 6.1.

Table 6.1   The 1970 and 1974 election results: ARENA, the MDB and blank/null percentages, and their increase or decrease between 1970 and 1974

	Senate			*Federal Chamber*		
Years	*ARENA*	*MDB*	*Blank/null*	*ARENA*	*MDB*	*Blank/null*
1970	43.7	28.6	27.7	48.4	21.3	30.3
1974	34.7	50.0	15.1	40.9	37.8	21.3
1974/70	−9.0	+21.4	−12.6	−7.5	+16.5	−9.0

Source: My own calculations based on official figures from the Electoral Tribunal.

The figures shown in Table 6.1 lead us to conclude that the increase in the MDB vote in 1974 was due not only to the transfer of support to the MDB from those who had earlier protested by spoiling their votes but also to a withdrawal of support from ARENA.

In his interpretation of the 1974 elections, B. Lamounier[28] suggests that the electoral results also showed an erosion of support for the regime due to a reversal of the expectations created by the euphoria of the 'economic miracle'. After a long wait for the promised benefits of the country's economic prosperity, the population – particularly the middle and lower urban sectors – had begun to realize that they were not among the selected beneficiaries of the so-called miracle.[29] This change of expectations – Lamounier concludes – 'allows us to understand how a *diffuse* support for the policy of the 'economic miracle' was transformed into a no less *diffuse* opposition to the economic model and, by extension, to the bureaucratic-military regime which had enforced it'.[30] The major factor explaining the decrease of support for the government party was certainly the one suggested by Lamounier. But, in addition, it should be said that the decline of the ARENA vote must also have been a result of the internal dissensions existing within the government party, making it impossible to unite its factions in order to contest elections under circumstances in which the opposition had become an active and effective adversary. By underlining the failures of ARENA, we are not minimizing the more important feature of these elections, namely, the transformation of the MDB into a channel of opposition expressing the wide dissatisfaction of the population. What we also want to stress is that another feature that was clearly apparent in the 1974 elections was the failure of the political arrangement established by the regime, particularly as regards to the creation of a political party designed to provide support for the regime. By establishing a two-party system, the regime created the first condition for its defeat in the 1974 elections. On the one hand, the creation of a government party, which gathered together rival oligarchical factions whilst remaining powerless to decide even on its own internal business, made it impossible for ARENA to perform its role in a context of more competitive elections. After 1974, the regime would manipulate the election rules as freely as possible in an attempt to resolve ARENA's intrinsic problems, and to prevent it from suffering any further great defeat, as we will see below. On the other hand, the creation of an opposition party which was simply designed to be a facade, provided the legal means for the opposition forces to organize under a single banner. By keeping this legal means alive, despite its lack of power in its dealings with the all-powerful government, and by making use of the electoral process to carry out an effective opposition campaign, the MDB eventually managed to become an important political force that eroded the base on which the regime was constructed. In 1974, in a more relaxed political climate, the MDB was able to express, and thus to channel, the dissatisfaction of wide sectors of the electorate.

It should be stressed that electoral support for the MDB in 1974 had little to do with the effectiveness or responsiveness of the party's Congressional performance. The impact of the MDB was circumscribed by the role that it could play in the electoral process through the campaign that the party effectively developed in order to win votes. In fact, as we will show in the next section, even after 1974 the MDB's ability to participate effectively in Congress would remain very limited, whilst its ability to influence through the electoral process would continue to be its major feature.

THE MDB IN CONGRESS AFTER 1974

The increase in the MDB's representation in Congress as a result of the 1974 elections spread enthusiasm among the opposition; it was as if a new era had begun for the MDB. Although remaining the minority in Congress, the MDB held 44 per cent of the representation in the House of Deputies and 30 per cent in the Senate. This representation gave the party the possibility of creating Parliamentary Commissions of Inquiry and of influencing decisions on constitutional amendment bills proposed by the government, since an amendment to the constitution needed to be approved by two-thirds of the representatives in both Houses. As the ARENA no longer retained two-thirds of the representation in the Federal Chamber, amendments proposed by the government could only be passed if they had the support of MDB members. The strengthening of the MDB representation thus revived hopes that the opposition party would finally be able to participate more effectively in the legislative business.

Certainly the opposition party was a much more active participant in Congress after 1974. However, this was not translated into a more effective role. In fact, the MDB still exerted as limited an influence as it had before, since the party laboured under the same constraints which had blocked its attempts to have some impact on the political system through its performance in Congress. Under a process of political relaxation carried out from above, it is obvious that the dilemma between moderation and radicalization imposed on the party by the regime continued to be the major obstacle in defining the party's strategies. Although Geisel's administration had promised and had actually started carrying out a process of political relaxation – of which the 1974 elections under freer conditions and the partial revocation of press censorship were clear indications[31] – the rules of the game remained undefined and, in fact, the political process would follow a pendular movement of compression and decompression. Thus the MDB's problem continued to be how to accomplish its opposition role with determination while avoiding any threat to undefined limits on opposition tolerated by the regime. The question of human rights, raised by the MDB in the first months of the new legislature, gave the first indication of the dilemmas facing the MDB and the limitations of the party's performance in Congress after 1974.

The Human Rights Issue

The MDB inaugurated the new legislature, which convened in March 1975, by putting forward a petition in the Federal Chamber requesting the attendance of the Minister of Justice to answer questions from the House about the cases of political prisoners whose whereabouts were unknown. The problem of the disappearance of political prisoners, highlighting the excess of repression committed by the political police, was undoubtedly a very important issue for the, now revived, opposition party to tackle. The more militant elements of the MDB particularly saw the handling of this problem as a fundamental duty corresponding to the expectations that the opposition's electoral victory had created regarding the party's future conduct. Also, there had been requests from families of those who had disappeared asking the MDB to carry out an investigation into the fate of their relatives.[32] The abuse of human rights, however, was a relatively sensitive theme which was certainly regarded by the regime as 'prohibited territory'. Although a request for the presence of a minister to answer questions about his office's affairs was considered a normal procedure in the legislature, an inquiry on this matter was likely to meet the resistance of the government. It would imply passing judgement on the repressive practices committed by one of the pillars of the system sustaining the regime: the political police apparatus whose strength and autonomy had increased considerably with their actions to dismantle left-wing organizations. Moreover, those hard-line military elements linked to the repressive apparatus were not at all pleased with Geisel's moves towards political liberalization.[33] Signs that Geisel's government wanted to ensure its control over the political process were made clear in a radio and television broadcast made by the Minister of Justice in late January. In his speech, the minister not only announced the dismantling of the Communist Party's printing press by the police, but also claimed that in the last elections some candidates who had been elected had received support from the Communist Party (PCB). Although the minister did not supply the names, it seemed that he wanted to insinuate that 'those candidates who managed to be elected thanks to the PCB', were being watched and could be punished.[34] The press commented that the Minister's speech was certainly a reaction to the MDB's success in the elections, but it was aimed at two targets. On the one hand, it was intended to cool down the opposition's enthusiasm over the election results and warn them that the political relaxation promoted by Geisel would not dispense with punishment of whoever disregarded 'the rhythm determined by the government'.[35] On the other hand, it was aimed at appeasing the hard-liners who were worried about the path followed by Geisel and particularly about the strengthening of the opposition in the elections.

In these circumstances, the MDB's initiative in raising the question of human rights, and demanding the presence of the Minister of Justice to answer questions about missing persons would serve to increase the political temperature at the beginning of the new legislature. The government's counter-attack would start as soon as the petition was presented for the Federal Chamber's consideration. In early March the press reported that two recently elected MDB deputies from São Paulo (Federal Deputy Marcelo Gato and State Deputy Alberto Goldman) had benefited from the Communist Party support for their campaigns. In defence of the accused deputies, the MDB replied with a note of protest denying the accusations and providing assurances that all of its candidates were committed to the MDB programme of which the fundamental principle was the defence of a democratic regime, therefore, it rejected 'any form of non-democratic state'.[36] At that time, nonetheless, the government seemed to be more interested in intimidating the opposition than in putting into practice any action against the deputies accused. As regards the MDB's initiative to investigate human rights violations, the government preferred the battle to be fought between the two political parties in the Federal Chamber. In any case, the petition requesting the presence of the Minister of Justice had to be passed by the House, thus its approval depended on ARENA since the MDB was in the minority. ARENA therefore would be entrusted with the task of blocking the MDB's initiative. This task was rigorously performed by the ARENA's leader in the House, Deputy José Bonifácio, whose aggressiveness towards the MDB helped to aggravate an already tense political scene. The fierceness with which Bonifácio dealt with the case was such that it seemed he was either convinced that the MDB's petition might conceivably be supported by his party's colleagues, or that he was performing the role of spokesman for the hard-liners. Probably he was simply willing to show the party's loyalty to the government to compensate for its poor performance in the elections. In any case, his behaviour as leader of the government party would be marked by a deep-rooted anti-communism which he would frequently show to attack the MDB. In a press interview Bonifácio criticized the MDB's petition by characterizing it as a provocation. He accused the MDB of 'playing the game of the communists for having given in to the pressures of the radical groups in the party', and claimed that the MDB was not collaborating with the process of political relaxation.[37] On this subject, his views were particularly astonishing:

> It is, by the way, worth noting that the people are not interested in the political relaxation at all. This is a concern of ours, the politicians, the journalists, the elite. The people, either with or without political relaxation go on enjoying themselves, working, going to the cinema, to football matches, travelling, spending holidays in Europe [sic].[38]

The debate on human rights went on for a month in the Federal Chamber. Trying to get support for the interpellation of the minister, the opposition stressed the problems of the families who remained ignorant of the fate of relatives arrested by the police, while the government kept refusing to give information about what had happened to them. Denouncing the grave situation of the political prisoners, the MDB presented evidence, such as the letter sent by a retired general describing the situation of his son, the engineer Pedro Celestino da Silva Pereira Filho, who had been tortured in Rio de Janeiro's police headquarters.[39] But the MDB's initiative would not go much further. When in April, the petition was submitted to vote, ARENA's leader José Bonifácio not only worked against its approval but also made sure that the MDB would stop pressing the matter. In his speech against the petition he gave information, provided by the Ministry of Justice, about some of the missing persons mentioned by the MDB, thus intending to show that the presence of the minister was unnecessary. He also repeated his accusations against the MDB, claiming that it was well known that five deputies linked to the Communist Party were under the MDB's cover. The outcome was the defeat of the petition. The proposal for the creation of a Parliamentary Commission of Inquiry, to which the MDB would resort in case the petition was not approved, died away as a result of ARENA's intimidation. In fact, the deputies who had been most involved in the defence of human rights, tried to set up the Commission, but by then, they faced resistance from the MDB leadership. Instead of either supporting or refusing to carry on the issue, the leadership cautiously postponed taking a position, on the basis that the proposal for a Commission would require discussion by the party's caucus as to the merits of taking this step. Ultimately, before any decision could be taken by the MDB, ARENA moved faster and created a Commission on the land question, in order to prevent the MDB from using the fifth and final possibility of constituting a Parliamentary Commission of Inquiry. This provoked the protest of the MDB's militant deputies who blamed the party's leadership for giving both time and freedom of manoeuvre to ARENA's leader, and characterized the attitude of the MDB leaders as a retreat for fear of the reaction of the regime's hard-liners.

The human rights issue highlighted clearly the problems the MDB was to face after 1974 when the opposition party had to deal with a political situation of controlled liberalization while at the same time taking into account the support it had received at the polls. In fact, the party's continuing dilemma between moderation and radicalization would become more and more of a problem for the definition of the MDB's positions. First, because the opposition party had to cope with a situation of controlled political relaxation whose promoter – Geisel's administration – was also facing resistance from the inner circles of the regime. Those who were against a political opening undoubtedly represented a real threat to Geisel's policy. Clear signs that those forces – namely the military faction in charge of the repressive apparatus – wanted to destabilize Geisel's government would emerge in October 1975: in São Paulo, the journalist Wladimir Herzog who had reported to the police at their request, died from the effects of torture. The political police headquarters reported the case as 'suicide'.[40] Later, in January 1976, at the same place, another case of 'suicide' was reported with the killing of the metalworker Manuel Fiel Filho. This time, President Geisel reacted swiftly by dismissing the head of the army command in São Paulo and replacing him with a man loyal to his own group.[41] If it was evident that Geisel's policy had to cope with the problem of controlling and appeasing the hard-line sectors, it also seemed that this threat was used by the government as a means of keeping the opposition in check. In a political system in which hard information was the exclusive property of the ruling circle, rumours that the President was under heavy pressure would in any case become facts which served to prevent any unwanted opposition move.

But Geisel's attempt to put the opposition under his control would not be limited to the use of verbal intimidation. The resort to the dictatorial powers of the AI-5 to punish the opposition would be the main weapon used to keep it under control while appeasing the hard liners. In early January 1976, two MDB deputies from São Paulo (Nelson Fabiano and Marcelo Gato) had their mandates cancelled and their political rights suspended for alleged links with the Communist Party in a police inquiry about that party's underground activities. In late March, 1976, the same fate befell the deputies from Rio Grande Do Sul, Amauri Müller and Nadir Rossetti, for having criticized the Armed Forces during a party rally held in a small town in their state. Three days later, another MDB deputy, Lysaneas Maciel from Rio de Janeiro, was also punished, because of a speech addressed to the Federal Chamber protesting against the punishment of his colleauges from Rio Grande do Sul. The frequent resort to the AI-5 to punish whoever went beyond the strict limits of opposition permited by the regime,[42] would characterize Geisel's policy of 'political relaxation' which seemed to be based on the premise that the opposition was to be held fully responsible for the continuation of the same policy.

Obviously, under these circumstances it was very difficult for the MDB to pursue a determined opposition line. The concern that any supposedly audacious move could elicit a reaction from the hardliners and thus jeopardize the long-awaited liberalization, would become the major cause of dissension within the MDB when it came to defining the party's strategy. In this respect, a second factor aggravated the MDB's position on the political scene after 1974: the party's victory in the elections and, consequently, the concern with accountability. Among the MDB representatives there was apparently a general feeling that the party should not disappoint those who had made possible its first ever success at the polls. The fact that even the moderate leadership supported the initiative of the more militant elements in raising the question of human rights, was an indication of this concern with the opposition platform defended during the electoral campaign. The MDB president's statement in reply to ARENA accusations that the MDB had become radicalized, was quite significant; he said that after their success in the elections no one should expect the MDB to sit back and meekly conform.[43] It should however be said that the concern for the preservation of the opposition's image affected the diverse group of parliamentarians who had been elected on the MDB's ticket in different ways. Here we should point out that with the increase in the MDB's representation, the party's internal divisions also increased. If during the previous legislature the dissensions within the party were related basically to the division between *autenticos* and *moderados*, after 1974 this division would be complicated by the emergence of new groups placed further on opposite sides of the former division. On the one hand, a group of about 30 deputies elected for the first time – mostly with the support of trade unionists and students – would join the side of the re-elected parliamentarians of the *grupo autentico*, but would advocate a much more aggressive opposition line on the premise that the party should be responsive to those who had supported it at the polls. These new deputies who would soon be labelled the *neo-autenticos*, would on several occasions also disagree with the *autenticos* who, after four years of parliamentary activity, had become much more amenable to political negotiation, particularly regarding the party's internal affairs. On the other hand, a group of about thirty deputies whose electoral support was basically dependent on their clientelistic style,[44] would advocate such a cautious line that they would have been better suited to the government party. This group became known as the *adesistas* for being considered adherents to the government's positions or *fisiológicos*, for being concerned only with the preservation of their political mandates.[45] This much wider range of positions which placed the *autenticos* and *moderados* in the middle between the two more opposed groups – the *neo-autenticos* and *adesistas* – would certainly make it more difficult for the MDB to define a political line which would be accepted and followed by all its members. The human rights question had already exposed some of the divisions undermining the party's initiatives. In this case, on the one hand, the *neo-autentico* deputies were the most actively committed to the investigation of human rights violations and were those who insisted on the creation of a Parliamentary Inquiry Commission. On the other hand, the *adesista* deputies obviously adopted a diametrically opposed attitude: they simply did not attend the parliamentary session when the MDB's petition was put to the vote, so as to avoid following the party's line. They also worked against the creation of a Parliamentary Commission of Inquiry on human rights by exerting pressure on the party leadership to block the initiative of the more militant deputies.

The internal divisions in the MDB would become more acute when, in September 1975, the elections for the party's national directive board were scheduled to take place. For more than a month the MDB went through an internal crisis as the factions struggled for positions in the national directorate and executive committee. The attempts of the *autenticos* and *neo-autenticos* to increase their influence by gaining positions in the party's command would be followed by counter-actions by the *adesistas* demanding more positions and blocking the negotiations with the leadership. On the other hand, the predominantly moderate leadership, while trying to reach a solution acceptable to the different groups so as to keep the party united around a single list for ratification by the national convention, was also determined to preserve its dominant position in the party command. The dispute and long negotiations to reach a compromise ended only when the official list, which had been altered several times, was finally put to the vote in the national convention. In fact, the list ratified by the convention ultimately preserved the supremacy of the moderate group that had been leading the party since 1971. On the other hand, the party emerged from the episode completely disunited, with groups opposing one another in such a way that it seemed the state of the party's internal affairs was the major problem confronting the MDB.

The first year of the new legislature clearly highlighted the obstacles preventing the MDB from carrying out a more effective performance in Congress, since the party – as we have pointed out – not only had to cope with its internal divisions but also, more fun – damentally, with the regime's constraints. The possibility of the MDB presenting any successful legislative initiative was quite limited. Any relevant bill presented by the MDB was bound to be either rejected by the ARENA's majority vote, or sent to the parliamentary archives for not having been submitted to the vote. As a bill proposing a constitutional amendment had to be discussed and voted on within sixty days, otherwise it would be filed away, the ARENA could manoeuvre so as to avoid the bill being put to the vote. This happened particularly in cases of bills dealing with a socially or politically relevant matter where it was convenient for the ARENA not to commit itself to rejecting the bill. For example, the MDB's bills dealing with the regulation of pensions for retired workers, the re-establishment of parliamentary immunity, the re-establishment of political autonomy for state capitals and municipalities considered areas of National Security, had all been remitted to the parliamentary archives. Since it would have been unpopular for the ARENA parliamentarians to reject these bills, they instead blocked the MDB's initiatives by not attending the parliamentary sessions so as to prevent the formation of the necessary quorum for the voting procedure. Thus, the time limit expired and the bill was filed. In addition, there were also cases of MDB bills which, after having been either rejected or filed, were transformed into government decree-laws, thus enabling the government, rather than the opposition, to capitalize on the political and electoral benefits resulting from the implementation of the measure. A good example was the government's decree-law which extended the period of worker's holidays to thirty days. This law, passed by the government in April 1977, had been the object of ten bills presented by MDB representatives over a period of five years, all of which had been blocked by the government party.

As mentioned earlier, the MDB's representation in the Federal Chamber after 1974 (more than one-third of the House's members) made it possible for the party to create Parliamentary Commissions of Inquiry, the constitution of which required the signature of one-third of the House's representatives. Where this legislative activity was concerned, the MDB participated actively, creating Parliamentary Commissions to investigate relevant issues such as the role of multinationals in the economy or wage policy and its consequences. Interesting reports diagnosing the problems and their consequences, and suggesting alternative policies, resulted from the work developed by these Parliamentary Commissions.[46] Nonetheless, they did not result in the implementation of any legislation to tackle the problems, as this was a task which depended entirely on the government's will. But these Commissions served at least to stimulate debate on relevant issues, and the reports provided the opposition with substantial arguments to criticize specific government policies. Criticism was in fact the only activity that the MDB could perform with determination. In this way the opposition party became much more incisive in its criticism of the government's social and economic policies, particularly of specific government measures designed to cope with the worsening economic crisis. The MDB's reply to Geisel's speech in October 1975, announcing new measures to face the economic crisis, was quite significant. Amongst the government's measures, which were aimed mainly at coping with the country's oil problems, there was one in particular which drew loud protests from the opposition: the decision to allow foreign enterprises to prospect for oil through the so-called *contratos de risco* (risk contracts) established with Petrobrás (Brazilian State Oil Company). The official note issued by the MDB started by recalling the origin of the economic crisis. It argues that this crisis could have been prevented if the government had taken into consideration signs of crisis in the world's financial market suggesting an economic recession at the beginning of the 1970s. The decline of sterling and the franc at the end of the 1960s, and the dollar crisis in 1971 were important signals indicating that 'something serious in the financial world was to happen'. Then, in 1973, as a result of OPEC policy, the oil crisis broke out:

A prudent and responsible government would certainly have realized that the situation demanded the creation of large import substituting projects. . . . The opportunities were excellent and the mobilization of resources would not have been difficult, since the national economy was growing at substantially high rates, at the cost of heavy sacrifices from the poor and considerable benefits for the rich. . . . But . . . short-sighted pragmatism dominated. Import substitution was considered a heresy. 'The solution was to export'. . . . The policy adopted was to invest in the car industry and in the construction of roads and 'pharaonic' bridges, while the privileged few . . . dedicated themselves to luxurious consumerism . . . and speculative activities. . . . That the economic situation had already worsened, there was clearer and clearer evidence of earlier in 1974. The opposition pointed to the alarming growth of our foreign debt, but the government's technocrats replied by praising the supposedly scientific 'superiority' of the coefficients of vulnerability to demonstrate the tranquillity of a picture under absolute control.

After such a long time, with so many opportunities lost, so many mistakes accumulated, the gravity of the problem finally came to light with undisguised clarity. And then everything was attributed to the international crisis, and the rise in the oil price. . . . Regarding the specific theme of energy and petroleum, the MDB has defended measures for the conservation of gasoline consumption . . . It is a simple measure, adopted in several countries with significant results and without the cruel effects on the cost of living that the high rise of 25% in the price of gasoline announced by the government will certainly produce. Yet in this field, the MDB has advocated the immediate enforcement of a programme of alcohol production on a large scale. . . . The country received the news of the decision regarding this programme with the hope that fast implementation could at least partially compensate for the inexplicable delay of a year for its launching.

The restrictions on the import of superfluous goods, announced by the government, have always been demanded by the MDB.... Regarding the cut backs in imports, the MDB does not understand why the same measure was not applied to the multinational enterprises, since the weight that these companies have in the composition of the 'deficit' of our balance of payments is well known.... It is however, regarding the question of the *contratos de risco* that the opposition, as well as the nation, received with astonishment the government's decision, since this violates the national principle of the state monopoly on petroleum....

The MDB wants to manifest its vehement opposition to the *contratos de risco*, which is certainly condemned by all the Brazilian people.... The MDB reiterates its commitment to the democratic ideals and the principles adopted in its programme; one in particular is the protection of State monopoly on petroleum[47].

If the MDB was impotent when it came to carrying out any initiative in the legislative process and if its criticisms of government policics were taken by the government to be mere demagogy, the MDB was still left with the possibility of influencing the legislative process by refusing to give support to bills and constitutional amendments proposed by the government. An examination of this aspect would show nevertheless how the MDB's possibilities of performing this opposition role were severely limited. The government's bill aiming at altering the electoral law and the constitutional amendment bill to reform the judiciary are relevant cases for discussion.

The *Falcão Law*

In May 1976 the government sent a bill to Congress which was apparently aimed at regulating certain clauses of the electoral code so as to provide guidelines for the municipal elections which would take place in the coming November. The main point of the bill was the clause which dealt with party broadcasts during electoral campaigns for municipal elections. The bill established that in the electoral campaigning on conducted radio and television the political parties would only be allowed to present the candidate's names, numbers and curricula, and in the case of TV broadcasting, their photographs as well. This meant that the parties would be prohibited from broadcasting any kind of live propaganda, such as speeches and debates, during the campaign. The justification given by the author of the bill, the Minister of Justice Armando Falcão,[48] was that it would be impossible to provide equal access to the means of communication for all candidates and all municipalities, since the number of radio and TV channels was very limited and could not cover the large number of municipalities in the country. He also argued that radio and television broadcasts normally reached a large area, that is, different municipalities with different problems. And if discussions of the specific problems in the large cities, where normally the broadcasting stations were located, were transmitted to other municipalities, these would generate misinformation and confusion among the electorate. He concluded: 'to give to a few municipalities the right to discuss their specific problems on electoral broadcasts, whose range covers several municipalities, is to favour the few while injuring the majority'.[49] Thus, in the name of 'equality' and 'information', the government was proposing to abolish the politicians' right to speak through the mass broadcasting media. In any case, the government's actual concern was neither with equality nor with the electorate's misinformation. In fact the bill had quite a different objective, namely to enforce restrictions on the opposition party regarding its performance in the municipal elections. It should be said that the MDB's chances of winning the elections for mayors and concillors were already reduced, given its disadvantageous position in relation to ARENA. First, the MDB was not as strongly organized as ARENA, which had local directorates established in the majority of the country's municipalities. Second, there was an inherent disadvantage for the opposition fighting local electoral contests, in that voters customarily tended to support the government party, since the municipality – largely dependent on the state government – was usually unwilling to suffer the negative consequences of electing a mayor who did not belong to the state governor's party. Moreover, in the large urban centres, namely the state capitals, where the MDB had better chances, elections for mayors had been abolished in 1966. In spite of the fact that the MDB had little chance of repeating its success of 1974, the government wanted to ensure that the electoral campaign would not be freely used by the MDB to publicize its opposition message. It was generally acknowledged that the MDB's electoral campaigning on radio and television during the last legislative elections had contributed decisively to the party's victory. This therefore was sufficient reason to change the rules, thus preventing the opposition from again using the channel of mass communication to criticize the government, particularly when a serious economic crisis had already worsened.

Needless to say, the MDB was strongly opposed to this bill and would denounce the government's initiative as a *casuistic* measure designed simply to hamper the opposition. The party's chairman argued that:

> The so-called *Lei Falcão* (*Falcão Law*) is an affront which imposes on the electorate a choice based on photographs and party labels, rather than on programmes and abilities. The radio as an archive, and the television as an album of photographs, testify to the fear of ideas and the fear of criticism. The target was the MDB but the government has struck a blow against Brazil, by obscuring the elections, discouraging the renewal of leaders, and silencing the vigorous and constructive debate on the country's problems.[50]

The MDB parliamentarians also pointed out the retrogressive character of the measure which would reduce the electoral battle to a door to door campaign.

On ARENA's side, Senator Teotonio Villela would be the only parliamentarian to publicly assume a position against the government's bill. In a speech addressed to the Senate he stated:

> There would be nothing more soul-destroying for a politician than to vote for the restriction of his own rights merely because it is alleged that this must be done for his party's own benefit. It would be the same as to say that ARENA prefers political compression to freedom of speech, silence to communication.... If elections are judgements of acts related to man, they are also hope created through a message. This, above all, is the element to be suppressed. As it is a political proposition rather than a matter of security, we can openly say that the Bill does not serve the politicians' interests, nor does it serve the public's interests; unless one assumes that politicians do not need to communicate and that voters can dispense with information.[51]

Despite the persuasive argument made by the ARENA Senator, he would be a lone voice in his party, since the few others who were also opposed to the executive's bill preferred to remain silent.[52] In any case, the bill was designed to help the government party in the elections. Moreover, ARENA had received clear orders from the executive not to let the bill be subjected to any major alteration and to resort to the party discipline law if dissensions within the government party emerged.[53] On the other hand, the MDB was completely incapable of blocking the bill, since ARENA alone, as the majority party, could pass it. Thus, the opposition's only recourse was to resort to obstructing the legislative procedures. In fact, the MDB decided to participate in the committee created to examine the bill in an attempt to eliminate the clause restricting the use of means of communication. Their participation obviously could not result in any alteration in the bill, which, as expected, was approved by Congress, on 24 June 1976. During a tumultuous session that lasted seven hours, the so-called Falcão Law was approved with the votes of 186 deputies and 36 senators, all of them from the government party. The MDB participated in the discussion but abandoned the plenary when the bill was put to the vote. In this way, the opposition party wanted to register its protest and leave all the responsibility of enforcing this restrictive legislation to ARENA.

The Judicial Reform Bill and the April Package

In the examination of the MDB's role in Congress after 1974, we showed the limitations on the opposition's ability to exert influence on the legislative process, due mostly to its minority party status which gave ARENA the power to block the MDB's initiatives and to pass all the legislation proposed by the executive. Nevertheless, there was an instance in which the MDB could have a decisive role in the legislative process as a consequence of holding more than one-third of the representation in the House of Deputies. Any bill proposing amendment to the constitution could only be passed if it received the support of two-thirds of the members in the Senate and the Chamber of Deputies. This meant that any constitutional amendment proposed by the government could not be passed, unless at least 39 MDB Federal Deputies voted with the government party. Obviously, to get the support of 39 deputies from the MDB was not such a difficult task if one considers the heterogeneity of those parliamentarians representing the MDB. But it was possible for the opposition to prevent deviations from the party line, by resorting to the Party Discipline Law. This law established that a parliamentarian was bound to lose his seat if he opposed, by attitude or vote, the party's position which had been legitimately decided upon by the party's directorate. Thus, if the party decided to adopt a definite position on a particular issue, all its members were obliged to follow it.[54] This law had in fact been designed to prevent defections within the government party and had been passed by the executive as a consequence of the Marcio Moreira Alves episode in 1968 when several ARENA members voted with the opposition against the prosecution of that MDB deputy.

Practice would show, nevertheless, that the MDB was not to be allowed to use either its one-third representation to reject a constitutional amendment or the Party Discipline Law to guarantee party unity on a specific matter. This was clear from the episode of the *reform of the judiciary* in March 1977.

The executive sent a constitutional amendment bill to Congress aimed at promoting the reform of the judicial system. Despite the apparently technical nature of the bill, it would give rise to much controversy. The executive's proposal did not introduce any of the fundamental changes considered necessary by interest groups for the modernization of the juciidary's structure so as to speed up judicial proceedings. Moreover, these interest groups – particularly the active Brazilian Bar Association, (*Ordem dos Advogados do Brasil*)[55] – defended the re-establishment of *habeas corpus* and the autonomy of the judiciary suspended by the AI–5. The bill would be widely criticized, not only by the Bar Association but also by prominent figures in the judiciary. It was known that even some members of the Supreme Federal Court were dissatisfied with the executive's proposal. In fact, it had been the Supreme Court that had provided the executive with a study containing both diagnosis and suggestions designed to help the executive in drawing up the bill. The government claimed that this study – which was kept secret – had been the basis of its bill. Nonetheless, there were rumours that very little of this study had been accepted by the executive. In any case, the time taken by the executive to prepare the bill after receiving the Supreme Court's draft – more than a year and a half – indicated that the suggestions proposed by the Judiciary's senior institution had not been very well received. The bill was eventually sent to Congress in November 1976 and a committee to examine it was constituted with members from both parties. During the committee's work, it soon became evident that the executive's bill was quite unsatisfactory. Even the committee's reporter, the ARENA Senator Accioly Filho did not accept the executive's proposal. Attempting to improve it he spent three months consulting specialized institutions and preparing a second version of the bill. But the executive was not willing to accept any substantive change to its draft and warned that the bill would have to be approved, otherwise it would simply be enforced through the AI-5. Thus ARENA's members in the committee managed to defeat the second version proposed by the reporter of the bill, who then resigned from his position. Needless to say, the MDB's version of the bill was also rejected. In fact, the MDB supported the substitute draft proposed by Senator Accioly Filho, in spite of the fact that the Senator's proposal did not incorporate the opposition's main demand of reinstating *habeas corpus* and constitutional safeguards for the magistrates. Faced with the government's intransigent attitude, the opposition decided unanimously to vote against the bill. At a meeting of the national directorate, the MDB decided to close its ranks (*fechamento da questão*) against the bill, thus blocking any possibility of having the government's bill approved by Congress.

The major question raised by the episode of the Judicial reform concerned the inflexible attitude taken by both the government and the opposition regarding an issue which was not politically relevant as such. The government certainly contributed a great deal to the more radical attitude assumed by the MDB regarding the matter. The government's intransigence regarding alterations to the bill, threatening to resort to the AI-5 in case it was not passed by Congress, seemed to indicate that the government wanted to see how far the opposition would go. As noted by most political commentators, the government wanted to test the opposition party to assess the climate for the introduction of other reforms – the political reforms – which were intended to be sent to Congress later. In fact, it was precisely this issue which also motivated the MDB to assume a determined position against the Judiciary bill. To elucidate this we must refer to other events which took place at the same time as the Judiciary bill.

The year 1977 was envisaged as the year of institutional reforms, which were to be a further step in the policy of political relaxation. ARENA was to be charged with carrying out negotiations with the opposition party so as to reach a compromise for the approval by Congress of a constitutional amendment introducing political reforms. In early March 1977 the so-called *Portella mission* was announced: the president of the Congress, ARENA Senator Petronio Portella was entrusted by President Geisel with the task of negotiating the issue of institutional reforms with the MDB. However, even before Senator Portella had begun his 'mission', the real nature of the reforms intended by the government became known. They were basically aimed at changing the rules of the game to prevent the MDB not only from getting to power at state level through the scheduled direct elections for governors in 1978,[56] but also from obtaining a majority in the Senate (quite possible in view of the MDB's victory in 1974). During the months of January and February 1977, comments in the press invariably drew attention to the fact that the political reforms did not envisage any political arrangement which would allow the opposition to share power, even at gubernatorial level. As one political commentator predicted:

> It is even possible that the arbitrary powers of the AI–5 will be diluted in a collegiate in which the executive power would retain the majority. But the Revolution will not give up power, because it does not think that the MDB is prepared for it. . . . The reforms will come. As the ARENA's president, Deputy Francelino Pereira likes to make clear: they will come, either by political means or by revolutionary means, and, as everybody knows, to guarantee the continuity of the Revolution and to restrain the growth of the opposition.[57]

Added to the MDB's discouraging prospects regarding the long-promised institutional reforms, there was the continuation of repression against the party's members. As soon as 1977 began, the opposition party was again beaten with the stick of the AI–5. This time the target would be the recently elected municipal councillors. In Rio Grande do Sul state, two MDB members of the council of the state capital (Porto Alegre) lost their mandates and had their political rights suspended: on 3 February, the opposition leader Glenio Peres was punished, supposedly because of a speech made during the inauguration of the new Council; two weeks later, his substitute in the leadership, Marcos Krassmann, suffered the same fate for protesting against the punishment of his colleague.[58] The repression of the MDB councillors provoked vehement protest from the very active section of the MDB in Rio Grande do Sul. That MDB section also criticized the national leadership for not taking any initiative to protest against the punishment of their colleagues. In fact, the national leadership only issued a note of protest when the second councillor was punished. If the silence and moderation of the MDB leadership were intended to cool down the political climate, so as not to provide any motive which might jeopardize the party's hopes regarding negotiations on the political reforms, it seemed that the government party was trying to achieve the opposite result. The

MDB leadership's cautious note of protest against the *cassações*, was followed by an aggressive response from ARENA through an official note which insistently accused the opposition of keeping links with 'well-known communists', of having become an agent of communist subversion and of stimulating radical opposition under the inspiration of 'activists whose task was to undermine the institutions'.[59]

The comment made by journalist Carlos Chagas, remarking on the state of disillusionment and exhaustion that the opposition party was reaching, was quite appropriate. He wrote on 19 February 1977:

> The MDB has been – by the way less for its national leadership, than for some of its regional sections and federal parliamentarians – reaching the limit of political exhaustion. Not only the recent *cassações*, but especially the information about the scarce prospects on the institutional reforms (the AI–5 does not change and the opposition cannot reach power) lead the main figures of the party to discouragement and even to the temptation to less orthodox initiatives. Its leaders are becoming aware of the impossibility of participating once again in a game of marked cards, that is, of carrying on its role of sheep faced with the wolf and, at the same time, having to explain this attitude to the party's base. Deputies and senators coming back from their constituencies where they spent the parliamentary recess, could only register the profound gap between public opinion and political reality, not to mention the parliamentarians' own behaviour. Notes of protest against the government's acts of force no longer cause any effect. They do not have repercussions. Rather, they just reveal the impotence of the opposition which is restricted to rhetoric. The hopes and expectations created with the 1974 elections were thwarted ... because of the forced immobility imposed on the party and on the nation. This does not mean that the nation is the MDB, rather, that both have been limited by the same constraints: while disagreeing with the government's attitudes, politics and general orientations, everybody has his hands tied down to keeping any action or reaction within the regime's orthodox pattern'.[60]

Despite the discouragement regarding the prospects of institutional reforms, the MDB was still willing to participate in negotiations with the government. In March 1977 official talks between the government and the opposition had begun so as to enable Portella to carry out his 'mission'. A meeting between Portella and the MDB president Ulysses Guimarães was held, although the subjects discussed showed already that the 'Portella mission' was not likely to result in any compromise. During those talks, the government communicated its intention not to permit direct gubernatorial elections in 1978, and of creating an organ for the state's defence that would later absorb the powers granted to the President by the AI–5. Not surprisingly the reaction of the MDB's national executive committee was the unanimous refusal of the proposed 'indirect' gubernatorial elections, although Ulysses Guimarães was authorized to continue the talks with Senator Portella. However, talks would not in fact be carried further in view of the friction which emerged over the question of the Judiciary Reform bill.

Given this background, it was not difficult to see that a state of animosity was emerging among the MDB parliamentarians. Thus the MDB's decision to challenge the government can be seen as a reaction to the government's inflexible attitude, not only regarding that bill but mainly regarding the political reforms which were to come later.

It should be also mentioned that the MDB's more militant deputies had their influence strengthened by the election of one of their prominent figures – Deputy Alencar Furtado – to the position of party leader in the House of Deputies. Alencar Furtado – from the *grupo autentico* – managed to defeat the moderate leader Laerte Vieira who, in attempting to be re-elected, had counted on the support of all the moderate leadership of the party. As party leader in the Federal Chamber, Alencar Furtado was to have an important role in the events which led to the MDB's decision to block the government's bill.[61] In fact, the position assumed by the MDB on this issue had resulted from a struggle within the party between those who advocated an attitude of strong opposition to the bill – namely the *autenticos* and *neo-autenticos* – and the moderate elements who defended the search for a compromise with ARENA so as to avoid a confrontation with the government.

The frictions within the MDB would come out when the MDB representatives in the Federal Chamber decided to oppose the government's bill, as a result of the ballot carried out by their leader in the House. This decision was not accepted by the more conciliatory group led by the then Deputy Tancredo Neves who had been carrying out talks with ARENA's leaders in an attempt to negotiate the acceptance of some of the opposition's amendments to the bill, in exchange for the party's support. Thus at a meeting of the national directorate attended not only by the parliamentarians but also by the presidents of the regional directorates, the issue was raised and led to a long and agitated debate. At the meeting Tancredo Neves called upon the federal deputies to reconsider their position, arguing that the political situation was 'very delicate' and that the consequence of an inflexible position against the bill would be a reversal of the political opening. He argued:

> If the MDB rejects the government's Bill it will have consequences which should be seriously examined. By the way, I belong to a school of politicians who advise prudence and moderation in such situations. If we carry out the decision taken by my colleagues in the Federal Chamber we will create an impasse, a confrontation. Confrontation, if one day we have to take it, it will be when we have public opinion, the press and the democratic conscience of the Nation at our side.... We are in a semi-democracy and we cannot escape from that. It is not time yet to expose ourselves to a test of confrontation.[62]

The deputy's speech helped to further aggravate the state of animosity against the issue, such was the controversy it provoked. It would be Senator Brossard's speech against the bill that would unexpectedly determine the outcome of the national directorate's meeting (which in fact had not been called for a decision on that specific matter).[63] The Senator started by pointing out that the MDB was not against the reform of the judiciary; it was rather against the government's bill since this was an ill-conceived reform. He argued:

> The controversy that this Bill has caused should be sufficient reason to convince the government that the proposed reform will be neither effective nor long-standing, since it is erected on a fragile basis, without the support of the judicial sector.... There is not a single movement in favour of this Bill. I cannot talk about the Supreme Court because this institution has maintained silence. It is known that there are judges from that Court in favour of the Bill. It is known, however, that there are also judges from that Court strongly opposed to the Bill.[64]

Brossard went on to mention all the judicial institutions and representative associations which had manifested their opposition to the bill. He also stressed the government's inflexible attitude in not accepting any proposal for the improvement of the bill, even those suggestions made by the committee's reporter who was a member of the government party. The Senator concluded his speech by asking: 'If the bill is not good, should we vote for it, hoping or aiming at appeasing the ire of the gods.'[65]

Encouraged by the long applause received by Senator Brossard, the parliamentarians who wanted to hold the position against the Bill, requested that the party chairman submit the issue to the vote of the national directorate. A ballot was held, and the outcome was that the directorate voted for the rejection of the bill unanimously. Even the parliamentarians who supported Tancredo Neves's position preferred to adhere to the clear majority. The Senate representatives who had earlier decided by vote to leave the question open, also changed their position. According to the resolution passed by the national directorate, the party's position should be respected by all MDB parliamentarians; the parliamentarian who voted against the party line would be subjected to the sanctions established by the Party Discipline Law.

Any possibility for the government to have its bill passed by Congress was therefore closed. The five days that followed the MDB national directorate's decision were spent in attempts by the moderates to reverse the decision, faced with the certainty that the government would react with the AI–5. Hours before the bill was submitted to the vote of the Congress, another meeting was held by the MDB representatives in the Federal Chamber, in a final attempt of the moderates to change the party's position. It was expected that a new ballot might reverse the decision, since the group which praised conciliation supposedly counted on the support of fifty deputies. Nonetheless, the situation had reached such a peak of animosity that the deputies once again confirmed the party's closing of its ranks against the bill, by 101 to 24 votes.

The bill was eventually put to the vote and received 241 votes in favour and 156 against, thus not reaching the quorum of two-thirds (283 votes) necessary if it was to be passed by Congress. It was 30 March, the eve of the anniversary of the 1964 Movement. On 31 March the signs that the consequences of the opposition attitude would come soon were clear in the speech that Geisel addressed to the Military Club in celebration of the 13th anniversary of the 'Revolution'. He referred to the episode in the Congress by saying:

Unfortunately, it was impossible to have those measures (the Judiciary reform) approved, ... because of the conduct of a minority which has practically become a dictatorship within the Congress; a minority which takes advantage of the circumstance that constitutional amendments require a quorum of two-thirds to be approved. ... Undoubtedly, this is a deplorable fact. It was not the government which was harmed by that attitude. Rather, it harmed the people, the Brazilian nation which needs a new Justice. And I assure you, this new Justice will be enforced.[66]

On 1 April, 1977, resorting to the AI–5, Geisel issued the Complementary Act Number 102 decreeing a recess of Congress. Less than two weeks were spent by Geisel and his selected loyal aides in the drawing up of the set of rules which would define a new political arrangement. Thus, apart from the decreeing of the bill on the Judiciary reform, which became the Constitutional Amendment Number 7, a set of political and economic measures were followed with the decreeing of the Constitutional Amendment Number 8 together with six decree-laws. These measures which became known as the *April Package*, introduced all the changes designed to assure the government's total control over the political process, thus cutting all the possibilities of the MDB to exert influence. The main measures were:

(1) Indirect elections for state governors through an electoral college composed by the State Assembly's members and delegates from municipal councils. This measure not only abrogated the earlier scheduled direct gubernatorial elections, but also made sure that the opposition would not get a state's government through the indirect electoral process either. By incorporating local delegates in the electoral college, the government prevented the MDB from electing five governors. This would have been possible if the previous practice of electing the governors by the State Assembly had been maintained, since the opposition had the majority in five state Assemblies: São Paulo, Rio de Janeiro, Rio Grande do Sul, Acre and Amazonas.[67]
(2) Indirect elections for one-third of the seats in the Senate through the same electoral college which would choose the state governors. This ensured 21 uncontested seats for the ARENA in the Senate.[68]

(3) The establishment of the *sublegenda* system for the direct senatorial elections. This meant that each party could contest a senatorial seat by running up to three candidates whose sum of votes would determine to which party the seat would go. Thus, the candidate who obtained more votes among his party's running-mates and whose party won in the sum of votes, would be elected. The *sublegenda* was designed to accommodate all the factions within the ARENA and to increase its chances in the senatorial contest.[69]

(4) The *Falcão Law*, that is, the restriction on electoral campaigning through radio and television which had been established just for municipal elections, was extended to the legislative elections.

(5) Alteration in the electoral college which was to choose the President of the Republic, and extension of the presidential term for the next President, from 5 to 6 years. This would guarantee military control over the political process for at least six years after Geisel had left power.

(6) As a consequence of the obstacles created by the opposition to the constitutional amendment on the judiciary, the quorum was reduced from two-thirds to simple majority, thus enabling the government to have a constitutional amendment bill passed by ARENA votes alone.

In addition to the political package, some measures on the social and economic sphere were also decreed such as permission for the executive to introduce new taxes which would be enforced automatically, changes in tenancy regulations, and the extension of paid holidays for salaried workers to 30 days.

The extensive nature and blatant unfairness of the reform issued as a result of the crisis of the Judiciary bill showed clearly that the judiciary question just anticipated a crisis which would have come anyway. The measures embraced by the April Package would be enforced by the government in any case. The government's realization that the opposition would not 'collaborate' in the legislative process made the government assume an intransigent attitude so as to exacerbate the crisis. As the *neo-autentico* Deputy João Gilberto commented on the episode of the judicial reform:

> Everything was already prepared. The government actually wanted to enforce the April Package, and whatever attitude we had taken, the government would have ended up by acting as it

did. ... Some people said 'the Congress was closed because of a question that was not political'. I think that this was the interesting thing in the episode. If it had happened because of an electoral or party issue, it would have been blamed on partisan passion. But it was an issue about an institution, the judiciary, and Congress just used its right to reject a bill![70]

According to the moderate Deputy Aldo Fagundes, the MDB's attitude was a reaction to the recurrent threat put to the opposition by the government:

Several times during the period of the AI-5 we heard rumours, threats ... then these sinister comments put ourselves practically face to face with a question of honour. Sometimes it was difficult to give in, to compromise, because sometimes this represented a retreat, a demoralization. ... Thus, although the rumors, the threats, were constant ... on certain occasions they served to make us face up to a question of honour. It was then impossible to compromise.[71]

7 1977–9: Attempting Popular Mobilization

THE POLITICAL PICTURE AFTER THE 1977 APRIL PACKAGE

The process of political relaxation introduced by Geisel seemed to have broken down in the face of the political measure established by the April Package of 1977. This was certainly the general feeling shared by all the liberal opposition forces who had earlier been so hopeful of the prospects for liberalization when Geisel first announced his policy of 'gradual and secure' political relaxation. For the promoters of this policy however, the April Package simply represented an indispensable readjustment so as to ensure that the gradual and secure character of the process of political relaxation was preserved. Political reforms leading towards liberalization were indeed planned, but nobody but the government itself was to define their content and lay down a timetable for their implementation. By decreeing the April Package, President Geisel, who had reserved for himself and his restricted circle of aides the role of sole promoters of the political opening, made sure that political reforms were not to be subjected to pressure from the opposition.[1]

In fact, the political measures established by the April Package which reduced still further the opposition's already limited possibility of influencing the political process, marked a redefinition of the government's strategy of relaxation as a response to the developments which had followed the first liberalization measure introduced at the beginning of Geisel's administration. As discussed earlier, Geisel's decision to reactivate the electoral process in 1974 by allowing a more liberal electoral campaign, resulted in a clear manifestation of opposition to the regime, channelled through the MDB. Furthermore, the 1974 election results had clearly shown that the regime lacked electoral support, particularly in the country's most urbanized and industrialized areas, precisely where the population had presumably benefited most from the economic boom of 1967–73. The partial liberalization of the press – another initiative of Geisel's political relaxation project – had also produced unpredicted

181

effects on the political process in so far as the press were starting to echo the demands for democracy and criticisms of the government's socio-economic policy coming from several sectors of civil society.

Moreover, the situation of economic adversity was far from being easily surmountable in the near future, despite the policy adopted by Geisel's government of maintaining economic growth through an ambitious programme of import substitution in the sectors of basic raw-materials and capital goods.[2] The economic problems and the policy adopted by the government were hardly likely to attract support for the regime. On the contrary, the economic question would undermine even the class coalition that had sustained the regime. The fact that the import substitution programme would necessarily involve large investments in the public sector and much stronger state control over the economy would provoke the concern of the private sector. It was not coincidental that in 1976 the entrepreneurs started to criticize the excessive participation of the state in the economy. The debate, transformed by the press into a campaign against State control of the economy (*campanha anti-estatização*) was a clear symptom of a process of disengagement from the regime by one of the former partners in the power coalition. From then on, statements in favour of a more democratic order would become part of the entrepreneurs' discourse. As Cardoso remarks:

> While Geisel's government stimulated the growth of the private and particularly the local industrial sector, it was proposing to give priority to economic policies which dissatisfied those sectors linked to the production of consumer durables.... Thus, the government's policy of industrialization – in line with what Guillermo O'Donnell calls the 'deepening of the economy' – alarmed the main partners of the system of alliances which had sustained the military-authoritarian regime. It alarmed not only the international companies linked to the production of consumer durables and to the sector of equipment importers ... but also the large local private sector producing complementary goods – structurally dependent on the internationalization of local production – and the local companies (of capital goods) even the large ones which initially supported the II PND (Geisel's Development Plan).... The government which most wanted to favour the interests of local sectors and which had already liberalized at least the press, was the target for the entrepreneurs's

angry criticisms which, initially aimed at the government, ultimately questioned the regime itself. . . . 1977 was the year . . . of the entrepreneurs' vocal re-encounter with criticism of government; that is why they started talking about democracy.[3]

If the liberalizing measures promoted by Geisel gave rise to increasing pressures in demand of democratization, they also produced a reaction from the military faction most opposed to the opening up of the regime. As mentioned in the last chapter, the intensification of police repression in 1975–6 by hard-liners in command of the Second Army in São Paulo was clearly perceived as a reaction against Geisel's policy of political relaxation. In this case, Geisel managed to neutralize the hard-line pressures by dismissing the head of the army in São Paulo after the killing of a journalist and a metal worker at the police headquarters, and, at the same time, by using the AI–5 to purge some MDB politicians so as to reinforce the President's authority over the hard-line sectors. But the struggle between the military factions was bound to become acute again in the face of the presidential succession issue. Although Geisel's term would not end until March 1979, speculation about the succession had already started in early 1977, and the ambition of the Minister of War – the hard-line General Sylvio Frota – to succeed to the presidential office was already known.

Therefore, as far as the engineers of the project of 'gradual and secure' political relaxation were concerned, two sources of pressure had to be controlled so as to guarantee its implementation and continuity: on the one hand, the pressures from the opposition sectors demanding prompt democratization; on the other hand, the pressures from the hard-liners against political relaxation. In other words, two conditions were indispensable for the implementation and continuity of the well-planned project of political relaxation advocated by Geisel's group. Firstly, the neutralization of the liberal opposition forces, particulary the MDB, so as to prevent MDB representatives from posing any threat to the controlled character of the liberalization which was to be implemented through political reforms approved by Congress. Secondly, the neutralization of the hard-liners so as to ensure that they would neither undermine Geisel's absolute command of the political process, nor interfere in the crucial question of the presidential succession.

The first condition was secured through the political reforms established by the April Package, which not only reduced the quorum for the approval of constitutional amendments, thus avoiding the problem of future reforms depending on MDB support for their approval, but also introduced a set of measures to control the electoral process so as to contain the increased electoral support for the MDB. The second condition would be assured by Geisel's determination to retain absolute control over the presidential succession. In the course of 1977–78, Geisel took a series of preventive actions to put all presidential aspirants out of the running so as to make sure that his appointee – the head of the SNI (National Information Service) General Figueiredo – would succeed him and carry on his political project. Geisel's determination to choose his successor led him, in October 1977, to sack the Minister of War, Sylvio Frota who, with the support of military hard-liners and radical right-wingers from ARENA, had been mobilizing support for his candidacy. With the same determination Geisel thwarted the presidential ambitions of Senator Magalhães Pinto, who had tried to present himself as the civilian alternative for the Presidency. Magalhães Pinto, who intended to partipate in ARENA's national convention to contest the nomination of the party's official candidate, gave up in face of the government's manoeuvres to guarantee that General Figueiredo would be nominated presidential candidate.[4] Geisel also neutralized the attempt of his ex-head of the Presidential Military Household – General Hugo Abreu – to mobilize military support for the opposition's candidate General Euler Bentes Monteiro, as we shall discuss later.

If President Geisel was able to control parliamentary politics and the presidential succession, thus assuring that his political project was carried out as planned, he would not be able to control the re-emergence of a growing opposition movement in civil society. From 1977 onwards, the country witnessed manifestations of opposition from several sectors of civil society, all joining the same chorus demanding substantial and prompt democratization. It is not part of the scope of this study to examine the important opposition movement which emerged from civil society during the mid–1970s and which found its expression in the voice of the Catholic Church and liberal professional associations, in the re-emergence of the student and trade union movements, and in the emergence of social movements with a strong popular base, such as the *Movimento do Custo de Vida* (Movement against the Cost-of-living). Nonetheless certain events should be mentioned here as an indication of the growing presence of the opposition movement during 1977 and 1978:

In February 1977, the National Conference of Brazilian Bishops (CNBB) – the principal organ in the Brazilian Catholic Church's hierarchy – issued a manifesto in which, by examining the country's institutional crisis, the bishops assumed a clear political position in support of the demands of the liberal opposition and called for a regime of social justice and democracy.[5]

In April, the Federal Council of the Bar Association (*Conselho Federal da OAB*) issued a note of protest against the government's April Package, asked for the return of the rule of law, the revocation of the AI-5 and a wide constitutional reform based on the convocation of a national constituent assembly.[6]

Also in mid-April, student demonstrations in São Paulo, Rio de Janeiro, Porto Alegre, Belo Horizonte and Recife, marked the re-emergence of the student movement on the political scene. This was the beginning of a series of demonstrations and strikes which spread throughout the country in 1977 and 1978, demanding not only solutions for the student's specific problems but also a political amnesty and genuine democratization.[7]

In June, during the official visit of Rosalyn Carter to Brazil, the president of the Women's Movement for Amnesty managed to break through the congressional security guard and give her a report on the victims of repression signed by the families of political prisoners, of the disappeared and of the people in exile. The Women's Movement for Amnesty, set up in 1975 under the leadership of Terezinha Zerbini – the wife of a general purged in 1964 – gained momentum with the creation in 1978 of the Brazilian Committee for Amnesty. Also supported by the Church, several left-wing groups and liberals, the committee organized a country-wide campaign with a slogan demanding a 'wide, general and unrestricted amnesty'.[8]

In July 1977, the Brazilian Society for Scientific Progress (SBPC), ignored the restrictions imposed by the government for the organization of its annual meeting to be held originally in Fortaleza and, with the help of money collected from students, professionals and the academic community to replace the financial support denied by the government, organized its conference in São Paulo. During the society's annual meeting the same demands were voiced; democratization, a national constituent assembly, an amnesty and the re-engagement by the university of several academics purged by the regime.

In August, during the celebration of the 150th anniversary of the establishment of juridical courses in Brazil, 200 jurists signed a manifesto entitled '*Carta aos Brasileiros*' (Letter to the Brazilian People), calling for the return of the rule of law and a national constituent assembly.

Also in August 1977, it was the turn of the workers to emerge onto the political scene as evidenced by their 'campaign for 34 per cent compensation'. The Metalworkers Union of São Bernardo do Campo and Diadema, led by Luis Ignácio da Silva (Lula), organized a broad campaign demanding that the government pay back 34 per cent in real wages lost as a result of a miscalculation of the inflation index. This campaign marked the prelude of the reemergence of the trade union movement which, given the novelty of the workers' strategy, would have in the first strikes of 1978 its most remarkable expression. As M. H. Moreira Alves describes:

> In May of 1978, without apparent prior notice, workers of the Saab – Scania automobile factory in São Bernardo do Campo – the heart of the industrial belt of São Paulo – sat down in front of their machines, crossed their arms, and refused to work. Within a period of two weeks a total of 76 843 metalworkers had joined the strike.[9]

In the following months, strikes broke out in several places across the country in a mobilization which extended to other sectors of salaried workers, from unskilled workers in civil construction to salaried professionals such as medical doctors and teachers in the public sector.[10] If better wages and improved working conditions were the major demands of all the movements, democracy and freedom for trade union organization were also demanded by several sectors involved in the workers' movements. At the Conference of the National Confederation of Workers in Industry (CNTI) held in July 1978, a dissident group of independent and more combative unions marked its break with the official trade union structure by issuing a document of principles which not only established the basis for the organization of an independent trade union movement, but also demanded more participation in the distribution of national income and in political decision-making. It asked for direct elections for Presidency of the Republic and the convocation of a national constituent assembly.[11]

In September 1978, thousands of people gathered at São Paulo's Cathedral Square to attend a rally organized by the *Movimento do Custo de Vida* – an authentic popular movement which had been built up on the initiative of the Ecclesiastical Base Communities (*Comunidades Eclesiais de Base*) and the Neighbourhood Associations (*Sociedades de Amigos do Bairro*).[12] That rally – the largest organized by the movement – was the result of a campaign which had collected 1.3 million signatures in support of a petition to be delivered to President Geisel, asking for an emergency cash bonus of 30 per cent for all workers, fair wage increases and a price freeze on all basic goods.[13]

The emergence of manifestations of opposition in civil society, however, did little to force any change in the 'gradual and secure' character of the process of political relaxation that Geisel was determined to push through. Nonetheless, it was undoubtedly important enough to ensure that the regime would be unable to rely on the electoral process as a source of legitimation. In this respect, the MDB continued to have an important political role in so far as it remained the only legal opposition party allowed to participate in elections. This is not to imply that the MDB and these opposition protest movements were closely related to one another in terms of undertaking joint and concerted actions against the regime. Notwithstanding the fact that the MDB was in contact with associations and institutions involved in the opposition movements and gave them its support, both the MDB and these movements were parallel opposition forces operating in different spheres. In any case, the growing opposition movement in civil society would certainly affect the MDB's performance. In order to maintain itself as a credible opposition party, the MDB could not ignore those movements, and would therefore seek new forms of political action and try to be more combative in Congress. The MDB's conduct however, would be also affected by the new constraints imposed following the restrictive measures decreed by the government through the 1977 April Package. In the light of these new circumstances, we will examine the MDB's participation in the political process during the last year of its existence as a single opposition party.

THE MDB AND THE POLITICAL PROCESS FROM 1977 TO 1979

Not surprisingly, the 1977 April Package brought discouragement to the ranks of the MDB. The abrogation once again of the direct gubernatorial elections scheduled for 1978 thwarted the aspirations

of several MDB politicians who had sought to contest state gover-
norships and had strong chances of winning the executive power at
state level by popular vote. The set of restrictive measures designed
to prevent the MDB from becoming a majority in Congress in the
next legislative elections buried all the MDB's hopes of influencing
the political process more effectively through its parliamentary
action. Yet, the impact that the MDB had had in the electoral
process in 1974 was bound not to be repeated on the same scale in
the next elections given the restrictions imposed on the electoral
campaign. Discouragement and disillusionment regarding the
party's prospect again encouraged the idea that the opposition party
had no alternative but to dissolve itself. But this was little more than
an emotional and short-lived reaction which merely reflected the
disillusionment of politicians with a party whose activities had once
again been curtailed. In fact, after so many years of restrained
opposition politics, most of the MDB politicians had got used to the
regime's storms and had developed a remarkable capacity for
tolerance and for working out ways to survive the thunderbolts.
Moreover, nobody would seriously consider dissolving the party
(which, after all, was the only legal channel for political participation) at a time when the MDB had at last created a positive image
among the electorate and when several sectors in civil society had
become much more involved in the movement opposing the regime.
It was after considering these factors that the more militant sectors
within the MDB maintained that the opposition party needed to
strengthen its links with civil society and try to mobilize public
opinion. This was in fact attempted by the MDB through the campaigns for a constituent assembly and for the presidential election,
developed through the National Front for Redemocratization.
Although neither of these campaigns had much impact on the political
process, they were significant opposition responses to Geisel's
project of implementing a limited political liberalization and of controlling the presidential succession

The Campaign for the Constituent Assembly and the Government's Political Reforms of 1978

The promotion of a popular campaign to gather support in favour of
the convocation of a national constituent assembly was suggested by
some MDB parliamentarians soon after the April Package was
decreed. On the 16 April 1977, in the newspaper *Journal da Targe*, an

article appeared under the heading: 'The MDB wants a Constituent Assembly. And the party will fight for it all over the country'. Despite this incisive headline, the article itself was simply an account of suggestions made by a group of MDB parliamentarians who were proposing a redefinition of the MDB's strategy in the face of the altered political picture following the political reforms recently imposed by the government.[14] Among the suggestions was the idea of promoting a wide-ranging campaign aimed at denouncing the real political situation of the country and mobilizing public opinion in support of a constituent assembly. Its advocates believed that, if the MDB intended to continue as a political organization, it could not remain limited to parliamentary activity which had proved so ineffective; rather, it should turn toward civil society, joining the opposition sectors so as to build a strong movement to pressure for substantial democratization. Thus, the call for a constituent assembly should be the MDB's alternative path to the government's policy of slow and secure political relaxation. On the 19 April, it was the Federal Council of the Bar Association (*Conselho Federal da Ordem dos Advogados do Brasil – OAB*) which raised the issue. In its note of protest against the April Package, the OAB asked for a sweeping constitutional reform which could only be achieved through a national constituent assembly. This theme had now become part of the political debate, presented as the only solution to the country's institutional crisis of which the recent measures imposed by the government had been a clear sign. But for months the issue would remain simply as a theme in the debate. Only in September 1977 did the MDB officially adopt the idea and decide to organize a campaign to mobilize public opinion in favour of a constituent assembly. In fact, the idea, which had actually been proposed by the more militant sectors of the party, did not initially raise much enthusiasm among the MDB's moderate leadership. Doubting the feasibility of promoting a campaign based on an issue which was totally unacceptable to the regime, they seemed to prefer to wait for further moves from the government regarding the much-heralded liberalizing political reforms. Moreover, as soon as the issue was raised by MDB parliamentarians, the leadership received warnings from the government about the danger of introducing the question of a constituent assembly. Certainly a campaign demanding a constituent assembly and involving popular mobilization, at a time of growing opposition in civil society and when the presidential succession question was at stake, was considered beyond the limit of the regime's tolerance of opposition activity. Not unexpectedly, the regime's supporters soon counter-attacked, making the MDB freeze, at least temporarily, its position regarding the campaign for a constituent assembly. On 28 May, the ARENA Deputy Sinval Boaventura – who would later become known for his involvement with the attempt to gather parliamentary support for the presidential candidacy of the hard-line Minister of War, Sylvio Frota – made a serious accusation against an MDB deputy. He produced evidence proving that a speech recently made by the MDB Deputy Marcos Tito had contained long passages reproduced from the Brazilian Communist Party's manifesto published in the party's official newspaper *Voz Operária*. The imprudence of the opposition deputy who had been careless enough to read out a speech prepared by one of his aides, embarrassed the MDB leaders and left the party without an adequate defence with which to respond to the accusations. During the following days, the radical right-wing elements of the ARENA attacked not only Marcos Tito but also three other MDB parliamentarians merely for having gone to the University of Brasilia campus to lend support to students on strike.

For twenty-one days the opposition party was kept in a state of uncertainty regarding the fate of its deputies amidst rumours that a wave of purges was again likely to hit the party. Eventually, only Marcos Tito was purged; but Geisel took twenty-one days to apply the AI-5 to cancel the deputy's mandate and suspend his political rights. Rather than a manifestation of Geisel's reluctance to punish the MDB deputy, the President's delay in using the AI-5 was interpreted as a carefully calculated move aimed at two targets. By not reacting promptly to the accusations against the MDB deputy made by an ARENA parliamentarian who was conniving with military hard-liners struggling for the presidential succession, Geisel wanted to show them his absolute political command which was not to be subjected to pressures from the regime's radicals. On the other hand, in delaying the decision regarding the fate of the MDB deputy, Geisel put the MDB on the defensive for almost a month, thus curtailing the opposition's offensive which had been gaining momentum, particularly on the issue of the constituent assembly.

But if the storm blew over after the punishment of the MDB deputy, another one would soon hit the opposition party when in June the AI-5 was used once more against the MDB. This time the victim was a leading party figure, the leader in the Federal Chamber, Deputy Alencar Furtado, who made a speech which, apart from touching on a sensitive theme – the victims of the regime's repressive apparatus – was heard by more than 21 million people who had tuned into an MDB radio and television broadcast. The MDB had promoted a symposium on 'Democracy and Liberty' in mid-June and had been allowed by the Electoral Tribunal to hold a nationwide party broadcast publicizing the closing session of the conference.[15] In fact, this party broadcast reproduced the speeches made by the MDB leaders ten days earlier at the end of the symposium. Thus, the content of the speeches that were broadcast had already been known, since they had been closely covered by the press during the symposium. The government's reaction against the MDB was caused by the fact that the party broadcast had actually reached public opinion, as indicated by the high audience figures obtained for the party broadcast in the opinion polls. The MDB's success, apart from resulting in the *cassação* of Alencar Furtado, led to judicial proceedings against the party president Ulysses Guimarães, initiated by an Electoral Procurator-General who intended to prosecute the party president for misuse of the free broadcasting time reserved for the Electoral Tribunal. The charge against Ulysses Guimarães was ultimately filed after four months of judicial procedures, but it was clearly intended to intimidate the MDB leadership at a time when the political temperature had risen considerably, with student's strikes and demonstrations, and with the ongoing struggle for the presidential succession.

After having disarmed the opposition so blatantly with the measures of the April Package and with the purges of MDB parliamentarians, in August the government announced its willingness to carry out a dialogue with the opposition aiming at negotiations for constitutional reforms towards liberalization. The 'Portella mission', which had died away during the crisis of the Judiciary Amendment bill, was to be revived. That is, Senator Petronio Portella was to resume his political mission of conducting talks with the opposition which, from then on, would not be restricted to the MDB but would also include representatives of all sectors of civil society. Within the ranks of the MDB, particularly the militant sectors of the party, the climate was far from receptive to a dialogue with the government when they were still feeling the impact of the regime's attacks. Moreover, the MDB could not easily enter into negotiations with the government and ignore the even louder voices of opposition coming from civil society, where professional associations, academics, students, representatives of the Church and even entrepreneurs were all joining in the same chorus demanding prompt and substantial democratization. As the MDB president Ulysses Guimarães commented, the MDB's old slogan – 'the voice of those without a voice' – no longer makes sense, because these voices have already made themselves heard all over the country'.[16] It was in this climate that the MDB national convention was held in mid-September 1977, and there was unanimous approval for the promotion of a campaign for a Constituent Assembly. The national convention marked the official adoption by the MDB of a clear position against the government's proposal for dialogue: it clearly stated that dialogue or political negotiation, could only be possible through a constituent assembly for which the party would fight through the mobilization of public opinion. In the manifesto approved by the convention, the MDB asked for an amnesty and proclaimed that a national constituent assembly was the only forum capable of establishing a truly democratic order in the country[17]. The decisions taken by the national convention marked a victory for the positions advocated by the more militant sectors of the party – namely the *autenticos* and *neo-autenticos* which by then had become known simply as the *grupo autentico*. Commenting on the MDB convention a journalist pointed out that the event showed that the two groups within the MDB – *autenticos* and *moderados* – seemed to have developed a capacity for sorting out their differences:

> The two extremes continue to exist . . . , but one fact became evident during the convention: the MDB managed to show a unity of command. Generally speaking, the division of the party into *autenticos* and *moderados* has become quite unrealistic. . . . Pressurized by opposition public opinion, as represented by several sectors of civil society, the moderate group has become more audacious and therefore closer to the position formerly occupied by the *autenticos*. The *autenticos*, on the other hand, have practically maintained within the limits of their initial performance or even adopted the tactic of discreetly retreating in the name of party unity.[18]

Despite the decisive line taken by the MDB at its national convention, the prohibition by the government of radio and television coverage of the Convention and the publicizing of its manifesto, was a clear sign that the MDB's strategy of popular mobilization for a constituent assembly was unlikely to be successful. This was indeed the case. Not only were radio and television stations forbidden from making any reference to the campaign, but public places which could have been the location for mass rallies were also prohibited from being used for the MDB's campaign. Thus the campaign was limited to speeches made by parliamentarians in the legislative chambers, a few public meetings held in some State Assemblies (for no more than a thousand people), and the publication of a special party document – the *Manual da Constituinte* – which explained in simple language what a constituent assembly meant and why the party was fighting for it. Less than two months after the party's national convention, the campaign had already died away and the constituent assembly became just one more item on the MDB's agenda. It must also be pointed out that one of the problems facing the campaign for the constituent assembly was the fact that the issue was not a sufficiently appealing theme which could in itself stimulate wide popular mobilization. As an MDB deputy remarked:

> One of the criticisms made of the campaign for the constituent assembly concerns its elitist character. Because it is a campaign directed at the elites, the intellectuals, in sum, those who understand that a constituent assembly is the historic solution for the country. ... The ordinary Brazilian is concerned with the condition that he lives in: low wages, unemployment, the cost-of-living, inflation ... Thus, to approach an ordinary Brazilian under these circumstances and tell him that our call is for a constituent assembly which would organize the juridical life of the country. ... This is quite difficult for him to understand.[19]

The government's initiative to put into practice the so called 'Portella mission' would also help to weaken the already faltering campaign for a constituent assembly. From late 1977 to mid 1978, Petronio Portella met most of the representatives of all sectors of civil society – heads of several professional associations, representatives of the Church, heads of entrepreneurs' associations, and even trade union leaders – to hold talks about the political reforms that the government intended to promote. The MDB was perhaps the last to participate officially in the Portella dialogue, since it was not until early June 1978 that Ulysses Guimarães met him to discuss the issue.

In late June, a Constitutional Amendment bill drawn up by Senator Portella with the blessing of President Geisel, was finally sent to Congress. The Bill was supposed to be the result of the 'national dialogue' promoted by Portella, but actually it was far from introducing substantial changes in the regime. Nevertheless, it was undeniably an advance, since it would revoke the AI-5 and other Institutional and Complementary Acts decreed after 1968, thus limiting the exceptional powers to which the next President of the Republic could resort. However, care was taken to ensure that the head of state would not be defenceless in the face of 'subversion', 'public disturbance' and 'threats to national security'. Instead of the AI-5, 'safeguards for the defence of the state' were incorporated into the constitution. Apart from the state of siege, the enforcement of which was subject to the approval of Congress, a new device was engineered: the state of emergency. Disregarding the need for prior consultations with Congress, the state of emergency could be decreed by the President who would simply be required to consult the Constitutional Council – a new organ composed of the President, Vice-President, the chairmen of the Senate and Federal Chamber, and Ministers of Justice and of the Armed Forces. The state of emergency could last up to ninety days and be extended for a further ninety days, during which parliamentary immunity could be suspended.[20] On this issue, the executive's bill was also limited: it did not re-establish full parliamentary immunity since 'crimes against national security' would be considered as exceptional cases. Thus, although the President would no longer be allowed, on his own, to cancel mandates and suspend political rights, parliamentarians could still be subjected to this punishment through prosecution. Another item of the Constitutional Amendment bill was concerned with the creation of political parties which would open the way for a future reform of the party system. It stipulated that the creation of political parties would require either the support of 10 per cent of the representatives in the Senate and in the Federal Chamber or the electoral support of 5 per cent of the electorate who had voted in the last elections, distributed throughout (at least) nine states, with the minimum of 3 per cent of the votes in each of the states. It also stated that, for a period of a year, legislative members were to be allowed to change their party affiliation within the existing parties.[21]

Needless to say, the amendments proposed by the MDB in an attempt to eliminate the Bill's more restrictive clauses, were all rejected by the committee which examined it. An amendment proposed by the ARENA Senator Accioly Filho would nonetheless create problems for the government in so far as the Senator's proposal had initially obtained the support, not only of the MDB, but also of forty parliamentarians from ARENA. This amendment proposed the reestablishment of direct elections for the one-third of senatorial seats which the government had recently decreed would be selected through 'indirect elections'. The MDB managed to put forward Accioly Filho's amendment as a separate item to be submitted to the vote. However, this attempt was also unsuccessful: the government succeeded in persuading ARENA's potential dissidents not to follow the opposition and, even persuaded some MDB parliamentarians to absent themselves from the Congressional session, thereby making it easy for the government to have the amendment defeated. On the 20th and 21st September the bill was submitted to the vote and it was easily approved, just with the support of the ARENA parliamentarians. In the first ballot, the bill received 241 votes to 145 from the opposition.[22] In the second round the Bill was again approved, by 227 votes. This time, the MDB left the plenary, thus abstaining from voting.[23]

In any case, in September 1978 the long promised political reforms had finally been approved by Congress which, in effect, merely ratified the bill proposed by the executive. The MDB was left without any possibility of influencing the decision in so far as the establishment of simple majority as a requirement for the approval of constitutional amendments, enabled the government to dispense with the MDB's support. In October 1978 another important event would take place: the indirect elections for the Presidency of the Republic. In response, the opposition would again try to influence the political process through the creation of the National Front for Redemocratization and through the MDB's candidacy for the Presidency.

The National Front for Redemocratization and the Presidential Succession

In 1978 another initiative to achieve popular support was attempted with the creation of the National Front for Redemocratization, the major aim of which was to influence the presidential succession. The movement was not an initiative of the MDB, although some MDB parliamentarians had participated in the setting up of the Front, and eventually the party adhered to the movement. The origins of the National Front for Redemocratization lay in the discontent created by Geisel's determination to impose his own choice on the presidential succession. It was a joint action by civilian and military dissidents of the regime and a reaction to Geisel's absolutist posture in imposing the candidacy of General João Baptista

Figueiredo to succeed him in office. Three prominent figures were the major participants in the creation of the Front: the ARENA Senator Magalhães Pinto – the self-proclaimed civilian leader of the '1964 Revolution' – , General Hugo Abreu – head of the Presidency's Military Household (*Casa Militar da Presidencia da Republica*) until his resignation in January 1978 – , and the retired General Euler Bentes Monteiro – ex-head of the SUDENE (the Northeast Development Agency).

Senator Magalhães Pinto – a stubborn aspirant to the office of President since 1964 – had his dreams once again thwarted with the appointment of General Figueiredo as the goverment's official candidate. After his unsuccessful attempt to gather support within his party so as to contest Geisel's appointee in ARENA's national convention, Magalhães Pinto had to find another way of entering the running for the Presidency. The creation of a Front which had the backing of the MDB – the only remaining legal channel through which to contest the presidential election in the electoral college – was a perfect strategy with which to put forward his candidacy as the civilian alternative. But there was also another aspirant for the job of opposition candidate in the presidential contest: General Euler Bentes Monteiro. The promotion of his name as the military alternative, committed to a nationalist policy and substantial redemocratization, had first got underway in July 1977 on the initiative of a Colonel in the reserve, Iese Rego Alves.[24] There had also been talks between General Euler Bentes and civilian politicians on the possibility of his participation in the presidential contest as the MDB's candidate. The third major participant in the formation of the Front was the recent dissident General Hugo Abreu. As the head of Geisel's Military Household, he had had a key role in helping the President to sack, in October 1977, the Minister of War – General Sylvio Frota – and dismantle the Minister's military support behind his attempt to impose himself as Geisel's successor. Nevertheless, General Hugo Abreu's loyalty to the President broke down when the government officially announced the candidacy of Figueiredo for whose appointment Geisel had disregarded consultations even with the Army High Command.[25] Disapproving of Geisel's handling of the presidential succession, and moreover, disapproving the choice of General Figueiredo, General Hugo Abreu resigned from his post and began initiatives to mobilize disaffected elements within the Armed Forces against Figueiredo's candidacy.[26] The search for a military leader who could contest the government's candidate led

Hugo Abreu to approach General Euler Bentes who, although already retired, had built up a positive image within the military establishment. The need for a channel through which to make a viable challenge to Fugueiredo's candidacy encouraged him to work for the creation of a National Front. Thus, in late May 1978, as a result of mediation by General Hugo Abreu and some MDB politicians, Senator Magalhães Pinto and General Euler Bentes Monteiro met to work out an agreement whereby they would collaborate in the same movement. As a result of this meeting, a note signed by Magalhães Pinto and Euler Bentes was issued, announcing the formal creation of the National Front for Redemocratization, designed to harness behind a single movement all the political forces committed to the redemocratization of the country. In the note, they also reiterated their commitment to the 'democratic ideals of the 1964 Revolution' and called for the MDB to join the Front.[27]

As regards the MDB, the opinions were sharply divided within the party as to the merits of party involvement with the Front and over the presidential succession issue. This resulted in the party delaying a month before deciding to officially join the Front for Redemocratization, and another two months before deciding to participate in the indirect presidential elections. The major question dividing the party was actually related to the presidential succession which, in any case, was the essential issue for which the Front's organizers intended to mobilize public opinion. In fact the MDB parliamentarians who were involved in the creation of the Front were also supporting the candidacy of General Euler Bentes Monteiro. The idea that the MDB should participate in the indirect presidential elections by backing a military candidate, had been advocated by some elements in the MDB as early as mid-1977.[28] This strategy and the name of Euler Bentes were advocated particularly by some parliamentarians from the *grupo autentico*. They saw in the candidacy of General Euler Bentes the possibility of attracting to the opposition the democratic and nationalist sector within the armed forces. Moreover, it was a 'way of provoking a division within the army'.[29] As Deputy Odacir Klein put it:

We knew that within the regime, grave dissension had emerged and, although the candidacy of Euler Bentes had a remote chance of winning, it had the possibility of aggravating those divisions and contributing to a weakening of the structure of government.[30]

But within the MDB there were also those who preferred not to touch on the military question at all. Among the more moderate elements, the idea of supporting the candidacy of Magalhães Pinto was thereby defended on the basis that, apart from representing a civilian alternative, he would possibly be more capable of attracting support from disaffected elements within the government party – an indispensable condition if the MDB's presidential candidacy was to have any chance of success. Moreover, the party's moderate leadership was cautious regarding the idea of adopting the candidacy of General Euler Bentes (who was actually the preferred name among the party's activists) given the unpredictable consequences which it might provoke, particularly following the initiatives undertaken by General Hugo Abreu in his attempt to mobilize military dissidents. In any case, in late August the MDB finally nominated General Euler Bentes and the MDB Senator Paulo Brossard as the party's official candidates for the Presidency and Vice-presidency.[31] Representing the opposition to Figueiredo's candidacy and to the government's policy of 'gradual and secure' political relaxation, General Euler Bentes Monteiro adopted a platform which promised the revocation of all the exceptional Institutional Acts and the re-establishment of the less authoritarian 1967 constitution, which would be replaced within a year by a new charter drawn up by a national constituent assembly.[32]

The campaign conducted by the National Front for Redemocratization was generally more successful in mobilizing public opinion than the MDB's previous campaign for the constituent assembly. The Front's activities certainly did not draw crowds but the meetings organized in several state capitals each managed to attract from two to three thousand people. Their impact was limited nonetheless, since radio and television broadcasts on the Front's activities were prohibited by the government. Moreover, the fact that the Front was to devote all its energies to the election campaign meant that organization would effectively fade away, once the presidential election was over.

As the election day approached, the government took steps to ensure that the opposition candidacy of General Euler Bentes would not pose any obstacle to the 'election' of General Figueirdo when the electoral college met on 15 October 1978. Not only was the government party instructed to resort to the Party Discipline Law to oblige all its members to vote for the government's candidate, but care was also taken to prevent any possibility of action from a military dissident movement: on 2 October, General Hugo Abreu was put under arrest for twenty days, in other words, for the period leading up to the presidential election.[33] As expected, on 15 October, General João Figueiredo was elected President of the Republic, receiving 355 votes from the ARENA parliamentarians while General Euler Bentes received 226 votes from the MDB representatives.[34]

Everything had happened as planned by Geisel's government: in mid-September, the 'indirect elections' for state governors and a third of the senatorial seats had taken place. These elections, in most cases, served merely to ratify the names of those candidates appointed by the central government.[35] In late September, the Constitutional Amendment proposed by the executive had been passed by Congress, introducing liberalizing political reforms in strict accordance with the gradual and secure character of the political relaxation policy. In mid-October, the new President, who for the next six years would be in charge of continuing that policy, had been elected. The last event to be handled by Geisel so as to complete the framework in which his successor was to rule, were the legislative elections scheduled for 15 November 1978. In this case, however, Geisel was unable to ensure full control of the electoral process.

The Outcome of the 1978 Legislative Elections

The 1978 election outcome, as a result of the restrictions imposed by the April Package, certainly did not give the victory to the MDB, but they did not give clear victory to ARENA either. ARENA obtained fifteen seats in the Senate while the MDB obtained only eight; and the government party got 55 per cent of the representation in the Federal Chamber, thus guaranteeing their majority in both Houses. However, in terms of the number of votes the MDB won the senatorial elections by a landslide of 4.4 million votes, and in the elections for the Federal Chamber, received as much electoral support as ARENA.[36]

Undoubtedly, the changes in the electoral rules, engineered by the government so as to ensure that ARENA retained its dominant position in the Congress, brought positive results. Apart from the one-third of senatorial seats guaranteed to ARENA through the 'indirect elections', the establishment of the *sublegenda* (sublabels) for the direct senatorial elections, and the restrictions imposed by the Falcão Law on campaign broadcasts, made it possible for the government party to obtain the majority of the representation in Congress. The *sublegenda* device which allowed each party to contest a senatorial seat by presenting up to three candidates, made it possible for ARENA to accommodate its divergent factions at local and state levels, and consequently, to participate more actively in the elections. For the MDB, on the other hand, the establishment of the *sublegenda* put the party at a disadvantage in several states where the opposition party was not able to run for the senatorial seat with the same number of candidates (in *sublegenda*) than ARENA. This led to cases in which an opposition candidate, who was the party's sole candidate for the Senate, was not elected although he alone obtained more votes than each of the three ARENA candidates. Instead, the seat was granted to ARENA which won in terms of the total number of votes obtained by the three ARENA candidates in the *sublegenda*. Moreover, with the prohibition on the free use of radio and television broadcast during the electoral campaign, the MDB lost its main weapon which had so decisively helped the opposition campaign in 1974. While the MDB was limited to showing just the photographs and brief curricula of its candidates on the television screens, the government, nonetheless, made extensive use of the media to publicize its achievements, openly campaigning for ARENA.

Undoubtedly, by imposing restrictions on the electoral process, the regime was to ensure for ARENA a majority in Congress. However, it was unable to avoid the MDB reconfirming yet again its supremacy at the polls, particularly in the most urbanized and industrialized areas of the country. The MDB won the elections for the Senate in the states of São Paulo, Rio de Janeiro, Minas Gerais, Rio Grande do Sul, Santa Catarina, Paraná, Goiás and Paraiba. In other words, apart from the states of Goiás and Paraiba, which belong to the Centre-West and North-East regions respectively, the opposition won in the majority of the states in the South-East region,[37] and in all the states of the South region.[38] These eight states together contained 69 per cent of the Brazilian electorate in 1978 (65 per cent if we consider only the Southern and Southeastern states – the most urbanized and industrialized area in the country). Moreover, the opposition candidates for the Senate obtained more votes than ARENA candidates in all the capitals of the federal states except three.[39] This meant that even in the urbanized areas of the less developed Northern and Northeastern states in which ARENA had its stronghold, the MDB had impressive electoral support. This also indicated that ARENA's electoral support was largely reliant on patronage politics and all kinds of political controls engineered to induce voter's support. These methods were widely used in rural areas where the electorate was still very dependent on local political bosses.

The examination of the MDB's experience during 1977 and 1978 underlines the limitations facing the party in its attempts to exert pressure for an acceleration of the liberalization process. Geisel's government was successful in engineering all sorts of devices to block the opposition's efforts, and to ensure that the process of 'gradual and secure' liberalization would not get out of control. Thus, in parliamentary activity, the MDB's hands were tied, and it could do little more than protest against the limited nature of the political reforms. The party's attempts to mobilize support in civil society, through the constituent assembly campaign and the National Front for Redemocratization, were unsuccessful. These were important initiatives, but they did not have an impact on the political system as regards accelerating the process of political opening. Certainly, much of the ineffectiveness of these undertakings was due to the regime's restraints which made the organization of public rallies difficult and prohibited mass media coverage of campaign activities. However, the failure of the opposition's experiment in popular mobilization was also related to the initiative's inherent limitations: the aims were not clearly defined and there was a lack of basic consensus amongst the actors involved regarding the adoption and implementation of this strategy. As for the campaign for the constituent assembly, apart from the fact that, in itself, the issue was not sufficiently appealing so as to arouse the support of the masses, (and perhaps because of that), doubts about the effectiveness of this undertaking were already present even before the movement was launched at the party's national convention. The adoption of the constituent assembly campaign was much more a reaction to the April Package than a plan of action with clear objectives. It was motivated by the militant sectors of the party and by the fact that the constituent assembly slogan was frequently recalled in the demands for a prompt and genuine democratization which came from the active sectors of civil society. The MDB moderates accepted this undertaking for fear that the party would otherwise be overtaken by the other protest movements, but without really regarding it as a viable strategy. With respect to the National Front for Redemocratization, it seemed potentially to be more capable of arousing popular support in so far as it had a clear aim: to contest the highest political office – the Presidency – universally perceived as the principal locus where changes could be made. However, the Front's campaign did not achieve better results than the constituent assembly campaign. Geisel moved quickly to prevent anything that might affect his determination to have Figueiredo appointed as his successor. On the other hand, the MDB's reluctance to define its position regarding the presidential candidacy left the movement for a long time without a leading figure who could attract popular support. Moreover, the adoption of a military candidate, although important in that it represented an attempt to provoke a division in the Armed Forces, was perhaps an imprudent choice in terms of arousing popular support.

It should also be said that one of the problems which may well have contributed to the minimal impact of these mobilization experiments was the fact that they were not organized through a joint initiative of the MDB and the active opposition sectors in civil society. As pointed out earlier, the links between the MDB and the sectors in society which were involved in protest movements, such as students, trade unions, professional associations and religious base communities, were based on mutual solidarity between distinct political forces rather than on an organic relationship aimed at developing a concerted action. This is clearly related to the fact that the opposition protest movements in civil society not only were (by 1977–8) a recent phenomenon in Brazilian political life under authoritarianism, but they had also emerged independently of the MDB which, engrossed in its own problems, had not dedicated much attention to the stimulation of political participation in society at large.

Referring to this separation between the opposition movement in civil society and the MDB, F. H. Cardoso remarks:

> From the point of view of civil society, the general distrust of the system of merely label-parties and of the politicians who emerged under a closed regime leads many leaders into an accentuated 'grass-rootism'. It also leads to a break between social movements and the state, and therefore between social movements and the parties which are their links with the state. This attitude is common in the sectors which are linked to the social movements motivated by the church, and it is relatively widespread in the union sector. The clear preference for mobilization around social

movements (the fight for amnesty, salary struggles, the fight for land, etc.) and the relative separation from the parties are due to the uprooting of the MDB, given the politicians' lack of interest in that type of movement under authoritarianism, and to the latent hostility of the civil society's intermediate-level leaders to present and future parties.[40]

The only events which brought together all opposition forces around a single objective were the elections. On these occasions the MDB, being the only opposition party, could count on the mobilization of the active sectors in civil society and monopolize political action with the aim of defeating the regime at the polls. This crucial role played by the MDB in capitalizing on the electoral support denied to the regime, would make it imperative for the military to promote the dissolution of the two-party system. This however would be a task undertaken by the fifth general-president, who would take office on 15 March 1979. A discussion of the political party reform will therefore be made in the penultimate chapter of this work.

8 The Political Party Reform and the Party of the Brazilian Democratic Movement (PMDB)

THE END OF THE MDB AS A SINGLE OPPOSITION PARTY

The question of a reform of the party system had been in the government's mind since the 1974 election results, when it was observed that the two-party arrangement had led to the elections taking on the character of a plebiscite. This implied that the two-party system would inevitably remain an effective means for opposition politics, rather than, as the government had hoped, a means for the regime to achieve legitimacy through the electoral process. Thus, the reform of the party system, intended to stem the growing electoral support for an opposition united under the MDB label, became imperative for the survival of the government's policy of gradual and secure political relaxation.[1] Nonetheless, if the implementation of party reform would solve the regime's problem regarding the electoral process, it would also lead to the opening up of a space for the creation of more representative political organizations. Whether or not to open this space was obviously a real problem in so far as 'the increase in representativeness is largely associated with effective democratic changes: with the increase in political participation and with the increased possibility of the political forces exerting much stronger and more clearly defined pressures'.[2] The fear of these consequences certainly contributed to the government's decision to postpone the implementation of party reform, although it had been considered as an option ever since the 1974 election results. In mid-1976, for example, it was stated in the press that the idea of dissolving the existing political parties had been meeting some resistance from within government circles.[3] This resistance was undoubtedly caused by the unpredictability, in terms of positive results for the regime, of implementing party reform without an efficient mechanism for controlling the creation of new parties. This would apply not only to the opposition side but also to the government side, since the objective was to provoke the disintegration of the MDB, but without causing the disintegration of ARENA. This was a difficult task if one considers that the government party could hardly be described as a united and cohesive organization. Therefore, before taking any step towards the reform of the party system, the government would work for the preservation of its base of support. In this regard, the changes in the electoral rules for the 1978 elections were aimed not only at ensuring a government majority in Congress but also at strengthening ARENA as a party organization. Also, the control exerted by the central government over the succession in the gubernatorial offices in 1978 had *inter alia* the intention of creating the conditions for a future party reform: the nomination of the state governors was based on the choice of politicians who, apart from displaying the 'quality' of being loyal to the central government, were figures of political prestige capable of creating a strong party base for the reorganization of the government party.

While trying to build up its base of support for a future party reorganization, the government encouraged speculation about a reform of the party system with the clear intention of provoking dissension within the MDB. Worried about the possibility of ARENA's defeat in the 1978 elections, the government adopted the strategy of fuelling the debate over the creation of new political parties, an issue which could well aggravate divisions among the ranks of the MDB and consequently harm the party's electoral performance. In this regard, we should point out that party reform was indeed a genuine demand of large sectors of Congress and of civil society. Notwithstanding the fact that the creation of more representative political parties was a fair demand of the opposition sectors dissatisfied with the excessively broad front represented by the MDB, this nonetheless served as a good weapon for the government given its strategy of dividing the opposition. Thus it was not coincidental that, from early 1978, there was mounting speculation concerning a possible party reform, to the point that it seemed that the demise of the two-party system was imminent. At the beginning of 1978, it was announced that Geisel had changed his position on the party system issue: from advocating the continuation of the two-party system, the President was now accepting the idea of dissolving the two parties. The announcement of the President's change of mind was certainly a signal sent by the government to fuel the debate. This would be confirmed later by the many statements made by Geisel's future successor, General Figueiredo, in favour of a reform of the party system. Moreover, the constitutional amendment proposed by the government and approved by Congress in September 1978 also touched on the party question by easing the requirements for the creation of political parties and by allowing members of the legislative houses to change their affiliation to the existing parties, that is, ARENA and the MDB. However, rather than providing clear and definite rules for party reform, that amendment was simply designed to provide an alternative should the MDB obtain a majority in the Federal Chamber in the November 1978 elections. As this did not happen, the government subsequently decided to postpone the implementation of party reform. Thus, after the 1978 legislative elections, instead of proposing changes to the Political Party Law, the government instructed the ARENA leadership to work for the consolidation of the existing government party.[4] Since the attempt to disintegrate the MDB had not yet produced the expected results, it was much more convenient to delay the reform of the party system. Moreover, the government was still uncertain about the preservation of a single and strong government party in the face of the difficulties created by dissident ARENA members who were wanting to create an independent party less submissive to the government. As for the measure allowing members of the legislative houses to change their party affiliation, designed to attract MDB politicians to the government party, it failed to produce any result in the short term. Most of the MDB's potential deserters (the so-called *adesistas* or 'joiners') preferred to wait for the definition of the rules concerning future party arrangements before taking the initiative to leave the MDB. In fact it was the ARENA which was the first to suffer the loss of some of its members, when prominent ARENA dissidents, such as Senator Teotonio Villela and Severo Gomes, a former minister, left the party to join the MDB.

If the government had been unsuccessful in provoking the disintegration of the MDB, it certainly helped to aggravate the party's internal dissensions regarding the party reform issue. During the course of the 1978–9, while the MDB persistently denounced the government for using this issue as a manoeuvre to weaken the opposition party, a considerable number of its members were openly working for the creation of other political parties.[5] By 1979 the MDB was divided between those who supported the creation of new parties and those who strongly defended the preservation of the MDB as a single opposition front. Led by the party's national chairman Ulysses Guimarães, the advocates of the maintenance of an opposition front argued that the creation of other opposition parties would actually help the government's strategy of dividing the opposition while keeping the nature of the regime unchanged. As Guimarães claimed in a speech addressed to the recently elected MDB Congressmen in February 1979: 'It is not yet time for the democratic forces to abandon the front of resistance and start to compete with each other. If we have an enemy that is depotism, how can we demobilize and even become adversaries, when this is only admissible and appropriate in a democratic system?.'[6]

Despite the persuasive arguments put forward by the advocates of an opposition front, it became increasingly difficult to keep the party united in the face of the wide range of tendencies – from right to left, from moderate to radical – separating the numerous groupings which were already tired of sharing the same political organization and were attracted by the prospect of more ideologically defined political parties. However, nobody was willing to leave the MDB before the government made a definite move towards the dissolution of the two-party system.

This move finally came in November 1979 when the party reform bill proposed by the government was approved by Congress despite the MDB's protests. Besides defining the rules for the organization of new political parties in accordance with the requirements previously laid down by the 1978 constitutional amendment, the bill explicitly determined the dissolution of ARENA and the MDB. Yet, in order to ensure that the MDB would not survive intact, at least under the same label, the bill made it compulsory to include the word 'party' in the names of all future political organizations. On the other hand, in order to prevent substantial defections from the government party, the bill maintained the possibility of creating opposing factions within a single party to adopt rival candidates for municipal and Senate elections – the so-called *sublegenda* mechanism. [7] For the government, this was an indispensable means of ensuring a strong party base in so far as the *sublegenda* made it possible to accommodate, within the existing party structure, divergent local factions which might otherwise have joined the new political party to be created by ARENA dissidents. With the approval by Congress of the party reform bill, on 22 November 1979, ARENA and the MDB ceased to exist as political organizations, after thirteen years of restrained participation in the political system under the military-authoritarian regime.

In 1979 the country had also witnessed the inauguration of a new presidential term with the accession of General João Figueiredo. With Figueiredo in power, the process of gradual and secure political relaxation continued its slow path. Thus began the era of *abertura* (political opening) – a new word coined to denominate the same process of controlled liberalization that Geisel's government had initiated under the label of *distensão* (detente). In any case, the regime had clearly moved further towards the liberalization of the political system. The government's Amnesty Bill, approved by Congress in August 1979, was undoubtedly an advance in that direction. Although the Amnesty Law was limited, since it excluded those who were in prison for alleged 'crimes of terrorism, robbery, kidnapping and personal offence',[8] it was estimated that about six thousand people were to be granted amnesty as a result of the law.[9] As for the party reform, despite the clear intention of provoking the fragmentation of the opposition, it was, nevertheless, a liberalizing measure, in that it allowed the creation of other political parties by those who were dissatisfied with the two existing parties.

Although dissolved by law, neither ARENA nor the MDB actually disappeared after party reform. Anxious to dispense with its unpopular label, ARENA changed its name to *Partido Democrático Social* – PDS (Social Democratic Party). On the other hand, eager to retain the popular image that the party's label had gained, the MDB simply added the word 'party' to its name, as required by the new law, thus becoming the *Partido do Movimento Democrático Brasileiro* – PMDB (Party of the Brazilian Democratic Movement). Apart from the reorganization of these two existing parties, four other political parties were created in 1980. The *Partido Popular* – PP (People's Party)[10] was set up by ARENA dissidents and moderates from the MDB under the leadership of Magalhães Pinto and Tancredo Neves, and was intended to represent the liberal-conservative forces. The *Partido dos Trabalhadores* – PT (Workers' Party) was set up by trade unionists under the leadership of Luis Ignácio da Silva, a metalworkers' leader, who, together with some sectors of the left, intended to organize a truly authentic political party for the working class. The attempt by ex-PTB followers to resurrect their old labour party resulted in a split of the *trabalhistas* and the creation of the *Partido Democrático Trabalhista* – PDT (Democratic Labour Party) led by the amnestied politician Leonel Brizola, and the *Partido Trabalhista Brasileiro* – PTB (Brazilian Labour Party) set up by Ivete Vargas who managed to inherit the old PTB label after a long dispute with Brizola's group.[11]

With the reform of the party system, the MDB obviously lost some of its parliamentarians who decided to join other parties. Table 8.1 records the affiliation of the ex-ARENA and ex-MDB federal deputies to the new parties as of January 1982. While only 37 deputies left the ARENA to join other parties, particularly the PP, 79 MDB deputies changed their party affiliation. Most of the parliamentarians who left the MDB joined either the PP (particularly the moderates who followed Tancredo Neves), or the pro-government PDS. This new alignment meant that the PMDB emerged as a more of a centre-left party, particularly since the two new parties more clearly identified with the opposition (the PT and PDT) managed to attract only a few MDB deputies. In fact, most of the militant and left-wing groupings within the old MDB ended up staying in the renamed PMDB and, as a consequence, forced the exit of the so-called *adesistas* who were inclined to support the government.[12]

Table 8.1 Affiliation to the new parties by the members of ARENA and the MDB – Federal Chamber, *January 1982*

New parties	Dissolved parties		
	MDB	*ARENA*	*Total*
PMDB	109	6	115
PDS	22	193	215
PP	41	28	69
PTB	1	3	4
PDT	10	–	10
PT	5	–	5
Undecided	2	1	3
Total	189	231	420

Source: List of members of the Federal Chamber (as of January 1982) provided by the *Câmara dos Deputados, Coordenação de Apoio Parlamentar, Setor de Informações.*

In the manifesto annnouncing the creation of the PMDB in December 1979, it was apparent that the party had opted for a more clearly defined ideological line. Apart from reiterating the party's fight against authoritarianism, the manifesto stressed the objectives of organizing a party for all salary- and wage-earning workers and of achieving enhanced political participation through the creation of a strong grassroots organization closely linked to the social movements in civil society. It stated:

> The PMDB will be the path for the opposition forces which understand that the fight against authoritarianism must result, not only in the re-constitutionalization of the state, but also in the democratization of society, through a combative and organized participation of all Brazilian people and especially of the workers and the middle class....
>
> The perseverance and nonconformity of many individuals transformed a defenceless party into a vigorous organization which the regime, if it was to prolong its survival, had to extinguish. This same perseverance and nonconformity will transform the successor of this party into a movement which will emancipate the country not only from the government but also from the despotic regime; not only from the despotic regime, but also from the current social order.[13]

The PMDB was however to be prevented from carrying out most of its intentions set out in its manifesto, as the liberalization process under Figueiredo followed an unforeseen pattern. Although an analysis of the period following the dissolution of the two-party system is beyond the scope of this work, we will end this historical reconstruction of the MDB's experience by examining briefly the events leading to the re-establishment of civilian rule in 1985.

THE PMDB AND THE RE-ESTABLISHMENT OF CIVILIAN RULE

As suggested in our analysis of the party reform, the emergence of the new party system did not coincide with the establishment of a new regime in Brazil. On the contrary, the new party arrangement had emerged from a well calculated strategy formulated by the military government aiming at dividing the opposition forces so as to keep the process of liberalization under control. Among the factors that needed to be controlled, the most crucial were undoubtedly those related to the presidential succession which would take place in 1985, when it was expected civilian rule would be re-established. As had happened in former presidential elections, Figueiredo's successor was to be elected by an electoral college rather than by universal suffrage, as the opposition had been pressing for. By keeping unchanged the rule for the presidential elections, the military wanted to avoid an unpredictable outcome in the succession to President Figueiredo. However, there was still a degree of uncertainty regarding the outcome of the presidential election, in so far as the composition of the electoral college would depend on the results of the 1982 elections when Congress would be renewed. As established by the 1977 *April Package*, the Electoral College would be composed of the members of the National Congress and of delegates from the State Assemblies. This meant that, if the PDS made a poor showing in the 1982 elections, the government would lose control of the presidential succession. It therefore became imperative to find a way of ensuring that those elections provided the government with a majority in Congress and hence in the electoral college. Thus, aiming at increasing the PDS's chance of victory, the government altered the electoral legislation in November 1981. The so-called November Package prohibited party alliance for the elections, required each party to run candidates for all the offices in contest in any one state (that is, state governor, senator, federal and state deputies, municipal councillors and mayors); and established the *voto vinculado* or 'tied vote', which meant that voters had to choose candidates of the same party for the several offices, from the local to the national levels. The introduction of the *voto vinculado* sought to ensure that the electoral support enjoyed by a candidate for one office, such as governor, would help to elect his or her colleagues running for other offices. This measure would be beneficial to the PDS in those states where it could count on the electoral superiority of a strong candidate for governor, for example. Thus, if the PDS managed to win the gubernatorial office in a particular state, it would also win the elections for the other offices.[14] As for the two other measures – the ban on electoral alliances and the obligation of parties' full participation in the electoral contest – the government's intention was to disperse the opposition vote among the several opposition parties, thus reducing the impact of a possible opposition victory. These measures were particularly damaging to the recently created parties, which had not had time to organize on a nationwide scale and were consequently unable to run candidates for all the offices in more than a handful of states. Had they been allowed to form alliances, they would certainly have refrained from contesting the gubernatorial elections in some states where they had little chance of victory, and would instead have supported or allied with the PMDB so as to join forces against the government.

In consequence of the government's November Package, the People's Party (PP) ceased to exist even before having been fully established. In order to cope with the difficulty of participating in the elections, its members opted for merging with the PMDB. This was consumated in February 1982, and as a result, the new party system once again changed its configuration, as shown by the party realignments as of August 1982 (Table 8.2). With the dissolution of the PP, some of its members joined the PDS or the PTB, but most of them joined or returned to the PMDB, thus making this party a broad front once again. In any case, the incorporation of the PP into the PMDB served as a reaction against the government's strategy and strengthened the position of the PMDB as the main party with chances of defeating the government in the elections.

The government's manoeuvres to control the political process did not stop at those alterations to the electoral legislation. In May 1982 other devices were engineered, this time aimed at safeguarding the

Table 8.2   Affiliation to the new parties by the members of ARENA and the MDB – Federal Chamber, *August 1982*

New parties	Dissolved parties		
	MDB	ARENA	Total
PMDB	136	32	168
PDS	28	196	224
PTB	11	3	14
PDT	9	–	9
PT	5	–	5
TOTAL	189	231	420

Source: R. Wesson and D. Fleischer, *Brazil in Transition* (New York, Praeger, 1983).

government against the possible consequences of the opposition obtaining a majority in Congress and in the electoral college. Firstly, in order to prevent an opposition majority from passing a constitutional amendment, the government re-established the requirement of a two-thirds majority for the approval of constitutional amendments.[15] Looking it from the regime's point of view, this was a sensible precaution which proved to be very effective in 1984, when the opposition parties attempted to pass a constitutional amendment restoring direct elections for the Presidency. Secondly, the government altered the composition of the electoral college for the presidential elections. As mentioned above, the College was to be composed of the members of the Congress and of state delegates. The change affected the number of state delegates: instead of the former criterion that determined the number of delegates per state according to population,[16] the new rule established a fixed number of six delegates per state, chosen among the members of the party which had the majority in the state legislature. As the electoral support for the opposition was particularly strong in the more populous states of the Southeast, by fixing an equal number of delegates for all states, the government intended to reduce the opposition's chance of electing a larger number of delegates for the electoral college.

The military government had, therefore, engineered all sorts of devices to ensure that the 1982 electoral outcome would not undermine its determination to keep the process of political opening under control. In spite of the government's interference, the process of liberalization continued its course, though at a slow pace, and the 1982 elections were an important step in that direction: new political parties had been created and participated in the electoral process, politicians who had lost their political rights under banning orders in the 1960s had resumed political life, and elections for state governors were held for the first time since 1965. Nonetheless, the election results provided proof of the efficacy of the government's strategy. Table 8.3 shows the results of the elections for governor, for the Senate and Federal Chamber. The PDS obtained 37.3 per cent of the total vote, less than the 39.6 per cent obtained by the PMDB and much lower than the 52.5 per cent of the vote obtained by all the opposition parties together. However, the PDS won 12 gubernatorial offices out of 22, 60 per cent of the Senate seats, and 49 per cent of the seats in the Federal Chamber; in addition, it obtained the majority in thirteen state assemblies. These results meant that the government

Table 8.3 National results for the 1982 elections and number of offices obtained by each party

Vote and seats	PDS	PMDB	PDT	PTB	PT	Blank/null	Total
Percentage of the vote[a]	37.3	39.6	5.4	4.2	3.3	10.2	48.214.344
Number of governors elected by parties	12[b]	9	1	0	0	–	22
Number of seats in the Senate	15	9	1	0	0	–	25
Number of seats in the Federal Chamber	235	200	23	13	8	–	479

[a] These are figures for the gubernatorial elections. The percentages for the legislative elections do not differ so much so as to be included in this table.

[b] In addition, the PDS won the gubernatorial office in the recently created state of Rondonia where the governor was appointed by the central government.

Source: Official figures from the *Tribunal Superior Eleitoral.*

had managed to guarantee its majority in the Electoral College for the presidential elections,[17] in spite of the fact that a majority of the Brazilian electorate had voted against the government.

As regards the opposition, the first electoral contest held under the new party system showed that the PMDB still maintained its position as the main political force in opposition to the regime. It received 40 per cent of the overall vote, was the outright winner in nine states and obtained 200 seats in the Federal Chamber, which was more than it held previously when it was the only opposition party. The PDT was the only other opposition party to elect a governor (in Rio de Janeiro). This was due largely to the personality of its candidate Leonel Brizola, a populist politician who had returned to politics after fifteen years in exile.[18]

Despite all the measures invented by the regime to restrain the opposition, the 1982 electoral results strengthened the position of the PMDB. The confirmation of its electoral support meant not only that it would be in state government for the first time and in some of the most important states in the federation, but also that it would still continue to play an important role in the political process. This was to be confirmed by later developments in connection with the presidential succession, when the opposition managed to undermine the government's plans for retaining full control over the process.

In 1984, a Constitutional Amendment Bill re-establishing direct elections for the Presidency was proposed by PMDB Deputy Dante de Oliveira and was to cause problems for the government. Aiming at raising support for the change, a campaign for prompt re-establishment of universal suffrage for the election of the President of the Republic was jointly organized by the opposition parties. The campaign resulted in a popular mobilization on a scale never previously seen in Brazilian political history: thousands of people carrying banners and wearing t-shirts with the slogan *Diretas Já* (Direct Elections Now!) attended the public rallies organized by the parties all over the country. From January to April 1984, the *Diretas Já* movement grew so fast that some PDS parliamentarians, worried about losing popularity as a result of their refusal to support the bill, started dissenting from the government which was determined to block the bill in Congress. However, the number of PDS dissidents was not large enough to enable the opposition to reach the two thirds majority that was necessary for the bill to be approved.[19] On the other hand, in order to defeat the opposition's initiative, the government not only exerted its full influence to keep the PDS in line, but also imposed a state of emergency in Brasilia, the capital, and blocked all the roads leading into this city to prevent a mass of people pressing for direct elections from rallying at the Congress building on the day that the bill was voted.

The military had refused to change the rules for the presidential elections. However, its command of the electoral process was to be undermined by the emergence of divisions within its own parliamentary support on the issue of the nomination of the government candidate for the Presidency. It was also to be undermined by the opposition's determination to influence the presidential succession. Following the military's refusal to hold direct elections, the opposition parties – with the exception of the PT (Workers' Party) – decided to participate in the presidential elections within the rules established by the government.[20] Led by the PMDB, negotiations took place with a view to increasing support for the candidature of Tancredo Neves, PMDB governor of the state of Minas Gerais and an exceptionally able politician. As a result of these negotiations, a group of PDS dissidents who had refused to accept the nomination of Deputy Paulo Maluf as the government candidate, agreed to vote for the opposition candidate whose chances of victory depended on their support in the Electoral College. The PDS dissidents who left their party and formed the PFL (Liberal Front Party) thus came to an agreement with the PMDB on the creation of the Democratic Alliance by which they would join forces to defeat the government candidate in the electoral college. In return for PFL support, Senator José Sarney – a dissident who had recently resigned the position of PDS national chairman – was nominated candidate for the Vice-Presidency.

On 15 January 1985 the electoral college met in Congress to elect General Figueiredo's successor. Tancredo Neves and José Sarney were elected President and Vice-President of the Republic, winning 480 votes out of 636, a remarkable victory which gave them a majority of 300 votes over the government candidate Paulo Maluf.[21] With this event, the Brazilian experience of military-authoritarian rule had finally ended, an end which was still marked by a compromise solution accepted by the moderate sectors of the opposition which agreed to participate in the indirect elections and established an alliance with the regime's dissidents.

Tancredo Neves was set to become, on 15 March 1985, the first civilian President after nearly twenty-one years of military rule.

Unfortunately however, on the eve of the inauguration of his government, he fell ill and had to be replaced by Vice-President José Sarney. By an irony of destiny, the (P)MDB which had waited for so long for the accession to the presidential office, ended up not only having to share the first civilian government with its old adversaries, but also having to accept, as the head of the new government, José Sarney – a former loyalist to the military governments – as a consequence of Tancredo Neves's death. Despite this outcome, the 'New Republic' – as the re-establishment of civilian rule became known – had restored a democratic climate[22] which it is hoped will develop towards the full institutionalization of a democratic system in Brazil.

As regards the PMDB, its nineteen-year history of resistance to the military-authoritarian regime enabled it to consolidate as a political party. However, the PMDB's difficulties in finding a new political identity in a changed situation in which it is now a partner in government has entangled it in many problems of internal dissent. And the position that the PMDB will hold in the new Brazilian political system remains to be defined.

9 Conclusion: Military-Authoritarian Rule and Party Politics

The intention of this study has been to look closely at a specific case of opposition politics in the authoritarian context of military rule. It has attempted to tell the history of the MDB, its problems, dilemmas, failures and successes as a legal opposition party operating under the constraints of Brazil's military-authoritarian regime. Although this has not primarily been a study of the regime established in Brazil after 1964, it has shown the major features of this regime as well as its development in so far as they affected or conditioned the way in which the MDB operated. We emphasized the hybrid nature of the political order that emerged after the so-called 1964 Revolution, and followed the different phases undergone by the regime, so as to provide the context in which the MDB operated, and to understand how this context affected and sometimes was affected by the opposition. Before making final remarks about this case of opposition politics under authoritarianism, we shall underline some points related to the Brazilian experience of military rule whose distinctive features must have contributed to make it difficult the institutionalization of the regime.

As was discussed in Chapter 1, the regime that emerged after the 1964 Movement was a combination of authoritarian and dictatorial rule with some mechanisms of a democratic system. The preservation of Congress, rotation of the executive, elections for the legislative houses, political parties, albeit formal, were bound to have an impact on the political system and were one of the sources of instability of the government. In fact, the difficulty of institutionalizing the new regime, which led J. Linz to characterize the Brazilian case as an authoritarian *situation* rather than an authoritarian regime,[1] was largely due to the fact that its political framework was bound to be undermined by its own contradictions. Some factors that may explain the adoption of this hybrid regime are suggested in this work, such as the need to preserve the new regime's image abroad, the need to secure a place for the civilians who were engaged in the 'Revolution', and the military instutition's need to preserve its unity

218

which could be eroded by internal conflicts resulting from direct military rule. We could also add to these factors, that the military's initial intention (at least of those high officers actively involved in the coup) was not the establishment of a typically military and authoritarian regime. Rather it was aimed at imposing on the country a 'democracy' with qualifications, that is a restricted or 'guided democracy'.[2] To affirm that the military did not intend to establish a permanent and overt military authoritarian system does not make the Brazilian case of military intervention unique. As S. Finer remarked in his work on the military written in 1962, direct military rule 'often pretends that it is transitional – a provisional form about to lead to something else'.[3] More recently, and referring specifically to the Latin American experiences of military rule, A. Rouquié argues in the same direction:

> In the Latin American normative and cultural context, those who hold military power know that, whatever they say, there still exists above them a superior legitimacy, that of the constitutional order. Not only can they not claim its support, but they also must ultimately pay lip service to it. In fact, military regimes are only really legitimized by their future. . . . [The military regime] is, in its essence, transitory. A permanent system of military rule is almost a contradiction in terms. The army cannot govern directly and durably without ceasing to be an army.[4]

The Brazilian military seems to have been aware of these problems and to have taken them into account even at the time when it seized power. This is shown not only by the respect paid to constitutional procedures in seizing power and maintaining it (Congress was convened to ratify the accession of the first general-president, the principle of rotation was respected),[5] but also by the attempt to transform a provisional form into a new political regime, evident during even the first military government. The constant reminder of the Revolution's commitment to the re-establishment of democracy was perhaps something more than a slogan used to claim legitimacy for military intervention. The 'institutionalization of the Revolution' and consequent restoration of democracy which was so often praised, meant, in the political sphere, nothing other than the establishment of a 'guided democracy'. In this project of an 'ideal democratic system', praised not only by the military legalist group but also by the civilians engaged in the coup, direct military rule was not expected to last for longer than was necessary to consolidate the basis for a safe and stable political system protected against the danger of 'subversion', populism and 'grave' dissent, whatever the meaning was given to these words.

Castelo Branco, the first general-president, seemed to be quite determined to go in this direction by trying to keep his government within the old constitutional order, and later reforming it so as to adapt it to the 'Revolution's ideals' before leaving the Presidency. Several moves of Castelo Branco's authoritarian performance reveal, in their ambivalence, an intention to found this protected political system. These are: his determination to hold the direct gubernatorial elections in 1965 as scheduled by the old constitution, albeit while making sure that 'subversive and corrupt' elements were left out of the contest; the decision to dissolve the old political parties but replace them by a new party system; his opposition to being succeeded by the Minister of War, General Costa e Silva, although he certainly expected to have a successor – military or civilian – who was closely identified with the 'Revolution's ideals' so as to continue his work; and his attempt to 'institutionalize the Revolution', by promulgating (in 1967) a new constitution which in fact was not exempted from ratification by Congress. This constitution was clearly marked by its authoritarian character and legalized an all-powerful executive. However it still retained, for example, direct elections for state governors and some level of independence for the Congress. In this regard, it should be remembered that the Institutional Act Number 2 (AI–2) which allowed Castelo Branco to carry out political purges, did expire at the end of his presidential term, and the 1967 Constitution guaranteed parliamentary immunity which could only be suspended (to allow the prosecution of a parliamentarian) if Congress gave permission. The Marcio Moreira Alves episode in 1968 was a clear example of the consequences of the establishment of this legal framework.

Needless to say, Castelo Branco was quite unsuccessful in his attempt to establish this 'guided democracy'. This is probably an impracticable project, particularly when it is implemented by actors who have recently seized power in the name of the military institution. Crises are bound to emerge and push the regime either to consolidate its authoritarian character (as happened after 1968), or to withdraw the military from power without effectively establishing guarantees that the new democracy would be protected against the dangers which had initially justified military intervention (as seems to have happened in 1984–5). Two problems contributed to the infeasibility of the institutionalization of a hybrid regime or 'guided democracy', at least in a society as complex as Brazil. The first problem, and perhaps the crucial one, is the internal conflict and power struggle within the military establishment intrinsic to direct military rule versus the structural imperative of unity to ensure the institution's survival. In the Brazilian case, the military group in charge of the first military government tried to protect itself against these consequences by maintaining as civilianized a regime, compatible with the old constitutional framework, as possible for a movement which called itself a revolution. But this did not prevent the emergence of an internal conflict between factions in the military corps, jeopardizing the unity of the organization. The conflict between hard-liners and legalists permeated all twenty-one long years of military rule and was a source of instability of the military governments. The AI–2, the inevitable acceptance of the candidacy of Costa e Silva, and the AI–5 – just to mention these more evident examples – were largely the result of an internal military conflict and were ultimately aimed at preserving the unity of the armed forces.

The second problem is the fact that if some space for civilian independence and opposition is tolerated and legalized by the regime, it would be inevitably used by the opposition forces and even by those civilians loyal to the regime who believed that the new legal order had to be respected. The crises of 1965 and 1968 were again good examples of this problem: in both cases Congressmen did nothing beyond their prerogative guaranteed by the constitution. These manifestations of independence and dissent were not just the product of an action undertaken by the opposition. They were also backed by parliamentarians who supported the regime and belonged to the government party. Therefore, two kinds of pressures were sources of instability for the government and made institutionalization of the regime difficult. They both affected one another in so far as they pulled the government in opposite directions: the internal hard-line faction of the military establishment pressured it to reinforce the authoritarian side of the regime, while the external, that is, civilian politicians, tried to make effective the liberal side of the regime.

As we have said, the first attempt to establish this kind of 'guided democracy' actually resulted in the regime's move towards a clearly authoritarian and military situation after 1968, and ended up by maintaining military rule for nearly twenty-one years in Brazil.

However, the original project of moulding the Brazilian political system into a tutelary democracy was not abandoned and was in fact resumed with the accession of Geisel to power in 1974. By 1973–4, the situation of the country seemed suited to the undertaking: 'subversion' had been neutralized with the dismantling of the guerrilla organizations, the legal opposition was under control and economic prosperity was achieved. To the military the country was apparently enjoying the ideal conditions for the establishment of the 'new democratic order' and the consequent return of the military to the barracks after so many years of direct rule. A policy of gradual and secure relaxation was the best formula for building this political order which had been so much desired. Having learnt from the unsuccessful experience of Castelo Branco, General Geisel protected his government and his policy against all intervening factors which had made Castelo Branco's project fail. The crucial defence was to keep the AI–5 which could serve as a weapon not only against opposition pressures but also to appease the hard-liners. However, the same, inherent, problems of consolidating this hybrid regime were bound to emerge again: the internal military conflict and the oppositional pressures. The first problem emerged with the unexpected results of the 1974 elections. Although expected to provide some legitimacy for the regime, these elections instead brought forth a generalized opposition sentiment which manifested itself in support for the legal opposition party that the 'revolution' had allowed to be created. Signs of the end of the economic miracle were also a complicating factor in so far as they aggravated the popular mood against the government. In the military area, radical authoritarian sectors which had been strengthened by the period of repression, tried to put into jeopardy Geisel's project.

More than Castelo Branco, Geisel made use of all his exceptional powers and his authoritarian and austere style of governing to neutralize both sources of pressure so as to carry out his policy. In order to cope with a stronger and more audacious opposition party, electoral rules were altered, the AI–5 was intermittently used to purge parliamentarians and legislative procedures were changed so as to block parliamentary opposition. On the other hand, military hard-liners were punished or appeased by the President's reinforcement of his absolute command of the political process. Regarding the internal struggle for power in the army, quite coincidentally, Geisel was on the verge of seeing the repetition of those events of Castelo

Branco's government concerning the presidential ambitions of the Minister of War. By learning from Castelo Branco's mistakes, Geisel moved faster to prevent an uncontrollable outcome and ensure that nobody but himself would choose his successor.

Geisel was quite successful in carrying out the project, at least in guaranteeing that it would have some continuity during General Figueiredo's term of six years. The establishment of the 'democracy' aimed at by the 1964 Revolution seemed finally about to become reality. The long duration of military rule and an aggravating and acute socio-economic crisis were certainly elements that helped to control attempts of the radical authoritarian sectors in pressing for a continuation of military rule. However, the problem still remained with regard to the other side of the coin: the pressures for a democracy without qualifications. The opening up of the political system, even when maintained within the limits of restricted democracy, implied that the enlarged space for political participation would be used by political forces demanding genuine democratization. The consolidation of a regime of 'protected democracy', or a semi-competitive system, seems to be only possible if it has as one of its basic pillars a political organization dominant and strong enough to control the demands of civil society. The Mexican system comes to mind and certainly must have evoked the military's envy. However, Brazil did not witness the emergence of a popular revolution, and its 'Revolution' took place in the relatively more complex Brazil of the mid-1960s rather than the Mexico of the beginning of the century. Nor did the ruling group make a sincere effort towards the creation of an authentic party of this 'Revolution'. Without this background, the opening up of a space for political participation had resulted in increasing pressures for a democracy without the protective components that the military had wished to enforce.

In the last eight years of military rule, Brazil witnessed a strong opposition movement which made difficult – and perhaps impossible – the viability of 'protected democracy'. It was necessary to dissolve the two-party system, originally conceived as the ideal formula, in order to cope with an opposition united in a single political channel. It was also necessary to change electoral rules several times to guarantee that the opposition would not have decisive power in the choice of the civilian president which would succeed military rule. In 1985 Brazil started a new era with the accession of the first civilian president after twenty-one years of military rule. To achieve this, the

country witnessed for two years an endless struggle for the presidential succession and a strong mass movement demanding direct elections. The outcome was still affected by the controls that the military
retained (indirect elections and a civilian acceptable to the military).
It is appropriate to quote here, the comments of one of the major
conspirators of the 1964 Coup, Marshall Cordeiro de Farias, who
truly believed in the 'democratic ideals' of the 1964 Revolution, witnessed the 'deviation' from them, and died before seeing the
outcome of so many years of military rule:

> What should we have done? It is simple: we would take over the
> government, as we did in 1964, but just for one or at most, two
> quadrennial terms. We then would *find a civilian of good character,
> oriented towards the great national commitments....* The transfer of
> power from the military to civilians is imperative. *But it is
> necessary that we have in government a man, a civilian, who has a
> correct viewpoint about Brazil and about the world surrounding us, a
> man capable of understanding that without development we,
> Brazilians, will be nothing.* The country has progressed a lot since
> 1964. Mistakes were made, but we have developed in a prodigious
> manner. We improved the transport network, communications,
> education. Yes, we improved, but the army is tired. The country is
> also tired. It is time to give the national destiny to civilians,
> enabling the army to return to its professional functions, *but ready
> to act at the request of the government in case of real necessity.*[6]

Having discussed some of the intrinsic problems in the Brazilian
experience of military-authoritarian rule, we shall now concentrate
our concluding comments upon the relation between the regime and
the legal opposition. In contrast to the experiences of several military
regimes in Latin America, the Brazilian case is almost unique in so
far as not only did the military never ban political party activity, but
it even created a new party system. During the long period of military
rule, the country witnessed three experiments with party politics.
First, the military tried to work with the political parties of the old
regime. The recognition of the impossibility of securing a solid and
stable congressional basis for the government made the dissolution
of the multiparty system imperative in 1965. Under the circumstances, the only choice available was the creation of a two-party system,
since the creation of a single party regime was not among the aims of
the 'Revolution', and a system of more than two parties would risk
reproducing the previous system of three dominant parties – PSD,

PTB and UDN. Thus, a formal two-party system emerged. It certainly served the regime during the phases of repression by keeping its democratic façade. However it became a problem for the regime during the phases of the decompression or attempts at moving towards a 'guided democracy'. In 1968 the political military crisis with the parliamentarians' show of independence occurred. In 1974 the electoral victory of the opposition gave the decisive proof of the non-viability of this two-party arrangement. Again the realization of the impossibility for the government to secure a solid congressional base of support, made the dissolution of the two-party system imperative. In 1979, therefore, the two parties were dissolved among the political reforms of the *abertura*. A new party system emerged in 1980 and it did not take two years to change its features as a consequence of the disintegration of the government party (PDS) and the consolidation of the renamed PMDB. As far as the party question is concerned, the military was unsuccessful in its attempt to create a political organization to serve as a pillar of the regime. The abolition of the multiparty system, its replacement by two new parties and their eventual dissolution in 1979 all resulted from unsuccessful attempts on the part of military governments to institutionalize a hybrid regime.

The second point to be noted is related specifically to the experiment of a two-party system. We have shown the electoral trends that marked the elections during the period and the process by which the MDB became an important political organization despite its being artificially created. In this respect, it should be underlined that the MDB's transformation into a real political force in opposion to the regime, had much to do with the establishment of an artificial two-party system. The artificial character of this system applied not only to the MDB but also to ARENA. The MDB was designed to function as a symbolic or loyal opposition. But ARENA was designed to function as a blindly loyal government party or an appendix to a powerful executive which kept control of all decision-making. In this sense, ARENA was almost as powerless as the MDB and had to play the role of securing parliamentary support for the ratification of legislation (originating in the executive) even when the party's members did not support a particular measure. This uncomfortable and subservient position made ARENA incapable of consolidating itself as a political organization, as was discussed in Chapter 6 in relation to ARENA's losses in the elections of 1974. Apart from the several alterations in the electoral legislation introduced by the government to help ARENA, the party was kept alive largely through patronage and clientelism, retaining its electoral stronghold only in the less developed and rural areas of the country. To some extent, the MDB was the beneficiary of this articifial party system. Since ARENA did not have the conditions for developing and becoming a real government party, electoral contests between ARENA and the MDB only favoured the former in controlled elections to ensure a majority for the government. However, when the control valves were relaxed, as in 1974, the consequence was ARENA's defeat. Moreover, the imposition of a two-party system forced the opposition to maintain unity despite the differences amongst liberals, conservatives and the left. The unity and consequent strength of the opposition party possibly would not have occurred had the opposition had the opportunity to create alternative organizations.

The major feature of the Brazilian military regime which made it a unique case is not only its hybrid character, but particularly the way in which it dealt with the question of political parties. In other Latin American cases of military rule the old parties were either kept under restricted control, or had their legal activity banned or suspended. The contrasting feature of the Brazilian case is the fact that the military *dissolved* the old party system and *created* a new one to replace it. Furthermore, it allowed the establishment of a *two-party system* which, by legalizing a channel for participation of the opposition, ended up by providing conditions for the consolidation of a new political party which seems to be capable of surviving after the military withdrawal from power. If we compare the Brazilian experience with the Argentine or Uruguayan which have recently returned to civilian rule, the contrast is quite clear. In both cases the redemocratization brought back to the political scene in essence the old dominant parties. In the Brazilian case, the replacement of the old party system by a new party arrangement which operated throughout the long period of military rule, resulted in the effective death of the party system of the 1945–1964 democratic period.[7]

The MDB was a single opposition party allowed to participate in the new political order commanded by the military. This political system was characterized by an undefined and hybrid situation which the military unsuccessfully tried to consolidate in the direction of a restricted democratic regime. The outcome was rather a process of repression and relaxation that the military regime went through. Under these circumstances the MDB continued operation, affected by the regime's pendular opening and closing movements and trying to survive as an opposition. Obviously its possibility of having some impact on the political process was ultimately conditioned by the space for opposition tolerated by the regime. Thus the MDB was always confronted with a difficult problem in defining its positions and actions: in other words, how to be an effective opposition without crossing the line of tolerance, precisely in a situation in which this line was not explicitly drawn, but varied in accordance with the opening and closing movements of the regime. Actually it was in the phases of decompression, that is after the wave of repression, that the MDB faced more acutely the problem of defining an effective strategy. The regime's signs of relaxation and the government's reiterated promises to return the country to democracy, provoked a wave of optimism at the same time that they put a difficult choice to the MDB: either to behave moderately for fear of provoking another authoritarian wave and jeopardizing the road towards democracy, or to take advantage of the enlarged space of decompression to exert pressures to accelerate the process of democratization. This was translated in what we called the dilemma between moderation and radicalization and which became the MDB's basic internal cleavage. We have shown that, although the MDB was dominated by its moderate faction, on several occasions the party assumed a more radical attitude, such as in the crisis of 1968 and in the judiciary reform episode of 1977. On these occasions two factors influenced the party to assume a more radical position: the ability of the minority group of militant deputies to pressure the party towards a more aggressive line, and the disillusionment and discontent of the moderate group (at least part of it) regarding the prospects for redemocratization, caused by faltering optimism after a long wait for clear signs from the government. In the 1968 and 1977 episodes, the regime's response was repression.

If the MDB was unsuccessful in trying to cross the lines of tolerance allowed by the regime, it proved to be also unsuccessful when it adopted a very moderate line. Quite certainly, by doing so, the opposition party avoided problems with the government. However, it hampered the opposition character of its public image. As we have discussed in this work, the moderate and conformist posture assumed by the MDB in 1969/70, served to discredit the party among the electorate. The outcome was the MDB's overwhelming defeat in the 1970 legislative elections. It is not our role to judge the merits of the MDB's conduct in any of the two directions which led the party to be punished either by the regime or by the electorate. Perhaps, under the circumstances of each event, the party suffered from a misunderstanding of the context in which it was operating, or perhaps the immediate political situation allowed no alternative. In any case, it is important to remark that after 1971 the MDB underwent a process of change which was to give some credit to its opposition image. Keeping itself within the rules of the game, the party started to work in that area which would make it a crucial weapon against the regime: the elections. In the 1973 'anti-candidate' campaign for the Presidency and the 1974 electoral campaign, the MDB was capable of using the space allowed by the regime, without threatening the system as a whole, and thereby gained electoral support. After 1974 the MDB's performance and success helped to reveal the problems of the military hybrid regime and highlighted the crucial role of this legal channel of political participation.

One could argue that the MDB became an important political force due only to the existence of a two-party system. The MDB's minimal influence through parliamentary activity would provide evidence for this assertion. As we have shown, the MDB's capacity to be an effective actor in Congress was limited as a consequence of being a minority. And on the occasions when the opposition posed problems for the government the party had to rely on the support of some elements of the government party. The only exception was in 1977 when the MDB was capable of blocking Congressional approval of the Judiciary Reform bill on its own. While the existence of a two-party system certainly provided the basis for the MDB's transformation into an important political force, the party's strength *was also due to its endurance in the political system*: in upholding conventional opposition politics and working to attract electoral support during the legislative elections. In other words, the MDB became an important movement or a genuine opposition party *also* because some politicians – liberals, conservatives and left wingers – worked for the creation of the party, kept it alive during difficult periods, and worked towards making it a credible opposition channel to voice popular dissatisfaction with the government and the regime which sustained it.

Apart from maintaining an opposition voice in the electoral contest, the MDB also helped to retain the option of party politics. Despite the limitations in the space for legal opposition politics, the existence of the MDB offered an instrument for those interested in opposing the regime through parliamentary politics. Even during the period when elections were held under strictly controlled conditions, several new parliamentarians were elected under the MDB label and used the legal political channel provided by the MDB to combat the regime. The emergence of the *grupo dos imaturos* in 1967 and the *grupo autentico* in 1971 are important examples to be remembered. Several politicians who became important opposition figures – belonging to the renamed PMDB or to the other new opposition parties – started their political career in the MDB. Therefore, the simple fact that the MDB kept operating during the long tenure of the military regime, made possible the emergence of a generation of politicians who will certainly have an important role in the process of democratization on which the country has finally embarked.

Notes and References

1 The Birth of the Legal Opposition in 1966

1. The President of the Chamber of Deputies was, according to the Constitution, next in line for succession. João Goulart was Vice-president to Janio Quadros and took over the Presidency when the latter resigned in 1961.
2. Even the constitutionally established period of thirty days allowed for a provisional government until a new President could be elected was not used, so as to avoid leaving the Presidency in the hands of Ranieri Mazzili, a PSD figure linked to ex-President Juscelino Kubitchek and to the previous regime. For details, see Ronald Schneider, *The Political System of Brazil* (New York: Colombia University Press, 1971).
3. In the election in Congress on 11 April, Castelo Branco received 361 votes. There were 3 ballots cast for Juarez Tavora, 2 for Eurico Dutra, and 72 abstentions (particularly from the Brazilian Labour Party (PTB)). Aside from the National Democratic Union (UDN), Castelo Branco received the support of the Social Progressive Party (PSP), the Social Democratic Party (PSD) and the Christian Democratic Party (PDC). Also, 53 PTB parliamentarians voted for Castelo Branco.
4. Castelo Branco's speech addressed to Congress on 11 April 1964. *Arquivo de Castelo Branco, CPDOC–FGV*, Rio de Janeiro. In a speech addressed to the Ministry of Foreign Affairs, Castelo Branco stated on 31 July 1964: 'we have made a basic option which stems from cultural and political fidelity to the Western democratic system. The interest of Brazil coincides, in any case, in concentric circles with Latin America, the American continent and the Western community'. Quoted in Alfred Stepan, *The Military in Politics – Changing Patterns in Brazil* (Princeton: Princeton University Press, 1971) p. 231.
5. The authoritarian features of the Brazilian case have been widely discussed. See mainly, Fernando Henrique Cardoso, *Autoritarismo e Democratização* (Rio: Paz e Terra, 1975), and 'On the Characterization of Authoritarian Regimes in Latin America', in David Collier (ed.) *The New Authoritarianism in Latin America* (Princeton: Princeton University Press, 1979); Alfred Stepan, (ed.) *Authoritarian Brazil – Origins, Policies and Future* (Yale: Yale University Press, 1973). In Stepan's book, see particularly Juan Linz, 'The Future of an Authoritarian Regime: the Case of Brazil', and Philippe Schmitter, 'The "Portugalization" of Brazil?'.
6. Letter sent to military ministers and distributed to all the army's commands regarding the presidential succession, as reported by Carlos Castello Branco, on 11 February 1966. Cf. C. C. Branco, *Os Militares no Poder* (Rio de Janeiro: Nova Fronteira, 1977), vol.1, p. 423.
7. The recognition of the new regime by the United States was almost instantaneous (2 April), and in the same day, conversations between the

230

American State Department and the Brazilian government concerning economic aid were started. On the United State's influence on Brazil and participation in the 1964 Movement see Moniz Bandeira, *Presença dos Estados Unidos no Brasil* (Rio de Janeiro, Civ. Brasileira, 1973), Phyllis Parker, *1964: O Papel dos Estados Unidos no Golpe de Estado de 31 de Março* (Rio: Civ. Brasileira, 1977).

8. The embarassment of being identified with Latin American military dictatorships is in fact very deeply rooted in the Brazilian military tradition, as we can see in this excerpt from a lecture given by Castelo Branco at the War School in 1955. Talking about the country's political problems and criticizing those who saw in a military dictatorship the only solution for Brazil, he argued: 'The Armed Forces cannot, so as to follow their tradition, make of Brazil another South American *republiqueta*, that is to lead the Republic to a straightjacket of totalitarian dictatorship. If we adopt this kind of regime, whoever takes power by force, will only be maintained by force and will only leave by force. What a backward and reactionary goal!' lecture addressed to the *ESG (Escola Superior de Guerra)* on 19 September 1955. *Arquivo Castelo Branco*, Rio de Janeiro, CPDOC – FGV. *Republiqueta* is a pejorative term using the diminutive form of republic. On the Castelo Branco government see J.F. Dulles, *President Castelo Branco* (Texas: A&M University Press, 1980).

9. Even if we consider the crucial role played by the ESG–IPES (War School – Institute of Economic and Social Research) in the 1964 Movement, as René Dreifuss emphasizes in his interpretation, the political forces which participated in the coup cannot be reduced to their links to the ESG–IPES complex. On the role of the ESG–IPES, see René Dreifuss, *1964: A Conquista do Estado – Ação Politica e Golpe de Classe* (Petropolis: Vozes, 1981).

10. In a meeting of the 'pro-revolutionary' governors led by Carlos Lacerda in the beginning of April 1964 it was decided that a prestigious military figure would be needed to carry out the difficult tasks ahead. Cf. Ronald Schneider, *The Political System of Brazil*.

11. On the UDN's views in favour of military intervention see Maria Victoria M. Benevides, *A UDN e o Udenismo – Ambiguidades do Liberalismo Brasileiro (1945–1965)* (Rio de Janeiro: Paz e Terra, 1981).

12. Carlos Lacerda's attempts to gather the support of hard-liners in the Armed Forces against Castelo Branco's government was a clear indication of the problems faced by the military in marginalizing politicians. See below in this chapter.

13. A detailed characterization of the military groups is found in Alfred Stepan, *The Military in Politics*. See also Edmundo Campos Coelho, *Em Busca de Identidade: O Exército e a Politica no Sociedade Brasileira* (Rio: Forense, 1976).

14. On the crucial role played by this group which had close links with the civilians through the IPES (*Instituto de Pesquisas Economicas e Sociais*), see the detailed study of René Dreifuss, *1964: A Conquista do Estado*.

15. A Stepan, *The Military in Politics*, p. 234.
16. *Ibid.*, p. 250.
17. Cf. A. Stepan, *The Military in Politics*, pp. 250–1. See also Sebastião Velasco e Cruz and Carlos E. Martins, 'De Castelo a Figueiredo: Uma Incursão na *Pré* História da 'Abertura'', in Bernardo Sorj and Maria Herminia T. de Almeida (eds) *Sociedade e Politica no Brasil pós-64* (São Paulo: Brasiliense, 1983); Eurico de Lima Figueiredo, *Os Militares e a Democracia* (Rio de Janeiro: Ed. Graal, 1980); and John W.F. Dulles, *President Castelo Branco* (Texas: A&M University Press, 1980).
18. We are developing a thesis asserted by Bolivar Lamounier concerning the Brazilian liberal representative regime. According to Lamounier, rather than just being an imported idea, liberal democracy in Brazil has an important function. During the First Republic (1889–1930), the use of *some* juridical formula was indispensable in order to establish a universal rule in the face of powerful and violent provincial groups who competed for public prestige and sinecures. Also, some general rule is necessary in a situation in which the military institution assumes power in the face of internal dissensions owing to the ambitions of succession and other disputes. He argues: 'No one contests that the generals, or a reduced number of them, held "real" power. It is known nevertheless, that the classic problem of "why not me?" is fatally presented in such situations'. Bolivar Lamounier, 'Representatação Politica: a importancia de certos formalismos', in B. Lamounier *et al.* (eds), *Direito, Cidadania e Participação* (São Paulo: T. A. Queiroz, 1981), p. 239.
19. This aspect is discussed in Chapter 5.
20. The Bill on the Statute of Political Parties was sent to Congress by the Executive on 22 April 1965 and became law on 15 July. Debate in Congress, nonetheless, was intensive with respect to the approval of the draft. The fact that this new legislation would prejudice the small parties by sharply raising the minimum requirements that the parties had to attain if they were to maintain legal status, was the major controversial point. See parliamentary debates in sessions of 19 and 20 May 1965.
21. *Estado Novo* is the denomination of the dictatorial period under Getulio Vargas, from 1937 to 1945.
22. This is a very summary description of the political parties from the period prior to 1964. The full list of the political parties that were presented in Congress is found in Table 1.1. The main works dealing with the parties of that period are: M. V. Benevides, *A UDN e o Udenismo* (Rio de Janeiro: Paz e Terra, 1981); I. Picaluga, *Partidos Politicos e Classes Sociais: A UDN na Guanabara* (Rio de Janeiro: Vozes, 1980); O. S. Dulci, 'A União Democrática Nacional e o Anti-populismo no Brasil' (Universidade Federal de Minas Gerais: Tese de Mestrado, 1977); L. Lippi de Oliveira, 'O Partido Social Democrático' (IUPERJ: Tese de Mestrado, 1973); L. Hipólito, *De Raposas e Reformistas – PSD e a Experiência Democrática Brasileira (1945–64)*, (Rio de Janeiro: Paz e Terra, 1985); R. Sampaio, *Adhemar de Barros e o PSP* (São Paulo: Global, 1982); R.H.

Chilcote, *The Brazilian Communist Party – Conflict and Integration, 1922–1972* (Oxford: Oxford University Press, 1974); L. W. Vianna, 'O Sistema Partidário e o Partido Democrata Cristão', *Cadernos CEDEC*, No.1, São Paulo: Brasiliense, 1978; M.C. Campelo de Souza, *Estado e Partidos Politicos no Brasil (1930–1964)* (São Paulo: Alfa-Omega, 1976); G. A. D. Soares, *Sociedade e Politica no Brasil* (São Paulo: Difel, 1973); D.V. Fleisher (ed.), *Os Partidos Políticos no Brasil* (Brasilia: Editora Universidade de Brasilia, 1983), vol. 1; O. B. de Lima Jr, *Os Partidos Politicos Brasileiros: a Experiência Federal e Regional: 1945–64* (Rio de Janeiro: Graal, 1983); P. J. Peterson, 'Brazilian Political Parties: Formation, Organization and Leadership, 1945-1959' (University of Michigan, Ph.D. thesis, 1964); A. A. de Mello Franco, *História e Teoria dos Partidos Políticos no Brasil* (São Paulo: Alfa-Omega, 1974).

23. The more important works – and the ones that we have used – dealing with the multiparty system's experience from 1945–64 are Glaucio A. D. Soares, *Sociedade e Politica no Brasil*; Simon Schwarzman, *São Paulo e o Estado Nacional*, (São Paulo, Difel, 1975); Maria do Carmo C. de Souza, *Estado e Partidos Políticos no Brasil (1930–1964)*; Wanderley G. dos Santos, 'Calculus of Conflict: Impasse in Brazilian Politics and the Crisis of 1964' (Stanford University Ph. D. thesis 1979). Regarding the political polarization of the party system before Goulart's fall, see especially W.G. dos Santos's thesis.

24. Governor Magalhães Pinto's letter to President Castelo Branco, on 13 May, 1965. *Arquivo de Castelo Branco*, Rio de Janeiro, CPDOC–FGV.

25. *Ibid.*

26. Lacerda was nominated candidate for the Presidency by the UDN National Convention in November 1964. He resigned from his candidacy in October 1965, after the results of the gubernatorial elections.

27. Castelo Branco's presidential term was supposed to end in December 1965. Thus presidential elections were scheduled for 3 October 1965 with the next president taking power in January 1966. But in July 1964 a constitutional amendment proposed by UDN's parliamentarians was passed in Congress, extending Castelo's terms until the end of 1966. In this episode, Carlos Lacerda seemed to be the only discordant voice in his party. Lacerda saw in the prorogation not only a threat to his candidacy but also to the return of civilians to power. He wrote to the UDN's chairman Bilac Pinto, in July 1964: 'We are rapidly marching towards an obscure and indefined "nasserism". By voting for the prorogation. . . . Congress is voting for a military dictatorship which will be fatally established in the country, remaining to know who is going to be the dictator, since this would not certainly be Marshall Castelo Branco. . . . *Bilac*, in one word: if the prorogation is passed, elections will not be held either in 1966 or in the short term', quoted in Daniel Krieger, *Desde as Missões . . . saudades, lutas, esperanças* (Rio de Janeiro: José Olympio, 1977), pp. 186–7. According to Juracy Magalhães, 'Lacerda's

game was just this: to have a person who would lead the revolutionary government during the shortest period possible, in order that he, Carlos Lacerda, could become the President'. Juracy Magalhães's Testimony (1977), in *Arquivo de Historia Oral*, Rio de Janeiro, CPDOC–FGV.

28. Carlos Lacerda's letter to Castelo Branco on 9 February 1965. *Arquivo de Castelo Branco*, Rio de Janeiro, CPDOC–FGV.

29. Carlos Lacerda's letter to Castelo Branco on 19 April 1965. *Arquivo de Castelo Branco*, Rio de Janeiro, CPDOC–FGV,

30. PSD deputy Mario Piva's speech, on 10 August 1965. *Anais da Camara dos Deputados*, 1965, vol. 19, p. 131.

31. The opposition's victory in those states reflected urban voters' dissatisfaction with the high cost-of-living and the economic crisis. Nevertheless, the ambiguous conduct of both governors during that time, may also have contributed to the government's defeat. As we have mentioned, both governors had been in disagreement with Castelo Branco's government. Moreover, their party's candidates were not outstanding figures in terms of electoral appeal. One can even question whether the governors had not intentionally worked for the electoral results to be unfavourable to the government so as to provoke a crisis. After the results came out, both governors blamed the government's policy for the defeat, stressing that the 'Revolution had been betrayed'. In a letter addressed to the UDN's chairman telling of his intention of resigning the candidacy for the Presidency, Carlos Lacerda stated: 'We fought against five ex-Presidents, the Communist Party and other forces, and in spite of that we obtained 40 per cent of the votes. We could not do more than we have done, because the government of the Revolution was condemned by the people. The UDN, I agree, cannot continue to support Castelo Branco's government while, at the same time, supporting my candidacy for the presidency of the Republic, since President Castelo Branco does not admit my candidacy. . . . I think I have the right to go to my party's National Convention to explain the reasons why I think that my candidacy does not make sense any longer. . . . I do not intend to participate in this sleight of hand act, in a revolution which, betrayed and led to betray the people, had just been defeated by the people, precisely for not being a true revolution', letter read in the Chamber of Deputies, on 8 October 1965. *Anais da Camara dos Deputados*, 1965, vol. 25, p. 765.

32. For details see Schneider, *The Political System of Brazil*. pp. 169–70.

33. By surveying the number of speeches and interventions on this issue, we verified that only three deputies defended the government measures. In turn, there were 43 speeches or interventions criticizing the bills: 19 from PTB representatives, 13 from PSD, 7 from UDN and 4 from representatives of the small parties. *Anais da Camara dos Deputados*, 1965, vols. 26–28. (Session from 11 to 26 October 1965).

34. Parliamentary speeches, sessions of 13, 20 and 21 October 1965. *Anais da Camara dos Deputados*. 1965, vols. 26–28.

35. Anais da Camara dos Deputados, 1965, vol. 27 (session of 25 October) pp. 241–4.

36. Carlos Castello Branco, *Os Militares no Poder*, vol. 1, p. 369.
37. Testimony of Juracy Magalhães (1977) *Arquivo de História Oral*, Rio de Janeiro, CPDOC–FGV.
38. Luis Viana Filho, *O Governo Castelo Branco* (Rio de Janeiro: Jose Olympio, 1975), pp. 370–1. Luis Viana Filho was head of the *Casa Civil* (Civilian Household) of the Presidency of the Republic during Castelo Branco's government.
39. Regarding the name chosen for the opposition party, Deputy Ulysses Guimarães (MDB National president since 1971), narrated: 'I remember that . . . we deliberately did not choose to include the term *party*. We adopted deliberately the word *movement* instead, because we were aware that there were no political parties in Brazil (even now there are not). Since there was no democratic normality, there could not be political parties. So we said: "let's be sincere and say to the public that it was a movement to achieve democracy, a Constituent Assembly, true political parties". By the way, at the beginning, there was sympathy for the word Action (Brazilian Democratic Action). I remember that when we were to decide, Tancredo Neves wittily said: "Look, Ulysses, let us find a masculine (*macho*) name (sic), because this UDN (which is a feminine name) has caused already so much trouble for the country and now is linked with this Revolution". Thus we substituted Movement for Action, becoming *Movimento Democratico Brasileiro*' interview with Ulysses Guimaerães, on 30 June 1982. Perhaps unknown for the MDB founders was the fact that *Movimento Democratico Brasileiro* or *MDB* was the denomination of a movement created in 1962 by members of the UDN (Adauto Lucio Cardoso, Men de Sá) and other right-wing figures such as Gustavo Corção, whose aim was to defend democracy against the 'claws of totalitarianism'. In July 1962 the movement distributed an official note calling upon 'true students, workers, democrats, civil servants and professional men' not to adhere to strikes, not to accept provocations and to support measures to guarantee public order. See, *Estado de São Paulo*, 9 February and 10 July 1962 and *O Globo*, 13 February 1962.
40. Several politicians that we interviewed remarked that the PSD Senator Rui Carneiro, who was a close friend of Castelo Branco, joined the opposition because the President had personally asked him so as to allow the creation of the opposition party.
41. We used as source, the list of Deputies of the *Anais da Camara dos Deputados*, 1965. Up to the dissolution of the multiparty system the names of the purged deputies continued to be mentioned with a footnote saying that they were *cassados*, Thus we identified 59 *cassados*: 25 from the PTB, 8 from the PSD, 3 from the PST, 1 from the PTN, 2 from the UDN, 4 from the PSB, 3 from the PSP, 2 from the PDC, 2 non-affiliated, and 9 alternates. According to another source, the list provided by Deputy Paes de Andrade, 65 deputies were purged. Cf. Paes de Andrade, *O Itinerario da Violência* (Rio de Janeiro, Paz e Terra, 1978).
42. Quoted in Luis Viana Filho, *O Governo Castelo Branco*, p. 371.
43. *Anais da Camara dos Deputados*, 1965–6, vol. 1 pp. 613–4.

44. The MDB gained the status of a definitive party in April 1967 when the Electoral Tribunal approved the MDB's petition requesting its transformation into a political party. See *Diário da Justiça* of 3 April 1967.
45. The electoral trends are examined in Chapter 3.
46. Interview with Mario Covas on 9/8/82. Mario Covas was a Federal Deputy from São Paulo and was *cassado* in 1969, after being the MDB's leader in the Chamber of Deputies during the episode Marcio Moreira Alves. After returning to political life in 1979, he was elected Federal Deputy in 1982, was mayor of São Paulo (1983–5) and was elected senator in 1986.

2   The MDB's Organization, Structure and Programme

1. This chapter is based on information collected from newspapers, extensive interviews with politicians and party militants and on the MDB constitution.
2. The fact that Oscar Passos was a general – although retired – certainly influenced his nomination for the position of president of the MDB. As Deputy Ulysses Guimarães told us: 'it would show that we did not have at all any prejudice or discrimination against the military'. Interview on 30 June 1982.
3. Cf. Carlos Castello Branco, *Os Militares no Poder* (Rio de Janeiro, Editora Nova Fronteira, 1977), vol. 1, p. 383.
4. Cf. *Lei Orgânica dos Partidos Políticos*, Law No. 4.470, 15 July, 1965. 1965.
5. The PSP created a very structured party organization but only in São Paulo state. The PTB was also very organised in some states such as Rio Grande do Sul. However none of the parties from the previous period had created a nationwide organizational network.
6. Data collected in *Jornal da Tarde*, 12 July, 1975, based on information provided by the Electoral Tribunal. All information about the number of directorates are approximate figures since the MDB did not have any archive with information about its local organization and its affiliated members.
7. According to information reported in *Jornal do Brasil*, 14 September, 1977.
8. In 1950, 53 per cent of the population of São Paulo state were classified by the demographic census as urban. More than a quarter of the total Brazilian urban population in 1950 were allocated in that state. Source: IBGE, *VI Recenseamento Geral do Brasil - 1950, Censo Demográfico* (Rio de Janeiro: IBGE, 1955).
9. This brief analysis is based on the study of Adhemar de Barros and the PSP produced by Regina Sampaio, *Adhemar de Barros e o PSP* (São Paulo, Global Editora, 1982). Sampaio examines the political career of Adhemar since his experience as an *interventor* of São Paulo during the *Estado Novo*, and shows in detail the building of the PSP organizational network in São Paulo.

10. As a consequence of Adhemar's purge, his son, Adhemar de Barros Filho decided to join the MDB. However, after having been elected federal deputy in 1966, Adhemar's son left the MDB and joined ARENA.
11. Lino de Mattos broke off with Adhemar de Barros in 1958. As a consequence he left the PSP and joined the PTN.
12. *Estado de São Paulo*, 14 September 1969.
13. *Estado de São Paulo*, 16 August 1973.
14. *Estado de São Paulo*, 24 November, 1974 and *Jornal da Tarde*, 12 July, 1975.
15. Lino de Mattos was then replaced in the presidency by the Deputy Natal Gale who remained in this position until 1979. Natal Gale's commitment to the opposition was so limited that when the political party reform took place in late 1979, he left the MDB and joined the PDS (the pro-government party).
16. Our description of the MDB structure is based on the MDB statute revised and approved by the party's National Convention of September 1975. Cf. Diretório Nacional do Movimento Democratico Brasileiro, 'Estatuto, Programa e Código de Ética', *Coleção Alberto Pasqualini*, vol. 10, 1976.
17. Before the 1971 revision of the Political Party Organization Law the requirement was 20 per cent of the affiliated members.
18. We must note here that the affiliated members who do not hold a position in the party's organization have the right to participate in the system of voting at the party's conventions *only* when the municipal conventions are held for the elections of the members of the directorate.
19. Cf. *Estado de São Paulo*, 13 August 1974.
20. A more detailed account of the MDB selection of candidates in 1978 can be found in, Shiguenoli Miyamoto, 'Eleições de 1978 em São Paulo: A Campanha', in Bolivar Lamounier (ed.) *Voto de Desconfiança – Eleições e Mudança Politica no Brasil, 1970–1979* (Petrópolis: Vozes / CEBRAP, 1980).
21. Interview with Deputy Marcio Santilli on 3 June 1982. The comment made by Deputy Euclides Scalco is also noteworthy: 'In Brazil, a political party is actually a party of parliamentarians, since they are the only ones who provide money for the party'. Interview on 27 April 1982.
22. On the characterization of factions, fractions and tendencies within a political party, see Giovanni Sartori, *Parties and Party Systems* (Cambridge, Cambridge University Press, 1976), Chapter 4.
23. For example, a member of the *PC do B* was elected federal deputy on account of his engagement in the social movement against the high cost-of-living (*Movimento do Custo de Vida*) which mobilized thousands of people in São Paulo. It should be remarked that the MR-8 (the ex-guerrila organization *Movimento Revolucionário 8 de Outubro*) also worked within the MDB but it joined the party only after 1979.
24. Actually, one of the consequences of the successful electoral performance of the MDB in 1974 was that a significant number of candidates

were elected simply because they had been included in the MDB list of candidates. Since the MDB lacked cadres up to 1974, anybody who wanted to run for a seat was accepted. This caused the inclusion in the party of several candidates who had little to do with opposition politics.

25. An empirical analysis of the deputies' electoral base in terms of its level of concentration or dispersion is found in the works of David Fleischer, 'Concentração e Dispersão Eleitoral: um Estudo da Distribuição Geográfica do Voto em Minas Gerais, 1966–1974', *Revista Brasileira de Estudos Politicos*, No. 43, 1976, pp. 333–60; and Maria Lucia Indjaian, 'Análise Preliminar da Bancada Federal Paulista Eleita pelo MDB em 1978', São Paulo, relatório de pesquisa apresentado à FAPESP, mimeo., 1981. A debate on the consequences produced by the electoral system on political representation in Brazil is found in Revista de Cultura e Politica, 'Debate sobre a representação proporcional: Bolivar Lamounier, Luis Navarro de Brito e Sérgio Abranches', *RCP*, Cedec, no. 7, pp. 5–74.

26. Teresa Caldeira's anthropological study of the people living in an area of the outskirts of São Paulo city remarks that the deputy is not regarded by the people as somebody who should represent it. She points out that those she interviewed either had a vague idea or did not know at all about the functions of the legislature. In any case, they attributed very little importance to the legislature and regarded those who hold a legislative mandate as having very little power. It is the executive that is perceived as having the monopoly of power. Cf. Teresa P. R. Caldeira, 'Para que Serve o Voto? (as Eleições e o Cotidiano na Periferia de São Paulo)', in B. Lamounier (ed.), *O Voto de Desconfiança*, particularly pp. 102–8.

27. In fact, in the only place where the MDB had been in government at state level (Rio de Janeiro), a very structured clientelist machine was built by the governor Chagas Freitas who retained full control over the MDB in Rio de Janeiro. See Eli Diniz, *Voto e Máquina Politica* (Rio: Paz e Terra, 1982). There is a vast literature dealing with the question of clientelism in Brazil. Some works should be mentioned such as: Victor N. Leal, *Coronelismo, Enxada e Voto*, (Rio de Janeiro: Forense, 1949); Orlando M. de Carvalho, *Ensaios de Sociologia Eleitoral* (Belo Horizonte: Edições da RBEP, 1958); Hélio Jaguaribe, 'Politica de Clientela e Politica Ideológica', *Digesto Econômico*, VI, no. 68, 1950; Pedro F. Couto, *O Voto e o Povo* (Rio de Janeiro, Civ. Brasileira, 1966); Paul Cammack, 'Clientelism and Military Government in Brazil', in C. Clapham (ed.) *Private Patronage and Public Power* (London: Frances Pinter, 1982); Alain Rouquie, 'Clientelist Control and Authoritarian Contexts', in G. Hermet et al. (eds) *Elections Without Choice* (London: Macmillan, 1978).

28. Interview with Deputy Samir Achoa on 5 May 1982.

29. As the MDB deputy Almir Pazzianotto commented: 'I can measure the influence of a deputy from the government party by the amount of people that wait for him at his office's door. (. . .) Anyway, in this House there must not have been a single deputy who has never been

asked for help for the solution to a personal problem. There is no way to avoid being asked particular favours.' Interview on 17 July 1982.

30. The MDB programme which we will use for this description is the one adopted and approved by the fifth national convention of 1972. Cf. Movimento Democratico Brasileiro, MDB, *Estatuto, Programa e Codigo de Ética*, Brasilia, MDB, 1972. This programme was not altered until the reorganization of the MDB into PMDB. Before the 1972 programme, there were only two others, the first programme of 1966 and the programme adopted in 1967.

31. Alluding to this problem the Deputy José Costa (PMDB) commented: 'The MDB, for example, does not have conditions to discuss deeply the land reform question, without taking the risk of splitting. The Brazilian political parties have programmes which actually are far from reflecting the average view of their representatives. . . . My party defends very advanced positions regarding the social question. But I do not think that we have conditions to put them into practice'. Interview on 30 April 1982.

3 Elections Under the Two-Party System

1. During the period of democratic rule, direct elections were held for all executive offices (President of the Republic, State Governors and municipal mayors) and for all representatives in the Legislative Houses (from the federal to the local level). The system of elections by absolute majority was (and has been) used in elections for executive offices as well as for the Senate. The proportional representation system is used in elections for the Federal Chamber, State Assemblies and Municipal Councils.

2. This restriction was also incorporated in the 1967 and 1969 constitutions. In 1976, 177 municipalities had mayors who had not been elected by their citizens. These cities comprised 30 per cent of the Brazilian electorate.

3. Initially introduced by the Institutional Act No. 3 of 1966 as a transitory measure which neither the 1967 constitution nor the much more authoritarian 1969 constitution had incorporated in their text, the 'indirect elections' for State Governors became part of the constitution when Geisel decreed in 1977 the so called April Package which also enlarged the electoral college by including delegates from the Municipal Councils.

4. We must point out that the Senate is composed of three representatives from each state of the federation. The senatorial term is eight years, but elections are held every four years for the renewal of one-third and two-thirds alternately.

5. Although we could not obtain the same data to calculate the rate of illiteracy in the Northeast among the adult population, the data on the population over 15 years old is a close indicator: 57.9% of the population over 15 years old were illiterate (1970) in the Northeast. Primary source: *IBGE, VIII Recenseamento Geral do Brasil – 1970: Censo Demografico* (Rio de Janeiro: IBGE, 1973).

6. My own calculations based on data from the 1980 demographic census. FIBGE, *IX Recenseamento Geral do Brasil – 1980, Tabulações Avançadas do Censo Demografico*, Vol. I, Tomo 2. Preliminary Results.

7. All literate citizens over 18 years old are supposed to have an electoral register card. In order to obtain this card an application form is completed and signed by the applicant in order to prove that he/she is literate. In some places the proof of literacy is not carefully considered since there are electors who are hardly able to sign their names.

8. My own calculations, based on primary figures from the *Censo Demografico* of 1970 (for the population) and from the Tribunal *Superior Eleitoral* (Electoral Tribunal).

9. All electors who abstain from voting and who do not justify their absence in the Electoral Courts within 30 days have to pay a fine of from three to ten per cent of the minimum-salary. Moreover, without having proof (a stamp registered in one's electoral card) that one has exercised the vote, or has justified one's absence, a person cannot apply for any public job (any job financed or linked with government functions), cannot borrow money from banks and saving societies associated with the government, cannot obtain either a passport or identity card, cannot matriculate in any official school and so on. See Article 7 of the Electoral Code: *Lei No. 4.737 – de 15 de Julho de 1965.*

10. PR is also used for elections to the State Assemblies and Municipal Chambers. This system has been used in Brazil since 1932, although several alterations have been made since. A study of the several electoral systems adopted in Brazil is found in Maria D'Alva G. Kinzo, *Representação Politica e Sistema Eleitoral no Brasil* (São Paulo, Editora Símbolo, 1980).

11. Cf. Electoral Code: *Lei No. 4.737 – de 15 de Julho de 1965*, Articles 106–9.

12. For an expanded discussion of this point see M. D. G. Kinzo, 'An Opposition Party in an Authoritarian Regime: the Case of the MDB (*Movimento Democratico Brasileiro*) in Brazil, 1966–1979' (D. Phil Dissertation, University of Oxford, 1985); and A. M. Carstairs, *A Short History of Electoral System in Western Europe* (London: George Allen & Unwin, 1980), Chapter 2.

13. For a full discussion of this problem and its political implications see M. D. G. Kinzo, 'An Opposition Party in an Authoritarian Regime'; and *Representação Politica e Sistema Eleitoral no Brasil* (São Paulo: Simbolo, 1980): Glaucio A. D. Soares, 'El Sistema Electoral y Representación de los Grupos Sociales en Brasil, 1945–1962', *Revista Latinoamericana de Ciência Politica*, vol. 2, no. 1, (1971) pp. 5–23.

14. This actually is the same method that is used in Finland. See A. Carstairs, *A Short History of the Electoral System in Western Europe*.

15. Paul Singer, 'A Politica das Classes Dominantes', in Octavio Ianni et al, *Politica e Revolução Social no Brasil*. (Rio de Janeiro: Civilização Brasileira, 1965), p. 91.

16. This section is a revised and more developed version of the first section of my article 'Opposition Politics in Brazil: The Electoral Performance of the PMDB in São Paulo', *Bulletin of Latin America Research*, vol. 3, no. 2, 1984, pp. 29–45.

17. In order to avoid the analysis and presentation of an excessive amount of statistics and tables we opted to base our analysis on the electoral results for the legislative elections at state and federal level. Thus, in this chapter we will not deal with the results of municipal elections during the period (1968, 1972 and 1976 elections). Since the major aim of this thesis is to show the role of the MDB in national politics, the disregard of municipal elections does not detract seriously from the main arguments.

18. We have used the electoral results for the Federal Chamber since they reflect more accurately the electoral tendencies than elections to the Senate, the State Assembly and municipal offices. Results of Senate elections, with the elimination of direct gubernatorial and presidential elections have come to reflect the national political mood. Elections to the Federal Chamber are not only based on the PR system, but are influenced by local as well as national political issues.

19. One must be careful in interpreting this increase as a change in sentiment toward the political parties and therefore as an expression of protest. This certainly occurred, but we must point out that in the 1970 elections, the establishment of a single ballot paper (*cédula unica*) was put into practice for the first time. This certainly must have contributed as well to the increase in the amount of spoiled ballots as a result of misinformation and the difficulty in filling out the ballot paper. The establishment of the *voto vinculado* (that is, voters must vote for candidates from the same party) in elections for the Federal Chambers and State Assemblies, a requirement which if disregarded can nullify the vote, also is a factor which may have contributed to the increase of spoiled ballots.

20. See Table 1.2 in Chapter 1 on the affiliation of the representatives from old parties to ARENA and the MDB.

21. A detailed analysis of the process of urbanization in the last thirty years is found in V. Faria, 'Desenvolvimento, Urbanização e Mudanças na Estrutura do Emprego: a Experiência Brasileira dos Ultimos Trinta Anos', in Bernardo Sorj and Maria Herminia Tavares de Almeida (orgs.) *Sociedade e Politica no Brasil pós-64* (São Paulo, Brasiliense, 1983). Vilmar Faria uses more precise criteria than the one used by the Demographic census, to define the rural population by also including the population of towns of less than 20 000 inhabitants. As our population figures were from the 1970 census, while V. Faria uses the data from the 1980 Demographic census, we can assert that the category of towns of less than 30 000 inhabitants in 1970 can be classified as rural areas.

22. Fabio W. Reis, 'Classe Social e Opção Partidária: As Eleições de 1976 em Juiz de Fora', in F.W. Reis (org), *Os Partidos e o Regime – A lógica do*

processo eleitoral Brasileiro, (São Paulo, Editora Símbolo, 1978), p. 217.

23. Glaucio Soares, using data on the party's share of seats in the Federal Chamber from 1945 to 1962, demonstrates that the two major parties, the UDN and the PSD, which held 81.5 per cent of the seats in 1945, suffered a systematic decline in the following years, holding only 51.1 per cent of the seats in 1962. Inversely, the PTB which had only 7.7 per cent of the representation in the Federal Chamber in 1945, increased its share to 16.8 per cent in 1950, 17.2 per cent in 1954, 20.2 per cent in 1958 and 28.4 per cent in 1962. The small parties also increased their representation during the period: holding only 5.6 per cent of the seats in 1945, they obtained 16.2 per cent in 1962. Moreover, in this last year, 62 per cent of the small parties' total representation were from parties which could be characterized as centre-left (PSB, PTN, MTR and PDC). Cf. Glaucio A.D. Soares, *Sociedade e Politica no Brasil* (São Paulo, DIFEL, 1973), Chapter 4. In Rio Grande do Sul where competition among parties had become polarized (*trabalhismo* versus *conservadores-liberais*), the same tendencies were found. Hélgio Trindade shows that the electoral strength of the PTB had increased in 56 per cent of the cities of this state, while the PSD, its main opponent, had declined in 85 per cent of the cities. See Hélgio Trindade & Judson de Cew, 'Confrontação Politica e Decisão Eleitoral: As Eleições Municipais de 1976 em Caxias do Sul', in F.W. Reis, *Os Partidos e o Regime*, particularly pp. 149–161. For the case of Rio de Janeiro see Olavo Brasil Lima Jr, 'Articulação de Interesses, Posição Sócio-Economica e Ideologia: as Eleições de 1976 em Niterói', in F. W. Reis *Os Partidos e o Regime*, particularly pp. 96–101.

24. Cf. Glaucio Soares, *Sociedade e Politica no Brasil*.

25. Bolivar Lamounier, 'O Voto em São Paulo, 1970–1978', in B. Lamounier, *O Voto de Desconfiança – Eleições e Mundança Politica no Brasil, 1970–1979* (Petropolis: Vozes/Cebrap, 1980).

26. The city of São Paulo is composed of 55 administrative units. These units were classified and regrouped in eight homogenous areas according to a set of socio-economic variables. In this classification family income was used as a basic criterion, along with the following variables: quality of sanitary installations, water connection services, demographic density, rate of population growth, mortality rate and residential use of land. For more details see B. Lamounier, 'O Voto em São Paulo, 1970–1978', pp. 22–31.

27. Cf. B. Lamounier, *ibid*, p. 29. The existence of a significant electoral support for the MDB in the poor outlying areas of the big cities is also demonstrated by Hélgio Trindade in the case of two cities in Rio Grande do Sul state. See H. Trindade, 'Padrões e Tendências do Comportamento Eleitoral no Rio Grande do Sul', in B. Lamounier and Fernando H. Cardoso (eds), *Os Partidos e as Eleições no Brasil* (Rio de Janeiro: Paz e Terra/Cebrap, 1975); and H. Trindade and J. de Cew, 'Confrontação Politica e Decisão Eleitoral: As Eleições Municipais de 1976 em Caxias do Sul', in F. W. Reis, *Os Partidos e o Regime*.

28. Cf. Fabio W. Reis, 'As Eleições em Minas Gerais', in B. Lamounier and Fernando H. Cardoso (ed.) *Os Partidos e as Eleições no Brasil*; Fabio Reis,

'Classe Social e Opção Partidária...', in. F. W. Reis (org.) *Os Partidos e o Regime*; and B. Lamounier, 'O Comportamento Eleitoral em São Paulo: Passado e Presente', in B. Lamounier and Fernando H. Cardoso (ed.), *Os Partidos e as Eleições no Brasil.*

29. Cf. B, Lamounier, 'Presidente Prudente: O Crescimento da Oposição num reduto Arenista', in F.W. Reis (org.), *Os Partidos e o Regime* and 'O Voto em São Paulo, 1970-1978', in B. Lamounier (org.), *O Voto de Desconfiança*; and Olavo Brasil Lima Jr 'Articulações de Interesse, Posição Sócio-Economica e Ideologia...', in F. W. Reis (org.), *Os Partidos e o Regime.*

30. B. Lamounier, 'O Voto em São Paulo', in B. Lamounier (org.), *O Voto de Desconfiança*, p. 61.

31. Cf. *ibid.*, p. 56.

32. Cf. Teresa Pires do Rio Caldeira, 'Para que serve o voto? (As eleições e o cotidiano na periferia de São Paulo)', in B. Lamounier (org.), *O Voto de Desconfiança.*

33. Cf. B. Lamounier, 'O Comportamento Eleitoral em São Paulo...', in B. Lamounier and F. H. Cardoso (ed.), *Os Partidos e as Eleições no Brasil*; 'President Prudente: O crescimento da Oposição...', in F. W. Reis (org,), *Os Partidos o e Regime*; F. W. Reis 'Classe Social e Opção Partidaria...', in F.W. Reis (org.), *Os Partidos e o Regime*; and O. B. Lima Jr, 'Articulação de Interesse, Posição Sócio-economica e Idealogia...' In F. W. Reis (org.), *Os Partidos e o Regime.*

34. B. Lamounier 'O Voto em São Paulo', in Lamounier (org.), *O Voto de Desconfiança*, pp. 39–40.

Part II: Introduction

1. According to the minimal definition of political party proposed by G. Sartori: 'a party is any political group identified by an official label that it presents at elections, and is capable of placing through elections (free or non free), candidates for public office', the MDB can be considered a political party. The peculiarity of the case in study is that the MDB was artificially created by the remnants of the dissolved parties from the prior party system. See Sartori, *Parties and Party Systems* (Cambridge: Cambridge University, Press, 1976), p. 63

2. Obviously the term democracy was used without any attempt of defining its meaning. The only clear feature was that this 'democracy' would not be anything which resembled the democratic period prior to 1964.

3. Marcus Figueiredo, 'A Politica de Coação no Brasil pós-64' in L. Klein and M. Figueiredo, *Legitimidade e Coação no Brasil pós-64* (Rio: Forense, 1978).

4 1966–8: Searching for Identity

1. On this event see Chapter 1.

2. He was transferred to the reserve in August 1966. In the November elections Amaury Kruel was elected MDB federal deputy.

3. Deputy from the State of Goias, he belonged to the PSD before 1965. In his speech made in the Federal Chamber (session of 3 May 1966), he stated: 'Having been asked by my colleagues of Goias to join the MDB, I did it because it was completely impossible for me to join ARENA. For, all the corrupt and subversive politicians of the PTB in my state are in ARENA'. *Anais da Camara dos Deputados*, 1966, vol. 7, p. 585.

4. Deputy Vieira de Mello, opposition leader of the Federal Chamber. *Anais da Camara dos Deputados*, 1966, vol. 18, pp. 915–8.

5. The Complementary Act. No. 20 established the use of the non-official ballot paper for the legislative elections in the municipalities of less than 100 000 inhabitants. This clearly facilitated fraudulent practices.

6. *Anais da Camara dos Deputados*, 1966, vol. 18, p. 918.

7. Up to 1971 parliamentarians were allowed to change their party affiliation.

8. *Jornal da Tarde*, 22 August 1966.

9. See Carlos Castello Branco's article in the *Jornal do Brasil*, 21 August 1966, republished in C. C. Branco, *Os Militares no Poder* (Rio de Janeiro, Nova Fronteira, 1977), vol. 1, pp. 545–6. The journalist Carlos Castello Branco has been a political commentator of the *Jornal do Brasil*. He has published three volumes of his daily articles written for that newspaper, and these books are important sources of information for the post-64 period.

10. *Anais da Camara dos Deputados* 1966, vol. 23 (session of 24 November 1966), pp. 197–8.

11. Quoted in C. C. Branco, *Os Militares no Poder*, vol. 1. p. 585.

12. On 11 November 1966, thus four days before the election day, President Castelo Branco suspended the political rights of 18 people; one of them was the journalist Helio Fernandes who was an MDB candidate for the Federal Chamber (Guanabara).

13. C. C. Branco's article of 20 November 1966, in *Os Militares*, vol. 1. p. 602. We should point out. nonetheless, that at least part of the spoiled ballots must have been due to the establishment of the single ballot paper for different elections and the *voto vinculado* for state and federal deputies. *Voto vinculado* means that voters have to vote for candidates of the same party for both state and federal deputies. Deputy Evaldo Pinto pointed out in his speech in the Federal Chamber about the elections that: 'only in one city, São Bernando do Campo, so close to São Paulo Capital, about 4000 ballots were nullified due to the fact that the voters did not know that they had to vote for candidates of the same party.' *Anais da Camara dos Deputados*, 1966, vol. 23, p. 188.

14. After the issuing of the AI–5 and consequent press censorship this newspaper developed a more sympathetic attitude towards the MDB.

15. *Jornal da Tarde*, 13 June 1967. *Communo-janguista* (communist-like) was the term that the right used to define João Goulart's reformist government. The *Jornal da Tarde* belongs to the *Estado de São Paulo* press company.

16. *Estado de São Paulo*. 16 December 1965.

17. *Estado de São Paulo*, 16 April 1966.
18. *Jornal da Tarde*, 3 September 1966. *Janista* means follower of the ex-president Janio Quadros.
19. See C. C. Branco's comments in his article of 17 November 1966, in *Os Militares*, vol. 1, p. 600.
20. See M. Figueiredo, 'A Politica de Coação', p. 155, and Ronald Schneider, *The Political System of Brazil*, particularly Chapter 7.
21. This measure, decreed by Castelo Branco, was intended to avoid delaying the approval of bills by the legislature.
22. Deputy Marcio Moreira Alves stated: 'Everybody recognizes, or says so, that the majority of the Armed Forces does not support the military elite which has perpetuated violence and maintained the country under an oppressive regime. After the events in Brasilia, I believe that the great moment of union for democracy has come. This is also the moment for boycotting: the Brazilian mothers have already manifested themselves; all the social classes have condemned violence. However, this is not enough. It is necessary (. . .) to boycott militarism. The 7th of September is coming. Taking advantage of the deep patriotic sentiments of the people, the military elite will ask the schools to parade along with the executioners of students. It is necessary that every father, every mother be conscious that the presence of their sons in this parade is a favour done to the torturers who beat them and shoot them in the streets. Thus, let everybody boycott this parade. This boycotting can be also achieved . . . by the girls who dance with the cadets or have romances with young military officers. It is necessary that . . . women . . . refuse to receive in their houses those who vilify, . . . who are silent and, therefore, become accomplices. . . . I believe . . . that it is possible to end this farce, this *democratura*, this false compromise, by boycotting. While the silent ones do not express their dissatisfaction, any contact between civilians and military officers must stop, because this is the only way to make this country return to democracy. This is the only way to make the silent, who do not agree with the misdeeds of their superiors, follow the magnificent example of the fourteen military officers, from Cratéus, who had the courage to publicly oppose an illegal and arbitrary act of their superiors', *Anais da Camara dos Deputados*, 1968, vol. 73 (3 September 1968), pp. 432–3.
23. As Deputy Mario Covas pointed out, Deputy Hermano Alves was less protected by parliamentary immunity since he was accused on the basis of his articles published in the press. Thus he could be prosecuted under the crimes of expression or manifestation. Interview with Mario Covas, on 9 August 1982.
24. Interview with a high civil servant of the Chamber of Deputies on 3 May 1982. His name is not mentioned by request of the interviewee.
25. Interview on 9 August 1982.
26. The *grupo dos imaturos* did not consist of more than 15 per cent of the MDB's representation in the Chamber of Deputies.
27. Deputy Davi Lerer's statement. Quoted in C.C. Branco *Os Militares no Poder*, (Rio: Nova Fronteira, 1978), vol. 2, p. 29.

28. *Jornal da Tarde*, 26 June 1967.
29. Quoted in C. C. Branco's article of 16 April 1967. *Os Militares*, vol. 2, p. 37.
30. *Petebista* and *Pessedista* were those politicians who had belonged to the Brazilian Labour Party and the Social Democratic Party, respectively.
31. The Committee of Popular Mobilization however did not manage to accomplish its task. According to Deputy Marcio Moreira Alves's (head of the committee) comment on 13 June 1968, the committee had not been able to mobilize even its organizers. C. C. Branco, *Os Militares* vol. 2, p. 380.
32. It must be remembered that the popular leaders Janio Quadros, Leonel Brizola and Miguel Arraes had not agreed to adhere to the *Frente*.
33. The Minister of Justice Gama e Silva was regarded as an ally of the radical sectors in the army and decisively worked in favour of this group by putting pressure on Costa e Silva to close the regime. Gama e Silva – as mentioned by the press – had a draft of an Institutional Act and a decree of state of siege which he had tried to convince Costa e Silva to adopt, since March 1968. See C. C. Branco, *Os Militares*, vol. 2, p. 329.
34. Carlos C. Branco pointed out that the prohibition of the *Frente Ampla* was actually a convenient measure for its leader's intentions: 'Lacerda realized that the *Frente* was sinking him into a radicalization process which was deflecting him from his aim while there was not any prospect of reaching it through violence. In any case, Mr Lacerda's intention was not to promote a change in the political scene in order to give the power back to the leaders deposed by the Revolution, but to re-establish a political process which would allow him – and whoever else wanted–to propose himself as the commander and executor of the "true" objectives of the Brazilian Revolution', C. C. Branco, *Os Militares no Poder*, vol. 2, p. 436.
35. C. C. Branco's article of 7 April 1968, in *ibid.*, p. 323.
36. C. C. Branco's article of 4 February 1968, in *ibid.*, pp. 273–4.
37. Cf. C. C. Branco's article of 5 April 1968, in *ibid.*, p. 320.
38. R. Schneider, *The Political System of Brazil*, p. 266.
39. Interview with Mario Covas, 9 August 1982. 216 deputies voted against the prosecution of Marcio Moreira Alves, 141 voted in favour, and 15 abstained. 94 ARENA deputies supported the opposition. Cf. R. Schneider, *The Political System of Brazil*, p. 273.
40. The Institutional Act No. 5 granted the President the power to decree the recess of the National Congress and local Assemblies, and during the recess period, to legislate on every matter; to decree intervention in the states and municipalities on the basis of the national interest; to suspend the political rights for ten years of any citizen and to cancel political mandates; to decree the state of siege; to confiscate properties; to issue Complementary Acts in order to put in practice the AI–5 determinations. Adding to those measures the Institutional Act suspended the guarantees of habeas corpus and stability in the exercise of public functions, and excluded from any judicial judgment the actions accomplished in the name of the AI–5.

41. C. C. Branco's article of 14 Dec. 1968, in *Os Militares*, vol. 2, pp. 562–3.
42. Later, the State Assemblies of Goias and Pará were also temporarily closed.
43. As a result of the political purges, the MDB lost 62 Federal Deputies, 4 Senators, 157 State Deputies, 293 councillors and 12 mayors. (*Estado de São Paulo*, 31 May 1974). The ARENA lost 26 Federal Deputies who also had their mandates cancelled.
44. For more information about the AI–5 purges see M. Figueiredo, 'A Politica de Coação'; Ronald Schneider, *The Political System of Brazil*; and Sebastião Velasco e Cruz and Carlos E. Martins, 'De Castelo a Figueiredo: Uma Incursão na Pré-história da Abertura', in B. Sorj and M. H. Tavares de Almeida (orgs), *Sociedade e Politica no Brasil pós-64* (São Paulo: Brasiliense, 1983).

5 1969–74: From Retreat to Rebuilding

1. Institutional Act No. 5, reproduced in A. Campanhole and H. L. Campanhole, *Todas as Constituições do Brasil*, p. 141 (our emphasis).
2. *Ibid.*, p. 141.
3. *Ibid.*, p. 141 (our emphasis).
4. M. Figueiredo, 'A Politica de Coação no Brasil pós-64', p. 143. According to a survey made by the Federal Chamber, from December 1968 to May 1969, the President of the Republic had already decreed 234 Decree-laws. *Jornal do Brasil*, 27 May 1969.
5. Quoted in C. C. Branco's article of 6 March 1969, republished in C. C. Branco, *Os Militares no Poder*, vol. 3 (Rio de Janeiro: Nova Fronteira, 1979), p. 90.
6. *Ibid.*
7. Colonel Jarbas Passarinho held the following positions: Minister of Labour during Costa e Silva's government; Minister of Education during Medici's government. Passarinho was also elected Senator in 1970. In 1978 he continued in the Senate thanks to the 'indirect elections' for one-third of the senatorial seats. When he was interviewed in 1982, Passarinho held the important position of president of the Senate. Later he lost his seat in the Senate in the 1982 elections. In 1986 he managed to be elected senator.
8. Interview on 20 May 1982. Before giving his interpretation, Jarbas Passarinho pointed out: 'naturally [this position] has made the left wing intellectuals think that I am a depraved person when I defend it'.
9. C. C. Branco, *Os Militares*, vol. 3, pp. 272–3.
10. Interview on 20 May 1982 (our emphasis).
11. C. C. Branco's article of 16 March 1969, in *Os Militares*, vol. 3, p. 104.
12. Article published in the *Estado de São Paulo*, on 23 April 1972. The journalist Fernando Pedreira published a collection of his newspaper articles in *Brasil Política* (São Paulo: Difel, 1975). See pp. 249–51.
13. Interview with Jarbas Passarinho, on 20 May 1982.

14. R. Schneider, *The Political System of Brazil*, p. 291. On the armed struggle actions see João Quartim, *Dictatorship and Armed Struggle in Brazil* (London: NLB, 1971); and Fernando Portela, *Guerra de guerrilhas no Brasil* (São Paulo: Global, 1979).
15. C. C. Branco, *Os Militares*, vol. 3, pp. 86–7.
16. Article of 1 August, 1969, in *ibid.*, pp. 274–5.
17. There is a vast literature about the class nature of the state and on the role of the technocracy. The main works are: Florestan Fernandes, *A Revolução Burguesa no Brasil* (Rio de Janeiro: Zahar, 1974); Octavio Ianni, *Estado e Planejamento Economico no Brasil (1930–1970)* (Rio de Janeiro: Civilização Brasileira, 3rd edn 1979); Fernando H. Cardoso, *O Modelo Politico Brasileiro e outros Ensaios* (São Paulo: DIFEL, 1972), and *Autoritarismo e Democratização* (Rio de Janeiro: Paz e Terra, 3rd edn, 1975); Sérgio Abranches, 'The Divided Leviathan: State and Economic Policy Formation in Authoritarian Brazil' (Cornell University Ph.D. thesis, 1978); Peter Evans, *Dependent Development: the alliance of Multinational, State and Local Capital in Brazil* (Princeton: Princeton University Press, 1979); Renato Boschi and Eli D. Cerqueira, *O Empresariado Nacional e o Estado no Brasil* (Rio de Janeiro: Forense, 1978); Carlos E. Martins, *Capitalismo de Estado e Modelo Politico no Brasil* (Rio de Janeiro: Graal, 1977); Carlos E. Martins (org.), *Estado e Capitalismo no Brasil* (São Paulo: Hucitec/CEBRAP, 1977); Luis C. Bresser Pereira, *Estado e Subdesenvolvimento Industrializado* (São Paulo: Brasiliense, 1977); *Tecnoburocracia e Contestação* (Petrópolis: Vozes, 1972); and *O Colapso de uma Aliança de Classes* (São Paulo: Brasiliense, 1978); Carlos E. Martins, *Tecnocracia e Capitalismo* (São Paulo, Brasiliense/CEBRAP, 1974); Alexandre Barros, 'The Changing Role of the State in Brazil: the technocratic military alliance', paper, Georgia, 1976; Barry C. Ames, 'Bureaucratic Policy Making in a Militarized Regime: Brazil after 1964' (Stanford University Ph.D. thesis, 1972).
18. The US Ambassador Burke Elbrick was kidnapped on 4 September 1969. He was released only after the government accepted the conditions of the kidnappers who demanded the publication of an opposition manifesto and the freeing of fifteen political prisoners. In 1970 two other diplomats were kidnapped: the Japanese Consul Nobu Okuchi in March and the German Ambassador Von Hollenben in June. See R. Schneider, *The Political System of Brazil*, Chapter 8.
19. For details see R. Schneider, *The Political System of Brazil*, and S. Velasco e Cruz and C. Estevão Martins, 'De Castelo a Figueiredo: Uma Incursão na Pré-História da Abertura', in B. Sorj and M. H. Tavares de Almeida (eds), *Sociedade e Política no Brasil pós-64* (São Paulo, Ed. Brasiliense, 1983).
20. Quoted in C. C. Branco, *Os Militares no Poder*, vol. 3, p. 354.
21. The term radical/radicalization is used here in opposition to a moderate attitude, thus it does not imply any evaluative judgement on that attitude.
22. Quoted in C. C. Branco's article of 20 February 1969, in *Os Militares*, vol. 3, p. 72.

23. The unwillingness of the MDB politicians to give up their mandates is quite understandable. Aside from interrupting their political careers, the condition of a *cassado* (political non-person) involved not only the suspension of political rights but also limitations on the *cassado*'s private activities. The ex-deputy Mario Maia narrated his experience as a political non-person as follows: 'After my cassação I went to Rio de Janeiro state, I did not go back to Acre, my state.... They advised me not to go back to Acre. They did not prohibit me from going, but they "advised" me. (...) When I went to Rio de Janeiro (to live in Niteroi), I had to present myself to the political police, and then they asked me to go to military headquarters where I had to go every three months to confirm my home address. I went on like this for 2 years... then they relaxed this requirement... Well, now the personal consequences of the *cassação*: as a medical doctor I was employed by the Health Ministry and also had a civil servant's position in the state of Guanabara's administration. So, with my *cassação* I lost these jobs and I had to earn my living as a private doctor... I lived in Niteroi for 10 years. The first years were more restricted, "watched"... I could not even get a bank loan; it was not allowed. After living there for two years I went to the *Banco do Brasil* to ask for a loan and it was refused. I was impeded from making any transaction with Public Savings, public banks, etc... By the end of the ten years of suspension of my political rights things became more relaxed', interview on 23 April 1982.
24. Cf. C. C. Branco, *Os Militares*, p. 216 (article on 14 June 1969).
25. Quoted in I. M. Magalhães *et al.*, 'Cronologia – Segundo e Terceiro Ano do Governo Costa e Silva', *Dados*, no. 8, 1971, p. 182.
26. *Estado de São*, 26 October 1969.
27. Cf. C. C. Branco's article of 25 November 1969, in C. C. Branco, *Os Militares*, vol. 3, pp. 386–7.
28. *Jornal da Tarde*, E. C. Andrade's article on 25 February 1971. Adolfo de Oliveira ended up resigning from the position of general-secretary and left the MDB by July 1971.
29. Article of 8 April 1970, in C. C. Branco, *Os Militares*, p. 519.
30. C. C. Branco, *Os Militares*, vol. 3, pp. 528–9.
31. It must be underlined that in 1970 several State Assemblies and municipal chambers were still under imposed recess. The suspension of the recesses were decreed by the government on 27 April 1970 for the Sergipe's Assembly, on 20 May for São Paulo's and Pernambuco's Assemblies and on 8 July 1970 for Guanabara's, Rio de Janeiro's and Goias' Assemblies. In each of these occasions more *cassações* were made.
32. Article of 28 April 1970, in C. C. Branco, *Os Militares*, vol. 3, p. 537. See also *Estado de São Paulo*, 28 December 1969 and 24 March 1970, and *Jornal da Tarde*, 2 March 1970.
33. *Jornal da Tarde*, 19 November 1970. By 1970 the *Estado de São Paulo's* newspaper company which also owns the *Jornal da Tarde* had started to change its line towards the MDB. As we have shown in the last chapter, this newspaper was very opposed to the MDB during the first years of

this party. After 1969, with the imposition of the press censorship, the newspaper showed signs of discontent with the regime that it had actively helped to establish in the country.

34. In 1970 two-thirds of the Senate's representation was to be renewed, thus in each state the parties could run two candidates for the two seats being contested. In São Paulo, both ARENA and MDB managed to have a senator elected in the 1970 elections. Senator Lino de Matos (MDB's president in São Paulo) was defeated possibly due to his moderate attitude during the electoral campaign. He considered that the MDB campaign should avoid conflict, revenge or any kind of radicalism. *Estado de São Paulo*, 8 July 1970. Franco Montoro who won the MDB senatorial seat, based his campaign on a more critical attitude towards the regime, stressing themes such as, the abolition of the Institutional Acts, criticisms of the government's wage policy, of the process of increasing participation of foreign capital in the economy and so forth. He also stressed his 'identification' with the workers. One of his propaganda papers stated: 'Let us elect Franco Montoro, the senator of the workers'. It stressed that he was the author of the law of the *salario-familia* (family-wage), and that as a deputy he had fought against the government's policy of wage restriction and defended a fair share for the workers in the distribution of national wealth.

35. Cf. *Estado de São Paulo*, 16 July 1970.

36. The only exception was in ex-Guanabara state where the opposition, having a majority in the State Assembly could 'elect' the governor through the indirect process. It is not coincidental that in that state the MDB has never lost an election, and that the then Governor Chagas Freitas was able to build a very effective clientelist machine. On this case, see E. Diniz, *Voto e Máquina Política – Patronagem e Clientelismo no Rio de Janeiro* (Rio de Janeiro: Paz e Terra, 1982). On the extensive resort to patronage politics by the post-1964 governments, see C. Medeiros, 'Politics and Intergovernmental Relations in Brazil, 1964–1982' (London School of Economics, Ph.D. thesis, 1983).

37. Cf. C. C. Branco, *Os Militares*, vol. 3, p. 590.

38. See C. C. Branco's article of 5 Nov. 1970, in *ibid.*, pp. 709–10, and *Estado de São Paulo*, 4 November 1970. It was reported in the press that about 2000 people were arrested just in São Paulo state.

39. The PIS sought to 'give the workers a direct stake in productivity and in the expansion of the private sector. A gradually increasing proportion of the gross receipts of each enterprise was to be credited to the individual accounts of its employees with the federal saving bank and invested for them by the government in the stock market. This "participation fund" was expected to reach US $ 1 billion by 1974, easing the shortage of risk capital as well as, hopefully, leading the workers to identify their future with the regime', R. Schneider, *The Political System of Brazil*, p. 324.

40. Cf. F. J. L. Costa and L. Klein, 'Cronologia: Um ano de Governo Médici', *Dados*, no. 9, 1972, p. 209.

41. *Estado de São Paulo*, 13 November 1970.

42. The states where the MDB managed to put forth a number of candidates equal or superior to the state's entitled number of seats were Acre, Alagoas, Amazonas, Guanabara, Paraiba, Rio de Janeiro, Rio Grande do Sul and São Paulo. With regard to the ARENA, only in Santa Catarina state this party did not manage to fill the list of candidates for the Federal Chamber. There, 11 ARENA candidates and 8 MDB candidates contested the 13 seats for the state.

43. *Jornal da Tarde*, 19 November 1970.

44. Cf. *Jornal da Tarde*, 19 November 1970.

45. *Estado de São Paulo*, 18 February 1971.

46. *Ibid.*

47. *Estado de São Paulo*, 9 May 1971.

48. Cf. *Carta de Principios* published in *Estado de São Paulo*, 27 April 1971.

49. The slogan of the constituent assembly would be taken up as an important issue by the MDB only from 1977 onwards.

50. *Estado de São Paulo*, 7 February 1971.

51. His argument of the irreversibility of the 1964 Revolution would be emphatically sustained later in 1972, in the manifesto (the *Carta de Principios de Campinas*) launched by his group, in a meeting, in Campinas, of the recently elected MDB mayors. The manifesto criticized the party's poor electoral performance in the 1972 municipal elections and blamed the MDB's lack of ability to win electoral support. This manifesto received sharp criticisms even from the party's moderate sectors. It was regarded as too moderate and pragmatic, and a position of adhesion to the regime. See *Estado de São Paulo*, 31 December 1972 and 10 January 1973.

52. *Estado de São Paulo*, 7 February 1971.

53. *Ibid.*

54. The government had scheduled direct elections for state governors in 1974. However, in 1972 the rules changed again and those elections confirmed to be indirect. As a consequence, Quercia would try to guarantee his appointment as the MDB candidate for the Senate. On the government's change of rules regarding the gubernatorial elections see *Estado de São Paulo*, 5 April 1972.

55. Interview on 7 May 1982. The terms *contestação* and *sistema* had a special connotation at that time. *Contestação* was a much stronger word which meant opposition behaviour beyond the limits tolerated by the regime. *Sistema* became the current word to name the regime's strict circle of power in which the military and the technocracy controlled the decision-making process. On the so-called *sistema* see S. C. Velasco e Cruz and C. E. Martins, 'De Castelo a Figueiredo', and C. Lafer, *O Sistema Politico Brasileiro* (São Paulo: Editora Perspectiva, 1978).

56. Interview on 20 April 1982. João Gilberto (Federal Deputy from Rio Grande do Sul and president of the MDB's Institute of Studies (*Fundação Pedroso Horta*)), belonged to the group of new deputies, elected in 1974, which were named the *neo-autenticos*. These deputies regarded themselves as more ideologically oriented and they later

created the *tendencia popular* within the MDB. Most of the MDB deputies who left the party to join the PT belonged to this group.

57. Interview on 30 June 1982.
58. *Estado de São Paulo*, 20 February 1972.
59. In discussing the MDB's intentions to modify its line so as to give more attention to concrete themes related to the government's policy, an article of the *Estado de São Paulo* on 2 March 1972, properly commented: 'it is easy to identify a decisive influence of the *autenticos* in the MDB's change. But it would be unfair to deny the ability of the party leadership to realize the convenience of a substantive change'.
60. We were told by several deputies interviewed from the *grupo autentico*, that the group used to send copies of their speeches made in Congress to their electoral bases so that they could get to know their performance in Congress – the only means to cope with the press censorship.
61. See particularly the article of Carlos Chagas (*Estado de São Paulo* 23 November 1972) and of Flamarion Mossri (*Estado de São Paulo*, 3 December 1972).
62. It was only two months before the elections that the MDB attempted to carry out a concerted action in Congress by scheduling parliamentarians to speak on specific themes, such as unequal income distribution and the presence of foreign capital in the economy. See *Estado de São Paulo*, 23 August 1972 and *Jornal da Tarde*, 23 August 1972.
63. Cf. *Estado de São Paulo*, 27 June 1972 and 22 Oct. 1972, and the MDB's manual for the 1972 municipal elections.
64. One of the consequences of this is the frequent shift to the government party of the MDB mayors. By 1970 the MDB had about 505 mayors. Soon after 303 of them left the party and joined ARENA. These desertions had been one of the main problems of the party since they destroyed municipal bases which were vital for the party's organization across the country. *Estado de São Paulo*, 23 November 1972.
65. Cf. *Estado de São Paulo*, 18 August 1972.
66. *Jornal da Tarde*, 24 September 1973.
67. Speech made by Ulysses Guimarães at the 6th national convention, 21–2 September. Published by the MDB, ' "Navegar é preciso, Viver não é preciso" ', Brasília: Centro Gráfico do Senado Federal, 1973. Fifty thousand copies of this speech were distributed to the party organizations over the country.
68. *Ibid.* The term *denationalization* is used to indicate the increasing role of foreign investment (multinationals) in the economy and the relative weakening of the local sector.
69. *Ibid.*
70. 'Navegar é preciso. Viver não é precisco' means 'To sail is essential. To live is not essential'. The other quotation means: 'Today, standing on the deck, I hope to God that I can soon shout to the Brazilian people: well done, my Captain. Land is in sight! Without shadows, fears or nightmares, the clean and blessed land of liberty is in sight'.
71. *Estado de São Paulo*, 23 September 1973.

72. *Estado de São Paulo*, 29 November 1973. Actually the Deputy Francisco Pinto, one of the leading figures of the *grupo autentico*, had advocated in December 1972 that the MDB should present candidates for all offices, and had underlined the need to choose a military figure willing to commit himself to a programme of economic emancipation and the reestablishment of freedom in the country. Cf. *Estado de São Paulo* 3 December 1972.

73. *Estado de São Paulo*, 16 January 1974. This article had had some parts cut by the censor thereby it was not published in full in the press. However, the newspaper archives preserved its original form.

74. This manifesto was published, later, in Deputy Paes de Andrade, *O Itinerário da Violência* (Rio de Janeiro, Paz e Terra, 1978), pp. 141–3.

75. The MDB top leadership punished the dissident group by dismissing them from the positions of vice-leaders in the Federal Chamber. See *Estado de São Paulo*, 16 January 1974.

76. *Estado de São Paulo*, 16 November 1973.

77. Telling of the difficulties faced by the candidates during their travels across the country, Ulysses Guimarães recalled: 'In Campo Grande (state of Mato Grosso), the Electricity Company cut the light during the campaign's rally ... In Goiania (Goias), the person in charge of the sound equipment disappeared and, in Natal (RN), the Secretary of Security prohibited the rally but had to back down from his decision in face of the pressure of 15 000 people who were waiting for the rally. Anyhow, we created the conditions for publicizing our ideas and the party programme, thus creating a climate which certainly will have beneficial results in the legislative elections in November'. *Estado de São Paulo*, 12 Jan. 1974.

6   1974–7: Attempting to Consolidate Legal Opposition Politics

1. One of the explanations of the regime's political opening has been based on this change of the military group in control of the government. According to this view, the *abertura* was a project of the *castelista* group who, returning to power, intended to 'correct the course' of the 1964 'Revolution' which had been diverted from its original aims. It is not our intention to discuss the reasons that led to the regime's decision to promote a political opening. Certainly an explanation for that involves the consideration of a set of more complex factors than the one pointed to above. Surveying the debate on the *abertura* from 1973 to 1981, M. F. Figuiredo and J. A. B. Cheibub identified five lines of interpretation for the political opening. Besides the one which was mentioned above, the political opening has been seen as: a) a product of the economic crisis: given the economic crisis which the country had started to endure since the beginning of the 1970's it was necessary to establish a new political pact in order to guarantee the functioning of the economic model; b) a product of economic development: the complexity of social interests emerged as a consequence of the country's economic diversification,

requiring political development as a means of administering this new situation; c) the regime's search for legitimacy: the need for institutionalizing a political arrangement which would increase the level of participation, since the source of legitimation used by the regime – economic success (in addition to coercion) – had become excessively costly; d) the political opening as a product of a crisis of authority: a response to the excessive centralization of power which provoked a breakdown of the mechanisms of authority and rendered decisions taken at central level inoperative. Cf. M. F. Figueiredo and J. A. B. Cheibub, 'A Abertura Politica de 1973 a 1981: Quem disse o Quê, Quando – Inventário de um debate', *Boletim Informativo e Bibliográfico de Ciências Sociais*, Rio de Janeiro, No. 14, 1982, pp. 29–61. The main works which discuss the political opening are: W. G. dos Santos, *Poder e Politica: Crônica do Autoritarismo Brasileiro* (Rio de Janeiro, Editora Forense, 1978); B. Lamounier, 'O Discurso e Processo (da distensão às opções do regime brasileiro), in H. Rattner (org.) *Brasil 1990, Caminhos Alternativos do Desenvolvimento*, (São Paulo: Brasiliense, 1979); B. Lamounier 'Notes on the Study of Re-Democratization', *Working Papers of the Wilson Centre*, no. 58; B. Lamounier and A. R. Moura, 'Política Economica e Abertura Politica – 1973–1983', *Cadernos IDESP*, no. 4, 1984; B. Lamounier and J. E. Faria (orgs.) *O Futuro da Abertura: Um Debate*, (São Paulo, Cortez Ed., 1981); H. Trindade (org.) *Brasil em Perspectiva: Dilemas da Abertura Politica* (Porto Alegre: Sulina, 1982); S. C. Velasco e Cruz and C. E. Martins, 'De Castelo a Figueiredo: Uma Incursão na Pré-história da Abertura', in B. Sorj and M. H. Tavares de Almeida (orgs.), *Sociedade e Politica no Brasil pós-64* (São Paulo: Brasiliense, 1983); F. Henrique Cardoso, 'The Authoritarian Regime at the Crossroads: The Brazilian case', *Working Papers of the Wilson Centre*, No. 93, 1981.

2. Quoted in B. Kucinsky, *Abertura, a História de uma Crise* (São Paulo: Ed. Brasil Debates, 1982), p. 20.

3. Source: José Serra, 'Ciclos e Mudanças Estruturais na Economia Brasileira do Pós-Guerra', in L. G. Belluzzo and R. Coutinho (orgs.), *Desenvolvimento Capitalista no Brasil – Ensaios sobre a Crise* (São Paulo: Brasiliense, 1982), pp. 66 and 97. Without intending to give an exhaustive account of the works produced about the economic crisis, some works must be mentioned: Paul I. Singer, *A Crise do 'Milagre'* (Rio de Janeiro: Paz e Terra, 1976); Edmar Bacha, *Os Mitos de uma Década – Ensaios de Economia Brasileira* (Rio de Janeiro: Paz e Terra, 1976); Pedro Malan and R. Bonelli, 'The Brazilian Economy in the Seventies: Old and New Developments', *World Development*, 5 Nos 1/2, 1977; Carlos F. Lessa, 'A Estratégia de Desenvolvimento 1974–1976 – Sonho e Fracasso' (Faculdade de Economia e Administração da UFRJ, tese apresentada para concurso a Professor Titular, 1978); Celso Furtado, *O Brasil Pós 'milagre'* (Rio de Janeiro: Paz e Terra, 1981); L. G. Belluzzo and Renata Coutinho (orgs.), *Desenvolvimento Capitalista – Ensaios sobre a Crise*.

4. Cf. Geisel's speech on 19 March 1974 (*Estado de São Paulo*, 20 March 1974) and the politicians' comments on the President's speech, in *Estado de São Paulo*, 21, 22 and 23 March 1974.
5. *Estado de São Paulo*, 18 April 1974.
6. Interview on 27 July 1982.
7. See, C. R. Duarte, 'A Lei Falcão: Antecedentes e Impacto', in B. Lamounier (org.) *Voto de Desconfiança* (Petropolis: Vozes/Cebrap, 1980) particularly page 194.
8. *Veja* magazine, 25 September 1974.
9. According to the Electoral Code, two hours were reserved daily for the Electoral Tribunal which, in turn, granted the parties equal periods of time, during the normal programmes scheduled in the media. The law also established that one of the two hours had to be in the evening, between 8 and 11 pm. As there were just two parties, the MDB had thirty minutes during the day and thirty minutes in the evening to use for its campaign. It was regarding the evening broadcast that the deal was made, reducing it from thirty to twenty minutes. Thus the party used five minutes for short films and fifteen minutes for debates and speeches.
10. *Veja*, 9 October 1974.
11. The MDB candidate obtained 4,630,182 votes (65.1 per cent), the ARENA candidate obtained 1,696,340 votes (23.8 per cent). Data collected in the Regional Electoral Tribunal (TRE-São Paulo).
12. Calculations based on data from the Superior Electoral Tribunal (TSE) and the Regional Electoral Tribunal–SP (TRE–SP).
13. *Veja*, 27 November 1974.
14. The six Assemblies in which the MDB held the majority were in the important states of Rio de Janeiro, Guanabara, São Paulo and Rio Grande do Sul, and the northern states of Acre and Amazonas.
15. Interview with Ulysses Guimarães, on 30 June 1982.
16. *Estado de São Paulo*, 31 May 1974.
17. *Estado de São Paulo*, 13 September 1974.
18. *Estado de São Paulo*, 13 July 1974.
19. *Veja*, 16 October 1974.
20. When we talk about the freer conditions of the 1974 elections, we are taking as a point of reference previous elections under the military-authoritarian rule. It must be pointed out that, although they were freer than before, the press was still under censorship and the regime also used intimidation to keep the electoral campaign under certain limits. For example, the deputy Francisco Pinto, who had lost his mandate as a consequence of his prosecution by the National Security Law for having made a speech against General Pinochet, was prohibited from running for a seat in the Federal Chamber, although he had not had his political rights cancelled. See *Veja*, 28 August 1974. The MDB had also asked its candidates to avoid giving any pretext for being called 'radicals' or 'subversives' by the government. See *Estado de São Paulo*, 19 July 1974.

21. *Veja*, 25 September 1974.
22. *Estado de São Paulo*, 8 October 1974. Deputy Cantidio Sampaio was running for reelection in the Federal Chamber. Orestes Quercia was the MDB candidate for the Senate, and Senator Carvalho Pinto from ARENA was attempting re-election.
23. This was clearly shown in São Paulo where the candidate for the Senate, Orestes Quercia, counted on the help of all the groups within the party, in spite of the fact that Quercia represented an opposition to the party leadership in the state. Details about the nomination of Quercia can be found in *Estado de São Paulo*, 19 July and 13 August 1974.
24. Carlos Estevão Martins, 'O Balanço da Campanha', in B. Lamounier and F. H. Cardoso (eds.) *Os Partidos e as Eleições no Brasil* (Rio de Janeiro: Paz e Terra, 1975). The same line of interpretation is found in the article by F. H. Cardoso, 'Partidos e Deputados em São Paulo: O Voto e a Representação Politica', in B. Lamounier and F. H. Cardoso, *Os Partidos*.
25. C. E. Martins, 'O Balanço da Campanha', p. 80.
26. *Estado de São Paulo*, 19 November 1974.
27. It would be inaccurate to assess that all the blank and spoiled ballots mean manifestations of protest, since they can be also due to the voter's indifference or misinformation. On this question, see B. Lamounier, 'O Voto em São Paulo, 1970—8' in B. Lamounier, (ed.), *Voto de Desconfiança*.
28. B. Lamounier's articles 'O Comportamento Eleitoral em São Paulo: Passado e Presente', in Lamounier and Cardoso (eds), *Os Partidos*; 'O Discurso e o Processo (Da Distensão às opções do regime brasileiro)'.
29. Cf. Lamounier's article mentioned above, particularly 'O Comportamento Eleitoral em São Paulo: Passado e Presente', p. 44.
30. B. Lamounier, 'O Discurso e o Processo', p. 106.
31. In January 1975 the *Estado de São Paulo* reaped the fruits of the government's first step towards the gradual liberalization of the press, when preliminary censorship was lifted in this newspaper. In June 1976 the liberalization was extended to the magazine *Veja*, and later to other newspapers, with the exception of *Tribuna da Imprensa, Movimento* and *O São Paulo* which were under censorship up to June 1978. See C. R. Duarte, 'Imprensa e Redemocratização no Brasil', in DADOS, vol. 26, no. 2, 1983, pp. 181–195.
32. On this question, the movement for the defence of the 'disappeared' had in fact been carried out by the *Comissão de Justiça e Paz da Igreja Catolica* (Commission for Justice and Peace of the Catholic Church). In August 1974, the Archbishop of São Paulo, Dom Paulo Evaristo Arns met General Golbery de Couto e Silva to discuss the problem. At the meeting, the Archbishop gave a list of names of 22 missing persons and requested an investigation on their whereabouts. See B. Kucinsky, *Abertura*, pp. 44–6.

33. As S. C. Velasco e Cruz and C. E. Martins pointed out, one of the central aspects of the government's strategy to carry out political relaxation was to strengthen the authority of the President of the Republic, so as to control the increased power and autonomy of the repressive apparatus. This provoked the reaction of the military sectors linked to the repressive apparatus who tried to destabilize the government by intensifying repression towards political prisoners and the remainder of the organized left in the underground, particularly the Communist Party. Cf. Velasco e Cruz and Martins, 'De Castello a Figueiredo: Uma incursão na Pré-História da "Abertura"'. About the strong and authoritarian style of Geisel in governing, see Walder de Góes, *O Brasil do General Geisel* (Rio de Janeiro: Nova Fonteira, 1978).
34. *Jornal da Tarde*, 1 February 1975.
35. *Jornal da Tarde*, 1 February 1975.
36. *Estado de São Paulo*, 7 March 1975.
37. *Estado de São Paulo*, 11 March 1975.
38. *Ibid.*
39. *Jornal da Tarde*, 21 March 1975.
40. The death of Herzog provoked vehement protest as shown by the presence of 8 thousand people in the memorial service held at São Paulo Cathedral. See B. Kucinsky, *Abertura*, pp. 48–9.
41. See details in B. Kucinsky, *Abertura*.
42. Geisel also resorted to the AI-5 to punish politicians accused of corruption. In April 1975, a judge and two civil servants from Rondonia were sacked and had their political rights cancelled. In July, the Senator Wilson Campos from the ARENA lost his mandate and his political rights. Later in 1976 the AI-5 was again used to punish practices of corruption against ARENA politicians from the state of Rio Grande do Norte: ex-governor Cortes Pereira, four of his aides and Deputy Ney Lopes de Souza (Sep. 1975); and against the MDB state Deputy Leonel Julio (president of the São Paulo State Assembly) in December 1975.
43. *Estado de São Paulo*, 12 March 1975.
44. Twenty deputies from this group came from Rio de Janeiro's representation, namely the *chaguistas* – followers of the ex-governor Chagas Freitas – who created in that state a very powerful clientelist machine. See *ISTO É*, 6 April 1977. On the clientelist style dominating the MDB's section of Rio de Janeiro, see E. Diniz, *Voto e Máquina Politica – patronagem e clientelismo no Rio de Janeiro* (Rio: Paz e Terra, 1982).
45. See *Estado de São Paulo*, 18 May 1975, and *Movimento*, 22 September 1975.
46. The reports produced by the Parliamentary Inquiry Commissions were published by the MDB in *Coleção Alberto Pasqualini*, vol. 11, 1976.
47. *Estado de São Paulo*, 11 October, 1975.
48. That is why the bill became known as Falcão Law.
49. *Jornal da Tarde*, 19 May 1976.
50. *Estado de São Paulo*, 19 June 1976.

51. *Folha de São Paulo*, 3 June 1976.
52. Teotonio Villela was the only parliamentarian from ARENA to vote against the government's Bill. This in fact marked the start of Villela's opposition attitude towards his party and the regime. Later in 1979 when the party reform took place he left the ARENA to join in the MDB.
53. The Party Discipline Law determined that all party members were subjected to the party's line establishing that a parliamentarian could lose his mandate if he did not follow the decision taken by his party. See, *Lei Orgânica dos Partidos Politicos*.
54. *Lei Orgânica dos Partidos Politicos*. See Senado Federal, *Legislação Eleitoral e Partidária* (Brasilia: Senado Federal, 1974).
55. The Brazilian Bar Association (OAB) had become, after 1974, a very important opposition voice amongst the associations in civil society. About the role of the OAB, see, M. H. Moreira Alves, *Estado e Oposição no Brasil (1964–84)* (Petropolis: Vozes, 1984).
56. Direct gubernatorial elections had not been held since 1965, but according to the current rules they were to take place in November 1978.
57. Lustosa da Costa's article in the newspaper *Estado de São Paulo*, 12 February 1977. See also the articles of Villas Boas Corrêa, ESP, 19/1/77; Evandro Paranaguá, ESP, 19/2/77; Carlos Chagas, ESP, 19/2/77.
58. The punishment of the two MDB councillors was due much less to what they had stated than to the intention of the government to diminish the large majority that the MDB held in that municipal Council. As the ex-councillor Glenio Peres explained after his *cassação*, 'The fact that we had got 14 out of the 21 members of the Council put some of our heads in evidence; I was the one who was chosen, but it could have been any other'. *Estado de São Paulo*, 4 February 1977.
59. *Estado de São Paulo*, 19 February 1977.
60. *Estado de São Paulo*, 19 February 1977.
61. Furtado tried to innovate by consulting his colleagues. He asked the opinion of deputies on the judiciary issue through a questionnaire distributed to the MDB members of the Federal Chamber. The results of this questionnaire served to decide the position taken by the federal deputies.
62. *Estado de São Paulo*, 25 March 1977.
63. The party chairman tried to avoid a discussion on the judiciary issue at the Directorate's meeting. He wanted to leave the decision on the matter to the parliamentarians, so as to leave a greater possibility of negotiation with the government party.
64. *Jornal da Tarde*, 25 March 1977.
65. *Ibid.*
66. *Estado de São Paulo*, 1 April 1977.
67. The state of Rio de Janeiro would be the only case in which the MDB could get the governorship since the party held also the majority of the local delegates.
68. There are 22 states in the country, but the ARENA could not count on Rio de Janeiro which was in the MDB's domain.

69. All these casuistic measures regarding the senatorial elections intended to prevent the MDB from becoming a majority in the Senate. The concern with the strengthening of the MDB in Congress was due not only to the obstacles that the opposition could pose to the legislative works but mainly to the problem it could cause in the appointment of the next President of the Republic who was to be elected by the electoral college.
70. Interview with Deputy João Gilberto on 20 April 1982.
71. Interview with Deputy Aldo Fagundes on 24 May 1982.

7 1977–9: Attempting Popular Mobilization

1. Walder de Góes provides an interesting account of President Geisel's performance, stressing the President's austere and independent-minded posture which undoubtedly influenced the way in which he ruled the country. As Góes points out, if, on the one hand, Geisel was truly committed to a policy of political liberalization, on the other hand he was the general president who centralized power, and therefore the decision making process, in his hands more than any of his predecessors. Cf. Walder de Góes, *O Brasil do General Geisel* (Rio de Janeiro: Nova Fronteira, 1978), p. 106.
2. This policy was sustained on the basis of extensive borrowings from the international financial market at a time of easy money availability. Cf. B. Lamounier and Alkimar R. Moura, 'Politica Economica e Abertura Politica no Brasil – 1973–1983', *Textos IDESP*, No. 4, São Paulo, 1984.
3. F. H. Cardoso, 'O Papel dos Empresários no Processo de Transição: O Caso Brasileiro', *Revista Dados*, Rio de Janeiro, vol. 26, no. 1, 1983, pp. 9–27 (pp. 16–18). On this question see also S. Velasco e Cruz, 'Empresários e o Regime no Brasil: A Campanha contra a Estatização', (Universidade de São Paulo: Tese de Doutoramento, 1985).
4. In order to ensure that all delegates would vote for Figueiredo, the ARENA's president was instructed to request from the party's regional directorates previous declarations of votes for Figueiredo from the Convention delegates. Faced with this development, Magalhães Pinto eventually abandoned the contest. See *Jornal do Brasil*, 19 January 1978, *Folha de São Paulo*, 20 January 1978, *Estado de São Paulo*, 28 March 1978 and *Jornal do Brasil*, 9 April 1978. Details of the presidential succession can be found in the journalistic works of Getulio Bittencourt, *A Quinta Estrela – Como se tenta fazer um presidente no Brasil* (São Paulo: Livraria Editora Ciências Humanas, 1978); André G. Stumpf and Merval P. Filho, *A Segunda Guerra: Sucessão de Geisel*, (São Paulo, Brasiliense, 1979); and Walder do Góes, *O Brasil do General Geisel*, Chapters 2 and 3.
5. Since 1968, the Brazilian Catholic Church had become an important political force opposing the regime, not only through its defence of human rights and denunciations of the torture suffered by political prisoners but also through its work with the poor in neighbourhood communities (the Ecclesiastical Base Communities). On the role of the

Church see Thomas Bruneau, *The Political Transformation of the Brazilian Catholic Church* (London: Cambridge University Press, 1974); Marcio Moreira Alves, *A Igreja e a Politica no Brasil* (Lisbon: Livraria Sá da Costa 1978); Frei Betto, *O que é comunidade eclesial de base?* (São Paulo: Brasiliense, 1981); Maria H. Moreira Alves, *Estado e Oposição no Brasil, 1964–1984* (Petropolis: Vozes, 1984); R. Ireland, 'Catholic Base Communities, Spiritist Groups, and the Deepening of Democracy in Brazil', *Working Papers of the L. A. Programme of the Wilson Centre*, No. 131, 1983.

6. On the opposition role of the Bar Association in Brazil, see M. H. Moreira Alves, *Estado e Oposição no Brasil*, pp. 209–12.

7. On the reemergence of the student movement see Bernardo Kucinsky, *Abertura, A História de uma Crise.* (São Paulo: Ed. Brasil Debates, 1982), pp. 105–8.

8. Cf. Bernardo Kucinsky, *Abertura*, pp. 108–12.

9. Maria H. Moreira Alves, 'Grassroots Organizations, Trade Unions, and the Church – A Challenge to the Controlled *Abertura* in Brazil', *Latin American Perspective*, vol. 1. no. 40, Winter 1984, p. 87. On the trade union movement see also JosÃ© A. Moisés, 'O ciclo de greves do final dos anos setenta', São Paulo, CEDEC, 1979, mimeo; Maria H. Tavares de Almeida, 'Tendências Recentes da Negociação Coletiva no Brasil', *Dados*, vol. 24, no. 2, 1981: and 'O sindicalismo Brasileiro entre a Conservação e a Mudança', in. Bernardo Sorj and M. H. Tavares de Almeida (eds.), *Sociedade e Politica no Brasil pós-64* (São Paulo, Brasiliense, 1983); Leôncio M. Rodrigues, 'Tendências Futuras do Sindicalismo Brasileiro', in Henrique Ratner (org.), *Brasil 1990, Caminhos alternativos do Desenvolvimento* (São Paulo, Brasiliense, 1979); John Humphrey, 'The Development of Industry and the Bases for Trade Unionism: a case study of car workers in São Paulo, Brazil', (University of Sussex, Ph. D. thesis, 1977).

10. An analysis of the strikes in the various sectors during the period from 1978 to 1981 can be found in M. H. Tavares de Almeida, 'O Sindicalismo Brasileiro entre a Conservação e a Mudança'.

11. *Folha de São Paulo*, 29 July 1978.

12. Ecclesiastical Base Communities are religious organizations created around an urban parish or a rural chapel, comprising people who live in the same neighbourhood. These communities also have an important social and political role in working with the poor in the rural areas and in the outskirts of the cities. See M. H, Moreira Alves, 'Grassroots Organizations, Trade Unions and the Church' and *Estado e Oposição no Brasil. Sociedade de Amigos do Bairro* are secular associations organized by people of the neighbourhood. They are very important as a means of organizing the population to demand basic services which in the poor areas of the large cities are almost non-existent. On the origins and development of those associations see José A. Moisés, 'Classes Populares e Protesto Urbano' (Universidade de São Paulo, Tese de Doutorado, 1974). An interesting critical analysis of the social movements showing the limits of action of the base communities can be found in Ruth Cardoso, 'Movimentos Sociais Urbanos: Balanço

Critico', in Bernardo Sorj and M. H. Tavares de Almeida (eds), *Sociedade e Politica no Brasil.*

13. In September 1978 the representatives of the *Movimento do Custo de Vida* attempted to meet President Geisel, who refused to see them. They then left the petition, with 1.3 million signatures, at the Presidential Palace. Later, the government responded by questioning the authenticity of the signatures: it alleged that many of them appeared twice. Cf. *Folha de São Paulo*, 14 September 1978, B. Kucinsky, *Abertura*, pp. 103–5.

14. The document was drawn up by a group of deputies from São Paulo and Rio de Janeiro. They wanted to have their suggestions discussed by the party's Executive Committee. *Jornal da Tarde*, 16 April 1977.

15. The MDB took advantage of a clause in the Electoral Law that allowed the political parties to have, once a year, a radio and tv broadcast to publicize their programme. Later, as a consequence of the MDB's initiative, Geisel decreed the Complementary Act. no. 104 (30 July 1977) suppressing the clause from the Electoral Law.

16. *Jornal do Brasil*, 14 September 1977.

17. Manifesto approved by the MDB's National Convention held in Brasilia, on 14 September 1977. It was published in the Diretório Nacional do MDB, 'Manual da Constituinte', *Coleção Alberto Pasqualini*, vol. 14, Brasilia, 1977.

18. *Estado de São Paulo*, 15 September 1977.

19. Interview with the Deputy Aldo Fagundes (ex-leader of the MDB in the Federal Chamber), on 24 May 1982.

20. In the terms of the exceptional powers granted to the President during the State of Emergency, the only fundamental difference in relation to the AI–5 was the fact that the President is not allowed to legislate.

21. Given that the clause specifically referred to the 'existing parties', it had the clear intention of allowing those MDB members who were uncommitted to the opposition to join the ARENA. For details of the Constitutional Amendment see *Estado de São Paulo*, 21 September 1978 where the complete text of the bill is published. The measures established by the Amendment came into force on 1st January 1979.

22. The ARENA Senator Teotonio Villela joined the opposition in voting against the Bill. The MDB Deputy Dias Menezes voted in support of the government. Details of the discussion and voting process for the Bill, see *Folha de São Paulo*, 20 and 22 September 1978; *Estado de São Paulo*, 21 and 23 September 1978; *Veja*, 27 September 1978 and *Isto É*, 27 September 1978.

23. The MDB's decision to leave the plenary rather than vote against the Bill was actually intended to avoid the embarassing fact that about forty deputies had absented themselves from the congressional session.

24. A short article in the newspaper *Estado de São Paulo*, on 31 December 1977 reported that, for the previous five months, the Colonel of the Reserve Alves Neves had been publicizing the candidacy of Euler Bentes among entrepreneurs, politicians and military officers in the army's reserve. From Rio Grande do Sul, where the colonel lived, he had extended his contacts to prominent figures in other states; perhaps

most notable was his meeting with the ex-minister Severo Gomes in São Paulo, who was also a supporter of the candidacy of Euler Bentes. *Estado de São Paulo*, 31 December 1977.

25. On this question, Walder de Góes provides an interesting account of Geisel's behaviour suggesting that the presidential succession had become a matter of private decision for the President. He remarks: 'Geisel's choice of General Figueiredo, made without consulting the military establishment, represented ... another move by the President to underline the overpowering nature of his command and thus reduce the Army's influence over political decision making. In fact, this is an inseparable part of the strategy by which Geisel wants to achieve the political normality of the country'. Walder de Góes, *O Brasil General Geisel*, p. 64.

26. For details of the activities of Hugo Abreu see *Isto É*, 9 August 1978, Carlos Chagas' article in *Estado de São Paulo*, 13 August 1978 and Hugo Abreu, *O Outro Lado do Poder* (Rio de Janeiro, Nova Fronteira, 1979) and *Tempo de Crise* (Rio de Janeiro, Nova Fronteira, 1980).

27. See particularly Carlos Chagas's articles in *Estado de São Paulo*, 30 May 1978, and 13 August 1978, and *Isto É*, 9 August 1978.

28. The name of Euler Bentes Monteiro as a military presidential candidate who the MDB could possibly support, was mentioned by some MDB leaders such as Senator Franco Montoro and Deputy Alencar Furtado in mid-May 1977. See *Estado de São Paulo*, 13 May 1977. Moreover, in April 1977, elements from the *grupo autentico* announced that they wanted to initiate a campaign for the participation of the military in the MDB. They argued that there were some military sectors dissatisfied with the way in which the government was ruling the country, and that the conditions therefore existed for attempting to attract them to the opposition side and even for persuading them to run for election under the MDB label. *Estado de São Paulo*, 29 April 1977.

29. Interview with Deputy Francisco Pinto on 29 April 1982.

30. Interview with Deputy Odacir Klein, on 27 April 1982.

31. In the party's national convention, held on 23 August, the nomination of the presidential candidacy of Euler Bentes was approved by 352 votes out of 497. However, 107 delegates left their ballot papers blank and 25 votes were nullified. As regards Magalhães Pinto's candidacy, the Senator gave up competing with Bentes for the Front's candidacy, Later he was reconciled with the government and decided to run for a seat in the Federal Chamber in the 1978 legislative elections.

32. *Folha de São Paulo*, 7 July, 1978.

33. In fact, General Hugo Abreu had already been marginalized in the army, since he had been passed over in the military promotions when Geisel granted the 4th star to General Figueiredo rather than to Hugo Abreu, who was next in line for promotion. As a consequence of this, Abreu automatically went into the reserve. *Estado de São Paulo*, 1 April, 1978.

34. Three ARENA Senators – Teotonio Villela, Magalhães Pinto and Accioly Filho – did not attend the meeting of the Electoral College, and five MDB parliamentarians abstained from voting for Euler Bentes, *Jornal da Tarde*, 16 October 1978.
35. The central government chose the candidates which ARENA's convention, as well as the states' Electoral College, merely ratified. Rio de Janeiro was an exceptional case since here, the MDB, which was the majority party, nominated Chagas Freitas – who in any case was quite close to the government. Another exception was São Paulo where Paulo Maluf decided to run against the appointed candidate Laudo Natel at ARENA's convention. Maluf managed to win the nomination as a result of a successful campaign among the party's delegates based on the traditional clientelistic style.
36. Statistics collected from the Superior Electoral Tribunal. On the election results see Chapter 3.
37. The South-East region is composed of the states of Espirito Santo, Minas Gerais, Rio de Janeiro and São Paulo.
38. Rio Grande do Sul, Santa Catarina and Paraná.
39. The three exceptional cases were the states of Maranhão, Piauí and Mato Grosso. In Piauí the MDB did not contest the senatorial elections since they lacked a candidate. (Statistics collected from the Superior Electoral Tribunal).
40. Fernando H. Cardoso, 'The Authoritarian Regime at the Crossroads: The Brazilian Case', *Working Papers of the Latin American Program of the Wilson Center*, no. 93, 1981, p. 16.

8 The Political Party Reform and the Party of the Brazilian Democratic Movement

1. A more detailed analysis of this question can be found in Maria D'Alva G. Kinzo, 'Novos Partidos: O Início do Debate', in B. Lamounier (ed.) *Voto de Desconfiança*. Part of the analysis developed in this chapter is based on the above-mentioned article.
2. B. Lamounier, 'O Discurso e o Processo (da Distensão ás Opções do Regime Brasileiro)', in H. Ratner (ed.) *Brasil 1990*, p. 115.
3. *Estado de São Paulo*, 24 June 1976. '6.
4. Cf. *Jornal do Brasil*, 2 December 1978.
5. The various proposals for the creation of new political parties during 1978–9 are listed in M.D.G. Kinzo, 'Novos Partidos'.
6. *Folha de São Paulo*, 1 February 1979.
7. In the event, when the Party Reform Bill was put to the vote, the article referring to the *sublegenda* was suppressed, thanks to a joint move by the MDB representatives and PDS dissidents who voted against the preservation of the *sublegenda*. However, President Figueredo. when sanctioning the Bill, vetoed the decision taken by Congress on that particular article, thus re-introducing the *sublegenda* in Law. See *Estado de São Paulo*, 21 December 1979. On the debate and voting process for the

Party Reform Law, see *Estado de São Paulo*, 11, 15, 17 and 23 November 1979, and *Jornal da Tarde*, 22 Nov. 1979.

8. Article 1, Section 2. The Bill, however, allowed the return to Brazil, of exiles who had also been involved in these kind of 'crimes' but had not been prosecuted. It was estimated that about 500 people were excluded from the amnesty proposed by the government. Nonetheless, according to information disseminated by the *Estado de São Paulo*, the Military High Court had announced a list of only 31 political prisoners who would not be granted amnesty. The newspaper also reported that, within a month, this number would drop to about 10 after the completion of several judicial cases still in progress. These remaining individuals would probably be freed as a result of the government's pardon, to be announced at Christmas 1979. See *Estado do São Paulo*, 21 September 1979.

9. Another feature of the government's Amnesty bill was the clause which granted amnesty to those who 'had committed any crimes of a political nature or for political reasons'. In other words, the bill was intended to prevent the prosecution of all those who had tortured political prisoners. Details of the bill, the debate and the vote in Congress can be found in *Estado de São Paulo*, 28 June, 1 July, 2, 10, 17 and 23 August 1979.

10. The name *Partido Popular* was quite inappropriate for a party which was popularly referred to as the bankers' party, given that it enjoyed the support of several prominent politicians linked to the financial sector, such as the ex-mayor Olavo Setubal, the ARENA chairman in São Paulo, Cláudio Lembo (both from the Banco Itaú), and even ex-Senator Magalhães Pinto who was linked to the Banco de Minas Gerais. However, the PP was short-lived, since it was incorporated in 1982 into the PMDB. Later in 1984, these politicians would join the Liberal Front Party.

11. On the struggle between the two groups see M. D. G. Kinzo, 'Novos Partidos: O Início do Debate'.

12. During the negotiation for the re-creation of the MDB, the militant sector of the party managed to obtain the inclusion in the party's first declaration of intentions, of a clause stating that the party would not accept any kind of *adesismo* (conciliatory line towards the regime). This, which would strengthen the ideologically committed groups within the new MDB, was one of the reasons which made Tancredo Neves's group decide to leave this party and join the party that Magalhães Pinto was in the process of creating. (See *Jornal da Tarde*, 22 and 26 November, 1979). That clause, however, ended up having no effect at all, when in 1982 the PMDB opened its doors to the members of the dissolved People's Party.

13. PMDB, 'Manifesto dos Fundadores do PMDB á Nação', *Revista do PMDB*, No. 1, July, 1981, pp. 11–15 (pp. 12 and 15). The manifesto was signed by 20 Senators, 108 Federal Deputies and 22 distinguished public figures and intellectuals.

14. This effect however could also benefit the opposition parties in those states where they had strong candidates, as actually happened in the state where the opposition won the elections.

15. As discussed in Chapter 6, in 1977 this quorum had been reduced from two-thirds to simple majority in order to enable the government to have a constitutional amendment passed by the ARENA votes alone.
16. Every State Assembly should appoint three delegates (state deputies) plus one for every million population of the state.
17. The electoral college would be composed of 362 PDS members, 272 PMDB, 30 PDT, 14 PTB and 8 PT members. Calculations made by D. Fleischer, 'The Party System in Brazil's ''Abertura''', paper presented at the 12th International Meeting of the Latin American Studies Association (LASA), México City, 29 September to 1 October 1983.
18. Additional figures on the 1982 electoral results can be found in M. D. G. Kinzo, 'Opposition Politics in Brazil: the Electoral Performance of the PMDB in São Paulo', *Bulletin of Latin American Research*, vol. 3, no. 2, 1984.
19. See *Estado de São Paulo*, 23–6 April 1984.
20. The PT refused to take part in the indirect presidential elections since it considered the electoral college to be illegitimate and unrepresentative.
21. Three PT congressmen defied the party line and voted for Tancredo Neves. See *Estado de São Paulo*, 16 January 1985.
22. In this regard, Sarney's government promoted important political reforms in 1985, such as the freedom for party organization which not only led to the creation of more than 20 other political parties, but also to the legalization of the Communist Parties (outlawed since 1947); enfranchizement was extended to illiterates; a national constituent assembly will meet in 1987; and direct elections for all political offices were re-established.

9 Conclusion

1. Juan J. Linz, 'The Future of an Authoritarian Situation or the Institutionalization of an Authoritarian Regime: The Case of Brazil', in A. Stepan (ed.), *Authoritarian Brazil*.
2. As J. Linz remarks, many authoritarian systems claim to be 'selective' or 'guided' democracies. Cf. Linz, 'An Authoritarian Regime – Spain', in E. Allardt and S. Rokkan (eds), *Mass Politics-Studies in Political Science* (New York, Free Press, 1970), p. 254. We could also argue however that a 'guided democracy' might also be a political project whose promoters have an authoritarian view about democratic system, rather than a clear intention of disguising an authoritarian regime.
3. S. E. Finer, *The Man on Horseback: the Role of the Military in Politics* (London: Pall Mall Press, 1962), p. 179.
4. Alain Rouguié, 'Demilitarization and the Institutionalization of Military-Dominated Polities in Latin America'. *Working Papers of the Latin American Program of the Wilson Center*, no. 110, 1982, p. 3.
5. Another important detail was the fact that, already in July 1964, Castelo Branco proposed a Constitutional Amendment (approved by Congress) which compelled military officers to transfer to the army's reserve or to retire, after having held an elected office (which included

the Presidency). This certainly was aimed to protect the military institution against its politicization by preventing general-ex-Presidents from regaining power in the military institution and being able to influence government through their position in the army.

6. O. Cordeiro de Farias, *Meio Século de Combate: Diálogo com Cordeiro de Farias, Aspásia Camargo, Walder de Góes* (Rio de Janeiro: Nova Fronteira, 1981) pp. 612–3.

7. One must note however that the Brazilian party system of the 1945–64 regime was not deeply rooted as was the case, for instance, of the Argentine or Chilean system before military rule was established in those countries; and the long tenure of military rule in Brazil helped to destroy memories of that experience. As was underlined in Chapter 3, between 1966 and 1978 the Brazilian electorate increased by 51 per cent which meant that half of the potential voters in elections after 1978 had never experienced electoral contests other than the ones between ARENA and the MDB.

Bibliography

Manuscript Sources

CPDOC – FGV (Centro de Pesquisa e Documentação da História Contemporânea – Fundação Getúlio Vargas, Rio de Janeiro): *Arquivo do Marechal Castelo Branco; Arquivo de História Oral: Juracy Magalhães (depoimento, 1977).*

Tribunal Regional Eleitoral, São Paulo:
(Election results of the municipal, state and federal elections – 1966–1978).

PRODASEN (Sistema de Informações Eleitorais – Senado Federal, Brasília):
(Election results of the 1978 legislative elections by state and muncipality).

Interviews
Federal Deputy Airton Soares (MDB/PT – São Paulo), 6 May 1982.
Federal Deputy Aldo Fagundes (MDB/PMDB – R. G. do Sul), 24 May 1982.
State Deputy Almir Pazzianotto (MDB/PMDB – São Paulo), 13 July 1982.
Federal Deputy Bezerra (MDB/PMDB – Acre), 19 April 1982.
State Deputy A. Carlos Mesquita (MDB/PMDB – S. Paulo), 13 July 1982.
Antonio Roque Citadini (Regional Directorate of the MDB/PMDB – S. Paulo), 7 June 1982.
Federal Deputy Aurélio Peres (MDB/PMDB – S. Paulo), 28 June 1982.
Federal Deputy Carlos Bezerra (MDB/PMDB – Mato Grosso), 28 April 1982.
Claudio Lembo (São Paulo's ARENA ex-president), 26 November 1982.
Federal Deputy Cristina Tavares (MDB/PMDB – Pernambuco), 22 April 1982.
David Lima Oliveira (Youth Department MDB/PMDB – R. G. Do Sul), 18 May 1982.
Federal Deputy Epitácio Cafeteira (MDB/PMDB – Maranhão), 30 April 1982.
Federal Deputy Euclides Scalco (MDB/PMDB – Paraná), 27 April 1982.
Senator F. Henrique Cardoso (MDB/PMDB – S. Paulo), 23 July 1982.
Federal Deputy Fernando Lyra (MDB/PMDB – Pernambuco), 7 May 1982.
Federal Deputy Francisco Pinto (MDB/PMDB – Bahia), 29–30 April 1982).

267

Federal Deputy Freitas Dinis (MDB/PT – Maranhão), 10 May 1982.
Federal Deputy Freitas Nobre (MDB/PMDB – São Paulo), 28 April 1982.
Federal Deputy Fued Dib (MDB/PMDB – Minas Gerais), 22 April 1982.
Hélio Augusto de Souza (S. J. Campos municipal directorate – PMDB-president), 20 August 1982.
Senator Humberto Lucena (MDB/PMDB – Paraíba), 22 April 1982.
Senator Jarbas Passarinho (ARENA/PDS – Pará), 20 May 1982.
Federal Deputy João Gilberto (MDB/PMDB – R. G. do Sul), 20 April 1982.
Federal Deputy João Herculino (MDB/PMDB – M. Gerais), 22 April 1982.
Federal Deputy João Paulo Arruda (MDB/PDS – S. Paulo), 12 July 1982.
Federal Deputy José Costa (MDB/PMDB – Alagoas), 30 April 1982.
Federal Deputy José Santilli (MDB/PMDB – S. Paulo), 27 May 1982.
Luciano F. Pinho (São Paulo's district directorate of Santa Cecília e Campos Elíseos – MDB/PMDB president), 26 August 1982.
Luiz Paulo Costa (S. J. Campos' municipal directorate – PMDB general-secretary), 30 August 1982.
Federal Deputy Marcelo Cordeiro (MDB/PMDB – Bahia), 27 May 1982.
Federal Deputy Marcio Santilli (PMDB – São Paulo), 3 June 1982.
Federal Deputy Marcondes Pereira (MDB/PMDB – São Paulo), 30 August 1982.
State Deputy Marcos Aurélio (MDB/PT – S. Paulo), 1 July 1982.
Federal Deputy Mario Covas (MDB/PMDB – S. Paulo), 9 August 1982.
Federal Deputy Mario Frota (MDB/PMDB – Amazonas), 30 April 1982.
Senator Mario Maia (MDB/PMDB – Acre), 23 April 1982.
Federal Deputy Mario Moreira (MDB/PMDB – Espírito Santo), 5 May 1982.
Federal Deputy Max Mauro (MDB/PMDB – Espírito Santo) 29 April 1982.
Federal Deputy Mendonça Neto (MDB/PMDB – Alagoas), 4 May 1982.
Senator Nelson Carneiro (MDB/PMDB – Rio de Janeiro), 20 April 1982.
Federal Deputy Odacir Klein (MDB/PMDB – R. G. do Sul), 27 April 1982.
State Deputy O. Doreto Campanari (MDB/PMDB – S. Paulo), 24 June 1982.
Federal Deputy Otacílio de Almeida (MDB/PMDB – S. Paulo), 7 June 1982.
Federal Deputy Paes de Andrade (MDB/PMDB – Ceará), 7 May 1982.
Senator Paulo Brossard (MDB/PMDB – R. G. do Sul), 27 April 1982.
Federal Deputy Pedro Lucena (MDB/PP/PMDB – R. G. do Norte), 28 April 1982.
Percival Maricato (São Paulo's District Directorate of Bela Vista – MDB/PT), 9 June 1982.

Reinaldo J. Custódio (MDB/PMDB Mayor of Colombia - S. Paulo), 7 July 1982.
Federal Deputy R. Cardoso Alves (MDB/PMDB - S. Paulo), 7 July 1982.
Federal Deputy Ronan Tito (MDB/PMDB - M. Gerais), 20 April 1982.
Federal Deputy Samir Achoa (MDB/PMDB - S. Paulo), 5 May 1982.
Federal Deputy Ulysses Guimarães (MDB/PMDB - S. Paulo), 30 June 1982.
Federal Deputy Waldir Walter (MDB/PMDB - R. G. do Sul), 7 May 1982.
Top Civil Servant of the Federal Chamber (A), 3 May 1982.
Member of the Brazilian Communist Party's Committee (A), 26 August 1982.

Printed Sources

ABREU, H., *O Outro Lado do Poder* (Rio de Janeiro: Nova Fronteira, 1979).
BANDEIRA, M., *Presença dos Estados Unidos no Brasil* (Rio de Janeiro: Civ. Brasileira, 1973).
BENEVIDES, M. V. M., *A UDN e o Udenismo - Ambiguidades do Liberalismo Brasileiro (1945-1965)* (Rio de Janeiro: Paz e Terra, 1981).
BITTENCOURT, G., *A Quinta Estrêla - Como se tenta fazer um Presidente no Brasil* (São Paulo: Livraria Editora Ciências Humanas, 1978).
CALDEIRA, T. P. R., 'Para que Serve o Voto? (As Eleições e o Cotidiano na Periferia de São Paulo)', in Lamounier, B. (ed.) *Voto de Desconfiança* (Petrópolis: Vozes/CEBRAP, 1980).
CÂMARA DOS DEPUTADOS, *Anais da Câmara dos Deputados, 1965-1968* (Brasília: Diretoria de Documentação e Publicidade, 1966-69).
CAMMACK, P., 'Clientelism and Military Government in Brazil', in Clapham C. (ed.), *Private Patronage and Public Power* (London: Frances Pinter, 1982).
CAMPANHOLE, A. and CAMPANHOLE, H. L., *Todas as Constituições do Brasil* (São Paulo: Atlas, 1976).
CARDOSO, F. H., *O Modelo Político Brasileiro e outros Ensaios* (São Paulo: Difel, 1972).
———, *Autoritarismo e Democratização* (Rio de Janeiro: Paz e Terra, 1975).
———, 'Partidos e Deputados em São Paulo: O Voto e a Representação Política', in Cardoso, F. H. and Lamounier, B. (eds), *Os Partidos e as Eleições no Brasil* (Rio de Janeiro: Paz e Terra/CEBRAP, 1975).
———, 'A Questão dos Partidos', *Contexto*, no. 5, Março 1978, pp. 1-20.
———, 'On the Characterization of Authoritarian Regimes in Latin America', in Collier, D. (ed.), *The New Authoritarianism in Latin America* (Princeton: Princeton University Press, 1979).
———, The Authoritarian Regime at the Crossroads: the Brazilian Case', *Working Papers of the Latin American Program of the Wilson Center*, no. 93, 1981.

———, 'O Papel dos Empresários no Processo de Transição: O Caso Brasileiro', *Dados*, vol. 26, no. 1, 1983, pp. 9–27.

CARDOSO, R., 'Movimentos Sociais Urbanos: Balanço Crítico', in Sorj, B. and Almeida, M. H. T. (eds), *Sociedade e Política no Brasil pós-64* (São Paulo: Brasiliense, 1983).

CARSTAIRS, A. M., *A Short History of Electoral Systems in Western Europe* (London: George Allen & Unwin, 1980).

CARVALHO, O. M., *Ensaios de Sociologia Eleitoral* (Belo Horizonte: Edições da RBEP, 1958).

CASTELLO BRANCO, C., *Os Militares no Poder*, vol. I (Rio de Janeiro: Nova Fronteira, 1977).

———, *Os Militares no Poder*, vol. 2 (Rio de Janeiro: Nova Fronteira, 1978).

———, *Os Miltares no Poder*, vol. 3 (Rio de Janeiro: Nova Fronteira, 1979).

CHILCOTE, R. H., *The Brazilian Communist Party – Conflict and Integration, 1922–1972* (Oxford: Oxford University Press, 1974).

COELHO, E. C., *Em Busca de Identidade: O Exèrcito e a Política na Sociedade Brasileira* (Rio de Janeiro: Forense, 1976).

COLLIER, D. (ed.), *The New Authoritarianism in Latin America* (Princeton: Princeton University Press, 1979).

COSTA, F. J. L. and KLEIN, L. G., 'Um Ano de Governo Médici', *Dados*, no. 9, 1972, pp. 156–221.

COUTO, P. F., *O Voto e o Povo* (Rio de Janeiro: Civ. Brasileira, 1966).

DAHL, R. A. (ed.), *Regimes and Oppositions* (New Haven: Yale Univ. Press, 1973).

DIÁRIO DA JUSTIÇA, 'Eleições de 15.11.1982', *Tribunal Superior Eleitoral*, 28 November 1983.

DINIZ, E., *Voto e Máquina Política – Patronagem e Clientelismo no Rio de Janeiro* (Rio de Janeiro: Paz e Terra, 1982).

DREIFUSS, R., *1964: A Conquista do Estado – Ação Política, Poder e Golpe de Classe* (Petrópolis: Vozes, 1981).

DUARTE, C. R. 'A Lei Falcão: Antecedentes e Impacto', in Lamounier, B., *Voto de Desconfiança* (Petrópolis: Vozes/CEBRAP, 1980).

———, Imprensa e Redemocratização no Brasil', *Dados*, vol. 26, no. 2, 1983, pp. 181–95.

DULCI, O. S., 'A União Democrática Nacional e o Anti-populismo no Brasil' (Universidade Federal de Minas Gerais, Tese de Mestrado, 1977).

DULLES, J. W. F., *President Castelo Branco* (Texas, A & M University Press, 1980).

DUVERGER, M., *Political Parties – their Organization and Activity in the Modern State* (London: Methuen, 1955).

ELDERSVELD, S., *Political Parties: A Behavioral Analysis*, 2nd edn (Chicago: Rand McNally, 1966).

FARIA, V. E., 'Desenvolvimento, Urbanização e Mudanças na Estrutura do Emprego: a Experiência dos Últimos Trinta Anos', in Sorj, B. and Tavares de Almeida, M. H. (eds), *Sociedade e Política no Brasil pós-64* (São Paulo: Brasiliense, 1983).

FARIAS, O. Cordeiro de, *Meio Século de Combate: Diálogo com Cordeiro de Farias, Aspásia Camargo e Walder de Góes* (Rio de Janeiro: Nova Fronteira, 1981).

FIECHTER, G. A., *Brazil since 1964: Modernization under a Military Regime* (London: Macmillan, 1975).

FIGUEIREDO, E. de L., *Os Militares e a Democracia* (Rio de Janeiro: Graal, 1980).

FIGUEIREDO, M., 'A Política de Coação no Brasil pós-64', in Klein, L. and Figueiredo, M., *Legitimidade e Coação no Brasil pós-64', (Rio de Janeiro, Forense, 1978)*.

FIGUEIREDO, M. and CHEIBUB, J. A. B., 'A Abertura Política de 1973 a 1981: Quem disse o Quê, Quando – Inventário de um Debate', *Boletim Informativo e Bibliográfico*, no. 14, 1982, pp. 29–61.

FINER, S., *The Man on Horseback – The Role of the Military in Politics* (London: Pall Mall Press, 1962).

FLEISCHER, D., 'Concentração e Dispersão Eleitoral: um Estudo da Distribuição Geográfica do Voto em Minas Gerais, 1966–1974, *Revista Brasileira de Estudos Políticos*, no. 43, 1976.

―――― (ed.), *Os Partidos Políticos no Brasil* (2 vols, Brasília: Universidade de Brasília, 1981).

――――, 'The Party System in Brazil's *Abertura'*, paper presented at the 12th International Meeting of the Latin American Studies Association, Mexico City, 1983.

FLYNN, P., *Brazil: A Political Analysis* (London: Ernest Benn, 1978).

FRANCO, A. A. de M., *História e Teoria dos Partidos Políticos no Brasil*, 2nd edn (São Paulo: Alfa-Omega, 1974).

FUNDAÇÃO MILTON CAMPOS, *As Eleições Nacionais de 1978* (Brasília: Gráfica do Senado Federal, 1979).

GOES, W. de, *O Brasil do General Geisel* (Rio de Janeiro: Nova Fronteira, 1978).

GOMES, L. M. G., 'Cronologia do Governo Castelo Branco', *Dados*, nos 2/3, 1967, pp. 112–132.

――――, 'Cronologia do Primeiro Ano do Governo Costa e Silva', *Dados*, no. 4, 1968, pp. 119–220.

HIPPÓLITO, L., *De Raposas e Reformistas – O PSD e a Experiência Democrática Brasileira (1945–64)* (Rio de Janeiro: Paz e Terra, 1985).

INSTITUTO BRASILEIRO DE GEOGRAFIA E ESTATÍSTICA, *VI Recenseamento Geral do Brasil – 1950: Censo Demográfico* (Rio de Janeiro: IBGE, 1955).

――――, *VIII Recenseamento Geral do Brasil – 1970: Censo Demográfico* (Rio de Janeiro: IBGE, 1973).

――――, *IX Recenseamento Geral do Brasil – 1980, Tabulações Avançadas do Censo Demográfico, Resultados Preliminares* (Rio de Janeiro: IBGE, 1981).

JAGUARIBE, H., 'Política de Clientela e Política Ideológica', *Digesto Econômico*, (VI), no. 68, 1950.

JENKS, M. S., 'Political Parties in Authoritarian Brazil' (Duke University Ph.D. thesis, 1979).

JORNAL DA TARDE (São Paulo), 1965–79.

JORNAL DO BRASIL (Rio de Janeiro), 1976–9.

JORNAL FOLHA DE SÃO PAULO (São Paulo), 1976–9.

JORNAL O ESTADO DE SÃO PAULO (SÃO PAULO), 1965–85.

KINZO, M. D. G., *Representação Política e Sistema Eleitoral no Brasil* (São Paulo: Símbolo, 1980).

———, 'Novos Partidos: O Início do Debate', in Lamounier, B. (ed.), *Voto de Desconfiança* (Petrópolis: Vozes/CEBRAP, 1980).

———, 'Opposition Politics in Brazil: The Electoral Performance of the PMDB in São Paulo', *Bulletin of Latin American Research*, vol. 3, no. 2, 1984, p. 29–45.

KINZO, M. G. D. and MIYAMOTO, S., 'Eleições Municipais de 1976: Acompanhamento do Processo Eleitoral', Relatório de Pesquisa à FAPESP, mimeo., 1977.

KRIEGER, D., *Desde as Missões . . . saudades, lutas, esperanças* (Rio de Janeiro, José Olympio, 1977).

KUCINSKY, B., *Abertura, A História de uma Crise* (São Paulo: Ed. Brasil Debates, 1982).

LAFER, C., *O Sistema Político Brasileiro*, 2nd edn (São Paulo: Perspectiva, 1978).

LAMOUNIER, B., 'O Comportamento Eleitoral em São Paulo: Passado e Presente', in Cardoso, F. H. and Lamounier, B. (eds), *Os Partidos e as Eleições no Brasil* (Rio de Janeiro: Paz e Terra/CEBRAP, 1975).

———, 'O Crescimento da Oposição num Reduto Arenista', in Reis, F. W. (ed.), *Os Partidos e o Regime* (São Paulo, Símbolo, 1978).

———, 'O Discurso e o Processo (da Distensão ás Opções do Regime Brasileiro)', in Rattner, H. (ed.), *Brasil 1990, Caminhos Alternativos do Desenvolvimento* (São Paulo: Brasiliense, 1979).

———, 'O Voto em São Paulo, 1970–8', in Lamounier, B. (ed.), *Voto de Desconfiança* (Petrópolis: Vozes/CEBRAP, 1980).

———, 'Notes on the Study of Re-Democratization', *Working Papers of the Latin American Program of the Wilson Center*, no. 58, n.d.

———, 'Representação Política: a Importância de Certos Formalismos', in Lamounier, B. *et al.* (eds), *Direito, Cidadania e Representação* (São Paulo: T. A. Queiros, 1981).

LAMOUNIER, B. and KINZO, M. D. G., 'Partidos Políticos, Representação e Processo Eleitoral no Brasil, 1945–1978: Ensaio Bibliográfico', *Dados*, Boletim Informativo e Bibliográfico de Ciências Sociais, no. 19, 1978, pp. BIB 11–32.

LAMOUNIER, B. and FARIA, J. E. (orgs.) *O Futuro da Abertura: Um Debate* (São Paulo: Cortêz Editora, 1981).

LAMOUNIER, B. and MOURA, A. R., 'Política Econômica e Abertura Política – 1973–1983', *Textos IDESP*, no. 4, 1984.

LAPALOMBARA, J. and WEINER, M. (eds), *Political Parties and Political Development* (Princeton: Princeton University Press, 1966).

LAURO, P., *Código Eleitoral Comentado por Assunto e Lei de Inelegibilidades Explicada de Forma Prática* (São Paulo: Ed. Brasileira de Direito, 1975).

LEAL, V. N., *Coronelismo, Enxada e Voto* (Rio de Janeiro: Forense, 1949).

LEI No. 4.740, *Lei Orgânica dos Partidos Políticos*, 15 de julho, 1975.

LIMA Jr, O. B., 'Articulação de Interesses, Posição Socio-Econômica e Ideologia: as Eleições de 1976 em Niterói', in Reis, F. W. (ed.) *Os Partidos e o Regime* (São Paulo: Símbolo, 1978).

———, *Os Partidos Políticos Brasileiros: A Experiência Federal e Regional (1945–64)* (Rio de Janeiro: Graal, 1983).

LINZ, J. 'An Authoritarian Regime: Spain', in Allardt, E. and Rokkan, S. (eds), *Mass Politics: Studies in Political Sociology* (New York: The Free Press, 1970).

———, 'The Future of An Authoritarian Situation or the Institutionalization of an Authoritarian Regime: the Case of Brazil', in Stepan, A. (ed.), *Authoritarian Brazil* (New Haven: Yale University Press, 1973).

MAGALHÃES, I. M. *et al.*, 'Cronologia – Segundo e Terceiro Ano do Governo Costa e Silva', *Dados*, no. 8, 1971, pp. 152–233.

MARTINS, C. E., 'O Balanço da Campanha', in Cardoso, F. H. and Lamounier, B. (eds), *Os Partidos e as Eleições no Brasil* (Rio de Janeiro, Paz e Terra/CEBRAP, 1975).

McDONOUGH, P., *Power and Ideology in Brazil* (Princeton: Princeton University Press, 1981).

McKENZIE, R. T., *British Political Parties: the Distribution of Power within the Conservative and Labour Parties* (London: William Heinemann Ltd., 1955).

MEDEIROS, A. C., 'Politics and Intergovernmental Relations in Brazil, 1964–1982' (London School of Economics, Ph.D. Thesis, 1983).

MIYAMOTO, S., 'Eleições de 1978 em São Paulo: A Campanha', in Lamounier, B. (ed.) *Voto de Desconfiança* (Petrópolis: Vozes/CEBRAP, 1980).

MOREIRA ALVES, M. H. *Estado e Oposição no Brasil (1964–84)* (Petrópolis: Vozes, 1984).

———, 'Grassroots Organizations, Trade Unions, and the Church – A Challenge to the Controlled *Abertura* in Brazil', *Latin American Perspectives* Issue 40, vol. 2, no. 1, 1984, pp. 73–102.

MOVIMENTO DEMOCRÁTICO BRASILEIRO (MDB), *Coleção Alberto Pasqualini*, 21 vols, Brasília, 1976–81.

NEUMANN, S. (ed.), *Modern Political Parties – Approaches to Comparative Politics* (Chicago: The University of Chicago Press, Midway Reprint, 1975).

OLIVEIRA, L. L. 'O Partido Social Democrático (IUPERJ, Tese de Mestrado, 1973).

PAES DE ANDRADE, A. *O Itinerário da Violência* (Rio de Janeiro: Paz e Terra, 1978).

PARKER, P., *1964: O Papel dos Estados Unidos no Golpe de Estado de 31 de Março* (Rio de Janeiro: Civ. Brasileira, 1977).

PEDREIRA, F., *Brasil Política* (São Paulo: Difel, 1975).

PETERSON, P. J., 'Brazilian Political Parties: Formation, Organization, and Leadership, 1945–1959' (University of Michigan, Ph.D. Thesis, 1967).

PICALUGA, I., *Partidos Políticos e Classes Sociais: A UDN na Guanabara* (Rio de Janeiro: Vozes, 1980).

QUARTIM, J., *Dictatorship and Armed Struggle in Brazil* (London: NLB, 1971).

REIS, F. W., 'As Eleições em Minas Gerais', in Cardoso, F. H. and Lamounier, B. (eds), *Os Partidos e as Eleições no Brasil* (Rio de Janeiro: Paz e Terra/CEBRAP, 1975).

——, 'Classe Social e Opção Partidária: As Eleições de 1976 em Juiz de Fora', in Reis, F. W. (ed.), *Os Partidos e o Regime* (São Paulo: Símbolo, 1978).

REVISTA DO PMDB, No. 1, July 1981.

REVISTA ISTO É, 1977–9.

REVISTA VEJA, 1973–9.

REVISTA VISÃO, 1970–6.

RIBEIRO, F. *Direito Eleitoral* (Rio de Janeiro: Forense, 1976).

ROUQUIÉ, A., 'Clientelist Control and Authoritarian Contexts', in Hermet, G. et al. (eds), *Elections Without Choice* (London: Macmillan, 1978).

——, 'Demilitarization and the Institutionalization of Military-Dominated Polities in Latin America', *Working Papers of the Latin American Program of the Wilson Center*, no. 110, 1982.

SAMPAIO, R., *Adhemar de Barros e o PSP* (São Paulo, Global, 1982).

SANTOS, W. G. dos, *Poder e Política: Crônica do Autoritarismo Brasileiro* (Rio de Janeiro: Forense, 1978).

——, 'Calculus of Conflict: Impasse in Brazilian Politics and the Crisis of 1964' (Stanford University, Ph.D. thesis, 1979).

SARTORI, G., *Parties and Party Systems – A Framework for Analysis*, vol. I (Cambridge: Cambridge University Press, 1976).

SCHMITTER, P., 'The "Portugalization" of Brazil?', in Stepan, A. (ed.), *Authoritarian Brazil* (New Haven, Yale University Press, 1973).

SCHNEIDER, R., *The Political System of Brazil – Emergence of a 'Modernizing' Authoritarian Regime, 1964–1970* (New York: Columbia University Press, 1971).

SCHWATZMAN, S., *São Paulo e o Estado Nacional* (São Paulo: Difel, 1975).

SENADO FEDERAL, *Legislação Eleitoral e Partidária* (2nd edn, Brasília: Senado Federal, 1974).

——, *Legislação Eleitoral e Partidária e Instruções do TSE para as Eleições de 1982* (Brasília: Senado Federal, 1982).

SERRA, J., 'Ciclos e Mudanças Estruturais na Economia Brasileira do Pós-Guerra', in Belluzzo, L. G. and Coutinho, R., *Desenvolvimento Capitalista no Brasil – Ensaios sobre a Crise* (São Paulo: Brasiliense, 1982).

SINGER, P. I. 'A Política das Classes Dominantes' in Ianni, O. *et al.*, *Política e Revolução Social no Brasil* (Rio de Janeiro: Civ. Brasileira, 1965).

SKIDMORE, T. E., *Politics in Brazil, 1930–1964* (Oxford: Oxford University Press, 1967).

——, 'Politics and Economic Policy Making in Authoritarian Brazil, 1937–71', in Stepan, A. (ed.), *Authoritarian Brazil* (New Haven, Yale University Press, 1973).

SOARES, G. A. D., 'El Sistema Electoral y Representacion de los Grupos Sociales en Brasil, 1945–1962', *Revista Latinoamericana de Ciência Política*, vol. 2, no. 1, 1971, pp. 5–23.

———, *Sociedade e Política no Brasil* (São Paulo: Difel, 1973).

SOUZA, M. C. C., *Estado e Partidos Políticos no Brasil (1930–1964)* (São Paulo: Alfa-Ômega, 1976).

STEPAN, A., *The Military in Politics – Changing Patterns in Brazil* (Princeton: Princeton University Press, 1973).

——— (ed.), *Authoritarian Brazil – Origins, Policies and Future* (New Haven: Yale University Press, 1973).

STUMPF, A. G. and MERVAL, P., *A Segunda Guerra: Sucessão de Geisel* (São Paulo: Brasiliense, 1979).

TAVARES DE ALMEIDA, M. H., 'O Sindicalismo Brasileiro entre a Conservação e a Mudança', in Sorj, B. and Tavares de Almeida, M. H. (eds) *Sociedade e Política no Brasil pós-64* (São Paulo: Brasiliense, 1983).

TRIBUNAL SUPERIOR ELEITORAL, *Dados Estatísticos – Eleições Federais, Estaduais, realizadas no Brasil em 1960, e em confronto com as anteriores* (vol. 5) (Brasilia: Departmento de Imprensa Nacional, 1963).

———, *Dados Estatísticos – Eleições Federais e Estaduais realizadas no Brasil em 1965 e 1966* (vol. 8) (Brasilia: Departmento de Imprensa Nacional, 1971).

———, *Dados Estatísticos – Eleições Federais e Estaduais realizadas no Brasil em 1970* (vol. 9), (Brasilia: Departmento de Imprensa Nacional, 1973).

———, *Dados Estatísticos – Eleições Federais e Estaduais realizadas no Brasil em 1974* (vol. 11) (Brasilia: Departmento de Imprensa Nacional, 1977).

TRINDADE, H., 'Padrões e Tendências do Comportamento Eleitoral no Rio Grande do Sul', in Cardoso, F. H. and Lamounier, B. (eds) *Os Partidos e as Eleições no Brasil* (Rio: Paz e Terra/CEBRAP, 1975).

——— (ed.), *Brasil em Perspectiva: Dilemas da Abertura Política* (Porto Alegre: Sulina, 1982).

TRINDADE, H. and CEW, J., 'Confrontação Política e Decisão Eleitoral: As Eleições Municipais de 1976 em Caxias do Sul', in Reis, F. W. (ed.), *Os Partidos e o Regime* (São Paulo: Símbolo, 1978).

VALENZUELA, A. and VALENZUELA, J. S., 'Party Opposition under the Chilean Authoritarian Regime', *Working Papers of the Latin American Program of the Wilson Center*, no. 125, 1983.

VELASCO e CRUZ, S., 'Empresários e o Regime no Brasil: A Campanha contra a Estatização' (Universidade de São Paulo, Tese de Doutoramento, 1985).

VELASCO e CRUZ, S. and MARTINS, C. E., 'De Castelo a Figueiredo: Uma Incursão no Pré-História da "Abertura" ', in Sorj, B. and Tavares de Almeida, M. H. (eds), *Sociedade e Política no Brasil pós-64* (São Paulo: Brasiliense, 1983).

VIANA FILHO, L., *O Governo Castelo Branco* (Rio de Janeiro: José Olympio, 1975).

WESSON, R. and FLEISCHER, D., *Brazil in Transition* (New York: Praeger, 1983).

Index